THE CANADA–UNITED STATES FREE TRADE AGREEMENT: THE GLOBAL IMPACT

The Canada–United State.

JEFFREY J. SCHOTT AND
MURRAY G. SMITH, EDITORS

Free Trade Agreement: The Global Impact

INSTITUTE FOR INTERNATIONAL ECONOMICS
Washington, DC

THE INSTITUTE FOR RESEARCH ON PUBLIC POLICY
Canada
1988

Jeffrey J. Schott is a Research Fellow at the Institute. He was formerly a Senior Associate at the Carnegie Endowment for International Peace and an international economist at the US Treasury Department.

Murray G. Smith joined the Institute for Research on Public Policy in June 1987 as Director of the International Economics Program. Previously, he was with the C. D. Howe Institute and during the Tokyo Round of multilateral negotiations, he was Director of International Economic Relations in the British Columbia government.

The editors would like to thank Ann L. Beasley, Kimberly Ann Elliott, Lynda Lennon, and Cindy McKaughan for their assistance in preparing the manuscript for publication. Angela L. Barnes, Marina Horrocks, and Lisa Salaz provided tireless and expert secretarial support. J.J.S. and M.G.S.

INSTITUTE FOR INTERNATIONAL ECONOMICS
11 Dupont Circle, NW
Washington, DC 20036
(202) 328-9000 Telex: 261271 IIEUR
Fax: (202) 328-5432

C. Fred Bergsten, *Director*
Ann L. Beasley, *Director of Publications*

The Institute for International Economics was created, and is principally funded, by the German Marshall Fund of the United States.

Printed in the United States of America
92 91 90 89 88   5 4 3 2 1

Library of Congress Cataloging-in-Publication Data

The Canada-United States Free Trade Agreement.

Bibliography:
1. Tariff—Canada. 2. Tariff—United States. 3. Canada—Commerce—United States. 4. United States—Commerce—Canada. 5. Free trade and protection—Free trade. I. Schott, Jeffrey J., 1949- . II. Smith, Murray G. (Murray Gordon), 1952- . III. Institute for International Economics (U.S.)
HF1766.C285 1988 382.7'1'0973 88-9110
ISBN 0–88132–073–0

Contents

Preface   *C. Fred Bergsten and Rod Dobell*   **vii**

1   **The Free Trade Agreement: A US Assessment**   *Jeffrey J. Schott*   **1**

2   **The Free Trade Agreement in Context: A Canadian Perspective**
    Murray G. Smith   **37**

3   **Dispute Resolution Mechanisms**   *Gary N. Horlick,*
    Geoffrey D. Oliver, and Debra P. Steger   **65**
    Comments   *Robert E. Hudec*   87
                Frank Stone   95

4   **The Auto Sector**   *Paul Wonnacott*   **101**
    Comments   *Mustafa Mohatarem*   110
                O. Victor Lonmo   113

5   **Implications of the Energy Provisions**   *Philip K. Verleger, Jr.*   **117**
    Comments   *Marshall Crowe*   128
                James T. Jensen   131

6   **Services and Investment**   *Jeffrey J. Schott and Murray G. Smith*   **137**
    Comments   *Harry L. Freeman*   151
                J. H. Warren   153

7   **Implications for the Uruguay Round**   *Jeffrey J. Schott*   **159**
    Comments   *John Whalley*   173
                Julius L. Katz   177

8   **Political Perspectives**   **181**
    Barbara McDougall   181
    M. Peter McPherson   187

APPENDIX

Conference Participants   197

TABLES

1.1 US trade with Canada   9
1.2 Canadian dependence on US trade   10
1.3 Staging of FTA tariff cuts   16
1.4 Impact of tariff cuts on US exports to Canada   18
1.5 Impact of tariff cuts on US imports from Canada   19
5.1 US imports of petroleum and natural gas from Canada, 1973–87 120
6.1 US trade in services with Canada, 1985–87   138
6.2 Direct investment between the United States and Canada,
     1982–86   146

Preface

The Free Trade Agreement signed by the President of the United States and the Prime Minister of Canada on 2 January 1988 could, if ratified by the two countries, produce an historic linkage between their economies. Properly handled, it could also initiate path-breaking responses to some of the thorniest problems of international trade and the resolution of trade disputes among nations and thus pave the way for even more far-reaching arrangements at the global level.

To assess the major features of the agreement, the Institute hosted a conference in Washington on 11 January 1988 jointly with the Ottawa-based Institute for Research on Public Policy. This volume includes the papers prepared for that conference, the remarks of discussants on each paper, and a presentation by a leading representative of the US administration and a minister in the Canadian government.

The book also includes overall evaluations of the agreement from the separate perspectives of the United States and Canada. The Institute for International Economics is releasing the American appraisal simultaneously in the series POLICY ANALYSES IN INTERNATIONAL ECONOMICS.

The Institute for International Economics

The Institute for International Economics is a private nonprofit research institution for the study and discussion of international economic policy. Its purpose is to analyze important issues in that area and to develop and communicate practical new approaches for dealing with them. The Institute is completely nonpartisan.

The Institute was created by a generous commitment of funds from the German Marshall Fund of the United States in 1981, and continues to receive substantial support from that source. In addition, major institutional grants are now being received from the Ford Foundation, the William and

Flora Hewlett Foundation, and the Alfred P. Sloan Foundation. A number of other foundations and private corporations are contributing to the increasing diversification of the Institute's financial resources.

The Board of Directors bears overall responsibility for the Institute and gives general guidance and approval to its research program—including identification of topics that are likely to become important to international economic policymakers over the medium run (generally, one to three years) and which thus should be addressed by the Institute. The Director, working closely with the staff and outside Advisory Committee, is responsible for the development of particular projects and makes the final decision to publish an individual study.

The Institute hopes that its studies and other activities will contribute to building a stronger foundation for international economic policy around the world. Comments as to how it can best do so are invited from readers of these publications.

The Institute for Research on Public Policy/L'Institut de recherches politiques

Founded in Montreal in 1972, the Institute for Research on Public Policy is a national organization whose independence and autonomy are ensured by the revenues of an endowment fund supported by the federal and provincial governments and by the private sector. In addition, the Institute receives grants and contracts from governments, corporations, and foundations to carry out specific research projects.

The *raison d'être* of the Institute is threefold:

☐ To act as a catalyst within the national community helping to facilitate informed public debate on issues of major public interest

☐ to stimulate participation by all segments of the national community in the process that leads to public policy making

☐ to find practical solutions to important public policy problems, thus aiding in the development of sound public policies.

The Institute is governed by a Board of Directors, which is the decision-making body, and a Council of Trustees, which advises the Board on matters related to the research direction of the Institute. Administration of the Institute's policies, programs, and staff is the responsibility of the president. The Institute operates in a decentralized way, employing researchers located across Canada. This policy ensures that research undertaken will include contributions from all regions of the country.

The Institute's goal is to promote public understanding and discussion of issues of national importance, with clarity and impartiality. Conclusions or recommendations in the Institute's publications are solely those of the author and should not be attributed to the Board of Directors, Council of Trustees, or contributors to the Institute.

Without doubt 1988 will be a significant year in bilateral economic relations across the 49th parallel, and the decisions made by our two countries about the ratification of the Free Trade Agreement will have broad consequences for the global trading system. We hope that this publication will contribute to a more complete understanding of the implications of the agreement and careful consideration on both sides of a decision that will have enduring consequences.

C. FRED BERGSTEN	ROD DOBELL
Director	President
Institute for	Institute for
International Economics	Research on
February 1988	Public Policy

1

The Free Trade Agreement: A US Assessment

Jeffrey J. Schott

The main objective of the US–Canada Free Trade Agreement (FTA) is to create an increasingly open market for trade and investment in goods and services between the world's two largest trading partners. Both governments have proclaimed the FTA to be a "win-win" result.

This paper examines the substantive issues raised by the FTA and the economic implications for the United States. Two main criteria are used to evaluate the agreement: the economic effects on the United States; and the systemic effects, i.e., the implications of the FTA for bilateral relations and for the multilateral trading system. In so doing, I will assess the costs and benefits for the US economy of the major aspects of the FTA to determine whether the FTA is a good deal for the United States, and whether it should be ratified by the Congress.

Objectives and Achievements

When the United States and Canada embarked on the FTA negotiations, they had several specific objectives that were considered essential to secure political acceptance of the overall pact. For the United States, the objectives included, *inter alia,* the establishment of new rules to govern services and investment, which would preclude a return to the more interventionist investment policies of the past in Canada and could serve as building blocks for broader multilateral agreements; and the resolution of nagging trade and investment problems in sectors such as autos and energy.

Given the dependence of the Canadian economy on exports to the United States, the Canadian objective had a more singular focus: to attain greater security of access to the US market, particularly through reforms of US trade remedy laws. These goals were reshaped during the negotiations, as the

1

scope of possible agreements was clarified. In the end, the negotiators sought seven basic objectives:[1]

☐ promote trade liberalization

☐ improve the climate for bilateral investment

☐ resolve bilateral problems in the auto trade

☐ resolve problems arising from disputes over the use of subsidies and countervailing duties

☐ create new rules to govern trade in services and liberalize the financial services market

☐ create a better framework for the conduct of bilateral investment and trade relations

☐ promote multilateral cooperation on trade and investment issues in the General Agreement on Tariffs and Trade (GATT).

The FTA deals with each of these issues in a surprisingly satisfactory manner. Notable gains were achieved in each of the areas. Both countries undertake important commitments to liberalize barriers to trade and investment and to "level the playing field" for bilateral economic relations. Some differences in the level of protection remain in certain areas, but the FTA provides balanced changes in policy from the preexisting situation. As such, the FTA provides a truly reciprocal bargain for both the United States and Canada. While the results were suboptimal and disappointing in a few instances, the deal is clearly a good one and merits ratification by the Congress.

Overall, the United States will benefit from the extensive new trading opportunities that result from the elimination of tariffs and many nontariff barriers that affect bilateral trade, from the reduction in Canadian investment controls that have restricted US holdings in Canada and often distorted trade flows, and from the enhanced security of access to Canadian energy supplies. More generally, the FTA protects US interests against a return to the inverventionist policies of the Trudeau era that provoked numerous trade and investment disputes. The FTA will promote increased US exports to Canada, facilitate US investment, *inter alia,* in the Canadian financial

---

1. This list is similar to the five specific objectives of the negotiations set out in Article 102 of the FTA: to eliminate trade barriers to goods and services; to promote fair trade; to improve the investment climate; to establish joint procedures to administer the FTA and to resolve disputes; and to promote further cooperation on trade and investment issues both bilaterally and multilaterally.

services sector, and enhance US energy security—and with a slightly positive impact on overall US income and employment.[2]

Most important, the FTA will encourage increased efficiency and productivity in US industry and thereby enhance US competitiveness in world markets. This is an essential prerequisite for the sustained US effort needed to regain market share at home and abroad to bring the global US current account back into equilibrium.

Given the importance of sustained export-led growth for the US economy in the near and medium term, because of the unsustainability of the present deficit of $150 billion in the US current account, the systemic benefits that result from the FTA may perhaps prove more significant than the bilateral economic benefits for the United States. True to the "bicycle theory" of trade policy, the FTA maintains momentum for trade liberalization and thus helps counter the drift toward protectionism. The FTA puts the "bicycle" of trade liberalization upright and moving forward. In so doing, the FTA also provides a boost to the GATT and the new Uruguay Round of negotiations. In particular, dispute settlement procedures in the FTA set important precedents for GATT, particularly the resort to binding arbitration and surveillance of national trade policies. In addition, FTA provisions on services and investment are pathbreaking steps in the development of international rules to guide government policies in areas that have not been subject to extensive international discipline.

While the FTA provisions do not provide a complete model for a GATT agreement in these areas, they do contain elements—particularly the elaboration of specific rights and obligations on national treatment, right of establishment and performance and other requirements—that can help negotiators in Geneva to craft a multilateral accord. The importance of this should not be understated: the success of the Uruguay Round will depend importantly on the development of new rules on dispute settlement, services, and investment, as well as the resolution of agricultural trade disputes (see Hufbauer and Schott 1985).

As in any negotiation, there were disappointments that need to be weighed against the benefits noted above. In several respects, the agreement did not improve the existing situation to the desired extent—and, in some cases, the FTA did not change it at all. In none of these areas, however, does the FTA result in a situation less desirable than presently exists.

The FTA achieved suboptimal results in five main areas: subsidies,

---

2. The real income and employment gains for Canada will be relatively greater, as one would expect given the disparities in size between the two economies. However, that also means that Canada will face greater adjustment pressures as it reorients its economy to take advantage of the improved access to a market more than 10 times its size.

investment in the energy sector, government procurement, transportation, and intellectual property rights. The failure to develop new rules on the use of domestic subsidies is the most significant, leaving a wide range of practices (including investment incentives) subject only to the discipline of national countervailing duty laws. The FTA provides for continued bilateral negotiations in this area, but the more fruitful avenue for progress may lie in the multilateral talks in the GATT.

Similarly, the absence of provisions on transportation services and on intellectual property rights is disappointing because of the lost opportunity to achieve meaningful reforms and new guidelines for public policy. By contrast, the FTA provisions on government procurement do open up new trading opportunities, but fail to make progress in extending discipline to procurement of services, or of subnational governments, or of new entities whose merchandise purchases are currently not subject to GATT rules.

The FTA also exempts Canadian energy industries from several important investment reforms. In particular, the maintenance of the Canadian ownership requirement could have a dampening effect on the development of oil and gas resources and thus offset over the long term at least some of the FTA gains in terms of enhanced US energy security.

The benefits and disappointments of the FTA from the US perspective will be elaborated in the following sections. I will first discuss the FTA from a macroeconomic perspective, including a review of its relationship to the exchange rate issue. I then review the bilateral economic relationship and the issues involved in the ratification of the FTA. Finally, I analyze the results of the FTA and conclude with a balance sheet of costs and benefits for the United States.

The FTA In Macroeconomic Perspective

The FTA comes at a crucial juncture for the US economy and for the world trading system. The record trade and current account deficits of the past few years have dug the US economy into a deep hole. Over the next five years or so, the United States will need an improvement of $100 to $150 billion in its current account, with an even more substantial reduction in the merchandise trade deficit because of the growing deficit on services that results from interest payments on the rapidly increasing US foreign debt (see Statement 1987, p. 3, and Bergsten 1987). This massive adjustment will require a sharp increase in US exports (particularly manufactures) and a recapture of some of the domestic market lost to foreign competitors in the early to mid-1980s when the dollar became substantially overvalued. This in turn will require an enhancement in the competitiveness of American industry and a reduction in foreign barriers to US exports, and the FTA will contribute at least modestly to both objectives.

At the same time, the extensive application of quantitative trade restrictions (especially via voluntary export restraints) has contributed to a growing trend toward protectionism and an erosion in the discipline of world trading rules (see Bergsten et al. 1987). A reversal of this trend is essential both to provide the framework needed for an expansion of US exports, as noted, and to avoid all the economic and political risks associated with market closure around the world. The current "Uruguay Round" of multilateral trade negotiations now under way in Geneva is perhaps the best chance to reinvigorate the GATT trading system.

As shown below, the FTA should spur an increase in trade between the United States and Canada. Some of the increase will result from the reduction of barriers provided by the FTA itself. Some will reflect the improved competitiveness of North American firms due to productivity gains. Some will reflect the substitution of trade from third countries as a result of the removal of bilateral trade barriers.

Some trade diversion will occur as a result of the FTA. US exports to Canada, and Canadian exports to the United States, should grow at the expense of goods from Japan, Germany, and other countries that will still face tariff and nontariff barriers. The overall trade-creating effect of the FTA should compensate third countries for at least some of these losses, however. In other words, the FTA should result in an expanded economic pie: the FTA preferences should enable US and Canadian firms to capture a greater share of the expanding markets, but third countries, though they may lose market share, may still be able to maintain or even expand sales in absolute terms.

The FTA should lead to an improvement in the US bilateral trade deficit with Canada, not necessarily at the expense of Canadian trading interests, but rather because US exports should displace some Japanese and European exports to the Canadian market. As a statement by 33 economists on the global economic crisis noted in December 1987, the US adjustment will have to come at the expense of countries with *global* surpluses such as Japan, Germany, and some of the newly industrializing countries (NICs) in Asia— and not from countries like Canada with their own current account problems (see Statement 1987).

What will the FTA contribute to this adjustment process? The most significant benefits will come from the increased productivity that will result as firms take advantage of the reduced bilateral barriers to trade and investment. Firms in both countries will gain from a reduction in input costs and from improved market access, which will enable them to achieve greater economies of scale in production and to redirect resources to more competitive product sectors. As such, the FTA will promote intra- and interindustry specialization.

Some adjustment will have to take place in both economies, but the aggregate changes should be small. Moreover, the FTA should create a better environment for economic growth, thus facilitating the adjustment process. Inevitably, some problems will arise at the plant level. Such dislocations should be accommodated, as appropriate, through national adjustment programs. As such, the US trade adjustment assistance program should be reviewed to ensure that it can meet that need.

Econometric estimates of the effect of the FTA—done mostly in Canada—indicate that, for Canada, the FTA will push real income to a higher level by 2.5 percent to 3.5 percent of GNP; estimates for the United States are much smaller, and considerably less than 1 percent of GNP (see Canadian Department of Finance 1988 and Shea 1988). The asymmetry is understandable, given the fact that Canada will obtain better access to a market that is more than 10 times its size, while US producers gain only a small increment to their already large home market.

Some may be surprised at the relatively small size of the gains of the FTA to economic output in both the United States and Canada. Clearly, the FTA is not a panacea for all the ills of either economy. Nonetheless, the trade and investment reforms in the FTA are significant actions that can contribute to the resolution of those problems. Seldom do governments have the opportunity to take actions that by themselves have such permanently beneficial impacts on their economies.

The Exchange Rate Issue

Misaligned currencies effectively can subsidize or tax goods and services traded across borders.[3] Such effects could offset benefits derived from the FTA. Indeed, when the FTA talks began, the US dollar was generally considered to be substantially overvalued, and some felt that it was overvalued against the Canadian dollar as well. Questions were raised by US Trade Representative Clayton Yeutter and others as to whether the relatively low level of the Canadian dollar constituted an implicit barrier to bilateral trade, particularly when the Canadian dollar dropped below 70 cents in early 1986—despite the fact that Canada itself consistently was running a global current account deficit.

---

3. A country whose currency is undervalued sees its exports priced lower (in terms of the currency of the importing market) than would be the case if equilibrium exchange rates prevailed; similarly, imports into its market cost more. The reverse is true for an overvalued currency that "taxes" exports and "subsidizes" imports.

To address these concerns, John Williamson estimated the fundamental equilibrium exchange rate (FEER) of the Canadian dollar (see appendix to Wonnacott 1987a). He found that in mid-1985 the Canadian dollar was slightly undervalued; his mid-range estimate of the FEER was then about 74 cents. The Canadian dollar has since appreciated considerably from its trough to a level of about 80 cents in March 1988. Moreover, the FTA could well lead the Canadian dollar to strengthen further over time because of the real income gains that result from the FTA (Wonnacott 1987a).

Despite recent developments in the exchange markets, there are lingering concerns that currency misalignments could distort bilateral trade flows in the future. The National Association of Manufacturers (NAM) has called for a bilateral consultative mechanism on exchange rates; the AFL-CIO has taken a more extreme position, seeking parity between the Canadian and US dollars.[4] Both positions reflect the heightened sensitivity of business and labor to currency misalignments as a result of the devastating impact on US trade of dollar overvaluation in the mid-1980s.

In essence, the NAM would like finance ministers to focus more attention on the implications of exchange rate policies on trade flows, and perhaps to include trade ministers in their talks. Bilateral consultations are already a subset of the multilateral consultative mechanism of the G-7 countries, but setting up regular bilateral trade-finance contacts could reinforce that process. By contrast, the AFL-CIO demand for parity is completely without merit. The US and Canadian dollars were at parity at times in the early 1970s; since then, however, the economies have experienced significantly different results, including substantially higher rates of inflation and unemployment in Canada.

The FTA sidesteps the exchange rate issue and contains no provisions on bilateral consultations or management of the US and Canadian dollars. Both governments leave that task to the ongoing efforts of finance officials in their regular bilateral contacts, in multilateral consultative bodies, and in the International Monetary Fund. The current situation would seem to be satisfactory, at least from a US standpoint, and hence its absence from the FTA should not cause a problem for the ratification process.

The Bilateral Economic Relationship

For the United States, the FTA presents a long-overdue opportunity to refocus attention on the important economic relationship with Canada.

---

4. See, for example, statements by Alexander B. Trowbridge, president of the NAM, and by Rudolph Oswald, director of economic research of the AFL-CIO, before the Subcommittee on Commerce, Consumer Protection, and Competitiveness of the House Energy and Commerce Committee, 23 February 1988.

Although Canada is the largest US trading partner, and Americans have substantial holdings in the Canadian economy, US–Canadian relations have received less priority from US policymakers than relations with Japan or Germany or Mexico or even the NICs. In Washington the squeaky wheel attracts attention; it is perhaps a tribute to the strength and durability of the US bilateral relationship with Canada that it has been treated with such benign neglect in the past.

The United States and Canada conduct the world's largest bilateral trade in goods and services. As shown in table 1.1, merchandise trade totaled almost $133 billion in 1987; US exports reached almost $60 billion and US imports were about $73 billion. About one-third of this trade is in automotive products that is already substantially free of trade restrictions. Bilateral trade in services was also significant and approached $31 billion in 1987, with US exports of $20.5 billion and imports of $10.2 billion. The substantial US surplus results primarily from the investment income received from US investments in Canada, though the United States also runs a surplus in nonfactor services trade (see Schott and Smith 1988). The aggregate US bilateral trade in goods and services in 1987 was slightly in deficit, with US exports of $80.3 billion and US imports of $82.9 billion.

The narrowing of the US deficit in the bilateral current account since 1985 results from largely offsetting trade and income flows. For the past five years, the US merchandise trade deficit with Canada has averaged almost $14 billion. However, the US trade deficit with Canada peaked in 1985 at $15.7 billion and declined to $12.9 billion in 1987. By contrast, the US surplus on factor and nonfactor services has averaged almost $11 billion for the past five years. Both balances seem to be moderating, however, in light of the recent appreciation of the Canadian dollar vis-à-vis the US dollar, and the growth of Canadian direct investment in the United States since 1983 (which should bolster Canadian investment income in coming years).

A discussion of the balances also masks the enormous difference in importance of bilateral trade to the two economies. As shown in table 1.1, US trade with Canada accounts for less than a quarter of US exports and less than a fifth of US imports. The export market share has grown during the 1980s, however, from 18 percent in 1980 to 23.6 percent in 1987—and Canada remains America's largest trading partner. By contrast, the United States accounts for almost three-fourths and two-thirds of Canadian exports and imports, respectively. The US market also has been of growing importance for Canadian exports, accounting for almost 77 percent in 1985–1986 compared to 62 percent in 1980 (see table 1.2). Canadian exports to the United States account for almost 20 percent of Canadian GNP, while US exports to Canada represent only 1.3 percent of US GNP.

The increasing Canadian dependence on the US market helps explain

Table 1.1 US trade with Canada* (billion US dollars)

	Merchandise exports	Percent of total US exports	Merchandise imports	Percent of total US imports	Trade balance	Services exports	Services imports	Bilateral current account balance
1980	40.7	18.0	42.0	17.1	−1.3	15.2	6.6	7.3
1981	44.6	18.7	47.4	18.2	−2.8	15.1	5.8	6.5
1982	38.1	17.6	47.8	19.6	−9.7	14.6	5.1	−0.2
1983	43.1	21.0	54.8	21.2	−11.7	17.4	6.1	−0.4
1984	51.7	23.1	67.1	20.6	−15.4	18.6	7.3	−4.1
1985	53.9	24.6	69.6	20.2	−15.7	16.6	7.5	−6.6
1986	55.6	24.5	68.9	18.8	−13.3	18.1	7.0	−2.2
1987	59.8	23.6	72.7	17.9	−12.9	20.5	10.2	−2.6

* Data include adjustments for undocumented exports and other reconciliation adjustments. Imports are on a customs value basis. Services trade data for 1987 are at an annualized rate based on statistics for the first nine months of 1987.

Source: US Department of Commerce, Bureau of the Census, *Advance Report of US Merchandise Trade: December 1987, FT 900 ADV*, 12 February 1988; *Survey of Current Business*, various issues (Table 10: US International Transactions, by area).

Table 1.2 Canadian dependence on US trade (percentage)

	Exports to US as share of total Canadian exports	Imports from US as share of total Canadian imports	Canadian exports to US as percent of Canadian GNP	US exports to Canada as percent of US GNP
1980	62.0	66.7	16.3	1.5
1981	65.2	65.3	16.5	1.5
1982	67.1	67.2	16.3	1.2
1983	71.7	68.2	17.1	1.3
1984	74.4	68.0	20.1	1.4
1985	76.7	68.1	20.4	1.3
1986	76.8	66.5	19.4	1.3
1987	73.1	67.1	18.5	1.3

Source: IMF, *International Financial Statistics* (February 1988) and *Direction of Trade Statistics Yearbook* 1987.

Canada's strong interest in market access assurances—which subsequently led Canada to be the demandeur in the FTA negotiations. Until 1985, however, interest in bilateral trade negotiations was not particularly strong in either country.

In the United States, the focus of trade policy in the early 1980s was the launching of a new round of multilateral trade negotiations, under the auspices of the General Agreement on Tariffs and Trade (GATT), to extend or expand GATT coverage of services, trade-related investment and intellectual property issues, and agricultural programs. The failure of the 1982 GATT Ministerial prompted a search for alternative strategies, however. Bilateral trade agreements with "like-minded countries" were seen as both building blocks for potential GATT accords and a fallback in case GATT talks failed. Negotiations took place with countries in the Caribbean basin and with Israel. Indeed, the free trade agreement with Israel—though more important from a political than an economic perspective—established a precedent that could be applied to the much more substantial economic relationship with Canada.

The bilateral approach also seemed to fit better with congressional skepticism about the GATT. The 1982 GATT Ministerial badly damaged the credibility of the GATT (see Schott 1983) and led to efforts to develop new US trade legislation that would protect US trading interests more effectively and expeditiously than GATT procedures. This effort grew more strident and more protectionist as the record US trade deficits mounted in successive years. The Reagan administration successfully opposed domestic content and textiles legislation, but the omnibus trade bill of 1984 was salvaged at the last moment by the removal of numerous protectionist provisions, although new qualifications were added on the use of fast-track provisions for implementing bilateral trade agreements, which, as noted below, almost resulted in the early demise of the FTA process (see Destler 1986). However, these legislative "achievements" came at a high cost in administered protection, notably tightened controls on bilateral textile trade, new restrictions in the Multi-Fiber Arrangement, and extensive voluntary export restraints on steel and several other products. Indeed, Treasury Secretary Baker has boasted that the Reagan administration has defended American trade interests by imposing more protection than any other administration in the past 50 years (Baker 1987).

In this environment, and with growing Canadian dependence on exports to the United States, it is not surprising that the new Conservative government of Brian Mulroney reappraised its opposition to bilateral trade negotiations with the United States in early 1985. The Canadian economy was buffeted by high unemployment and a sharp decline in its terms of trade due to the slump in commodity markets.[5] It could therefore ill afford additional doses of US protectionism.

The "Shamrock" Summit between President Ronald Reagan and Prime Minister Brian Mulroney in Quebec in March 1985 set both countries on track for bilateral trade liberalization. The goal was "to establish a climate of greater predictability and confidence for Canadians and Americans alike to plan, invest, grow and compete more effectively with one another and in the global market."[6] To that end, they directed their trade officials to determine how to "reduce and eliminate existing barriers to trade" and to report back within six months, and to resolve a list of longstanding bilateral trade problems.

Following the recommendations of the report issued on 5 September 1985 of the Royal Commission on the Economic Union and Development Prospects of Canada, chaired by former Canadian finance minister Donald Macdonald, the Canadian government decided a few weeks later to broaden this effort to encompass the negotiation of a bilateral free trade agreement. President Reagan concurred and formally notified Congress on 10 December 1985 of his intention to negotiate a trade agreement with Canada under the fast-track implementing procedures as amended by the Trade and Tariff Act of 1984.

Under the new fast-track provisions as extended to bilateral arrangements in 1984, the House Ways and Means Committee or the Senate Finance

---

5. For further discussion, see the appendix by John Williamson in Wonnacott (1987a).

6. Declaration by the Prime Minister of Canada and the President of the United States of America Regarding Trade in Goods and Services, Quebec, 18 March 1985.

Committee had 60 legislative days to disapprove of the President's initiative. After a rancorous debate, the vote by the Senate Finance Committee in April 1986 ended in a 10-10 tie, thus allowing the FTA negotiations to proceed by the slimmest of margins. To achieve this result, however, the President had to commit to "finding a rapid and effective solution to the Canadian softwood lumber problem . . . independent of the comprehensive negotiations."[7] Action on softwood lumber, as well as the imposition of tariffs in May 1986 against Canadian imports of wood shingles and shakes pursuant to an escape clause case, created an inauspicious start for the FTA negotiations on 21 May 1986 in Ottawa. It did, however, provide Canada with a sharp reminder of the risks involved in *not* going forward with the FTA process.

One need not recount the vagaries of the negotiating process, which languished for more than a year before entering a final, frantic stage starting in the summer of 1987. This last push was driven by the need to conclude talks by 3 October 1987 to meet the 90-day prenotification requirement to qualify for the fast-track implementing procedures that expired on 2 January 1988. This deadline was met with only minutes to spare. However, the negotiators produced only the framework of an agreement, including a general description of the major concessions agreed to by both countries. The final text was not completed until 9 December 1987 and was signed by President Reagan and Prime Minister Mulroney on 2 January 1988.

The Ratification Issue

The governments of the United States and Canada now face the responsibility of ratifying and then implementing the historic agreement that they have negotiated. The ratification debate already has been joined in both countries.

In the United States, ratification of the FTA will be facilitated by the fast-track procedures of the Trade Act of 1974, which require an up-or-down vote on the entire FTA package without amendment within 90 legislative days of submission of implementing legislation by the President. Given the congressional calendar, it is possible that such a vote could be delayed until 1989, after the planned entry into force of the FTA on 1 January 1989. However, the procedure worked out in an exchange of letters in February 1988 between the administration and congressional leaders—which provides for the joint drafting of implementing legislation for the FTA—commits to a ratification vote in 1988. The administration promised to "accept the provisions worked out in the consultative process provided they are con-

---

7. Letter of President Ronald Reagan to Senator Bob Packwood, 8 May 1986.

sistent with the Agreement and its implementation and are appropriate to carrying out its fundamental purposes."[8]

By cooperating in this way with the Congress on the FTA legislation, the administration increases the probability that provisions of the omnibus trade bill (HR 3) will be modified in conference so that certain provisions of the bill that could upset the negotiated balance of concessions in the FTA—notably those relating to changes in the antidumping and countervailing duty law—will be dropped. If they are not, the President can still veto the omnibus bill as he frequently has threatened to do. The exchange of letters should lessen the threat that the FTA implementing legislation will be "held hostage" to administration acceptance of the omnibus trade bill, or that there will be a strong backlash against the FTA bill if the President vetoes the omnibus trade bill.

A more likely threat, however, may come from efforts by particular domestic interests to "claw back" reforms contained in the FTA, effectively amending the FTA package through provisions in the FTA implementing legislation.[9] Indeed, the US maritime industry already achieved a major clawback in the FTA while the final text was being drafted in November 1987 by forcing the deletion of provisions that could have exempted Canada from *future* changes in US maritime restrictions (such as the Jones Act). As a result, the entire transportation sector was eliminated from the services chapter. If provisions of the implementing legislation are inconsistent with the FTA, it could prompt reciprocal actions by Canada and result in the unraveling of the FTA package.[10] However, the President has the final word on the composition of the FTA implementing bill since he submits the proposed legislation to the Congress under the fast-track procedures, and has said he will not approve such provisions.

In Canada, the implementing process under the parliamentary system of government is more predictable. The ruling Conservative Party has a large majority in the House of Commons and will eventually prevail over the Liberal majority in the non-elected Senate, which can delay but not block acceptance of the FTA. Ratification is therefore almost assured as long as the Conservatives remain in power. The Liberal Party opposes the FTA,

---

8. Letter of James A. Baker III and Clayton Yeutter to Jim Wright, Dan Rostenkowski, Robert Byrd, and Lloyd Bentsen, 17 February 1988.

9. For example, auto parts manufacturers in both countries recently have called for an increase in the North American origin requirement in the FTA from 50 percent to 60 percent to encourage greater use of US and Canadian products. The impact of such a change is discussed below in the section on autos.

10. Clawbacks are not unique to the United States. A Canadian proposal for a duty remission scheme for textiles threatens to undercut FTA tariff concessions and to provoke reciprocal withdrawals in US concessions in the FTA.

however, and may seek to revise the agreement if it returns to office in an election that must be held by late summer 1989.

A more delicate problem remains, however, as to whether some provinces will abide by certain specific obligations (for example, on wine) under the FTA. Article 103 of the FTA commits both national governments to ensure compliance by state, provincial, and local governments. The failure of those subnational governments to comply would be considered a violation of a national obligation and could be subject to retaliation or compensation under FTA provisions.

What would happen if the FTA was not ratified by both countries? The domestic process is not without its pitfalls. The squeaky wheels are already sounding in Washington, Ottawa, and some states and provinces. Some argue that the FTA does not meet their expectations; others complain that the agreement is unbalanced, at least in particular sectors; and still others want more protection, not trade liberalization. These concerns will have to be weighed against the significant economic and systemic benefits of the FTA detailed below.

However, the issue facing both countries is more complicated than that. One cannot turn back the clock to the Shamrock Summit of March 1985 and continue bilateral relations as if the negotiations had never occurred. Expectations have been raised by the FTA process; having tried and failed would be much worse than not having tried at all. The rejection of the FTA at this stage *by either country* would have a substantial impact on US–Canadian economic and political relations, which has to be considered in the cost-benefit analysis of the FTA.

The failure to ratify would be costly to both bilateral relations and to the GATT process. A US rejection would likely provoke a nationalist response in Canada that would adversely affect bilateral relations. Furthermore, it would cast serious doubt on the willingness of the United States to pursue trade reforms. It would thus send a damaging signal to the GATT—if two countries with complementary economies, extensive bilateral trade and investment, and a long history of friendship cannot succeed in liberalizing trade, what hope is there for the more heterogeneous GATT negotiations? The "bicycle" would be seen to be toppling, and the GATT system would suffer a loss in terms of the effort to renew momentum toward trade liberalization.

Canadian rejection of the FTA also would have profound implications for bilateral trade relations. As the leading US trading partner, Canadian exports could be affected by changes over time in US antidumping and countervailing duty laws, which could provoke a wave of new trade disputes. In addition, the United States could resort quite possibly to 301 actions against discriminatory trade and investment practices in Canada, following the precedent of US policies vis-à-vis Japan, Korea, and Taiwan. As such, the trend toward process protectionism in the United States would be reinforced. A key reason for Canada to ratify the FTA is to subscribe to an important insurance policy against potential trade problems with the United States.

Analysis of the FTA Results

The FTA covers a wide range of sectors and functional issues. The following sections detail the specific benefits and shortcomings in each area.

Trade Liberalization

Both the United States and Canada will benefit from the elimination of tariffs on bilateral trade, the opening up of more government contracts to competitive bidding, the liberalization of energy trade, and the removal of some barriers to agricultural trade. The following subsections provide preliminary estimates of the economic consequences of the FTA reforms in these areas.

Tariffs—One of the major achievements of the FTA is the elimination of all tariffs—without exception—between the two countries over a ten-year period. Tariffs on some products will be eliminated immediately, but most of the cuts will be phased in over five to ten years in equal annual installments.

Existing tariffs are generally low in the United States, though high tariffs remain in sectors such as apparel and some chemicals. The average duty collected on dutiable imports from Canada in 1985 was only 3.3 percent, or 0.9 percent of the total value of Canadian imports (most of which already enter duty-free). Canadian tariffs are substantially higher, averaging 9.9 percent on dutiable US imports. Including duty-free US imports, however, the average Canadian levy on US goods falls to 2.4 percent. Given the current relatively low tariff barriers, one should not expect dramatic trade gains *in the aggregate* from the FTA tariff cuts. Despite the low average tariff, however, some industries currently are protected by high tariffs and thus substantial shifts in trade could occur in specific sectors.

As shown in table 1.3, based on 1985 data for dutiable imports, 35 percent or $6.7 billion of US dutiable imports from Canada, and 53.4 percent or $7.2 billion of Canadian dutiable imports from the United States, will be subject to a 10-year phase-out. The products with the longest phase-out generally are also those with the highest tariffs: almost 50 percent of US

Table 1.3 Staging of FTA tariff cuts

	1/1/89		1/1/94		1/1/99		Total	
	US	Canada	US	Canada	US	Canada	US	Canada
Value of trade affected (million 1985 US dollars)	1,105	1,760	11,281	4,549	6,670	7,230	19,056	13,540
Percentage of dutiable imports for which tariffs are eliminated*	5.8	13	59.2	33.6	35	53.4	100	100
Value of duties affected (million 1985 US dollars)	43.7	82.9	272.7	447.9	307.6	806.2	624	1,337
Percentage of duties collected on bilateral trade	7	6.2	43.7	33.5	49.3	60.3	100	100

Source: US Department of Labor. (Preliminary data as of February 1988)
*Excluding petroleum and products, subject to 5-year US staging, the US cuts are 9, 47, and 44 percent in 1989, 1994, and 1999 respectively.

duties collected and 60 percent of Canadian duties collected come from products with a 10-year phase-out. However, the dollar value of the duties affected by the cuts—i.e., the revenue foregone from the tariff cuts—was more than twice as large for Canada in 1985 as for the United States ($1.3 billion versus $624 million).

The tariff cuts should lead to increased *bilateral* exports by both countries. The size of the increase and the impact on the bilateral trade balance are difficult to estimate, however. Much depends on the trade-creating effect of the increase in real income for producers and consumers that results from the economies of scale, lower production costs, and increased productivity generated by the trade and investment reforms.

Part of the effect can be estimated, however, through a partial equilibrium analysis of the impact of the tariff cuts. Tables 1.4 and 1.5 contain preliminary calculations that indicate that US exports to Canada should increase by about $2.4 billion compared to a Canadian gain of $1.1 billion (both figures in 1985 US dollars) after all the tariff cuts are implemented fully.[11] These figures represent only the tip of the iceberg of the trade effect of the FTA and undoubtedly underestimate the total trade creation and overestimate the bilateral gain for the United States that will result from the growth in both economies. For example, the calculations capture only increases in products already traded. In some instances, new opportunities will be created for products that have not been exported in the past; these gains are not included in the above estimates. Moreover, the calculations do not reflect the potential increase in intraindustry trade. As has been demonstrated in the auto sector since 1965, trade can grow substantially within the same industry as companies specialize in particular product lines.

In many sectors, exports grow in both countries, indicating that the FTA cuts will result in *intra-* as well as *inter*industry specialization. As shown in tables 1.4 and 1.5, bilateral trade in machinery, chemicals, and scientific instruments should grow substantially when the tariff cuts are phased in. Exports will increase in both countries, but in these sectors and others the growth in US exports should be higher. In other sectors such as paper, the reverse is true, and Canada should gain proportionately more than the United States.

What this means is that the tariff cuts will promote the adjustment of industries on both sides of the border. Some dislocations may occur but they are likely to be small. Moreover, adjustment should be eased by the extended phase-in period of the tariff cuts. In addition, since much of the adjustment will be intraindustry, the impact on labor should be eased somewhat because skills should be similar and relocations should often take place within the same firm and/or close geographic area.

Where particular adjustment problems exist, affected industries can benefit from national adjustment assistance programs to facilitate worker retraining and relocation. Existing programs should be reinforced to better accommodate adjustments that may result from the FTA.

In the aggregate, there should be net employment gains in both countries as trade expands and real income grows over time. For the United States, however, the gains should be quite small in almost all sectors and barely noticeable from existing labor market fluctuations—according to recent

---

11. These figures are highly sensitive to the assumptions of the import demand elasticities. US imports probably are underestimated because the elasticity of demand for imports from Canada should be higher than the global import elasticity used in the calculation for each sector of US imports at the two-digit level.

Table 1.4 Impact of tariff cuts on US exports to Canada*

SIC	Industry	1985 Canadian dutiable imports from US (million dollars)	1985 Duties paid (million dollars)	Average duty (percent)	Import elasticity	Increased imports (million dollars)
35	Machinery	2,838	209	7.4	−2.07	404.8
36	Electrical machinery	1,661	172	10.4	−2.07	323.9
28	Chemicals	1,283	139	10.8	−2.07	258.9
34	Fabricated metals	1,013	104	10.3	−2.07	195.8
37	Transportation equipment	943	96	10.2	−2.07	180.7
38	Instruments	829	59	7.1	−2.07	113.8
30	Rubber	741	97	13.1	−2.13	182.8
33	Primary metals	724	50	6.9	−2.07	96.7
20	Food products	701	62	8.8	−0.76	43.1
26	Paper	513	45	8.8	−2.07	85.9
	Subtotal	11,246	1,033	9.2	−1.99	1,886.4
	Other industries	2,294	304	13.3	−2.07	557.4
	Total	13,540	1,337	9.9	−2.00	2,443.8

* Based on data as of October 1987. Minor revisions to conform the data with the new harmonized system of tariff nomenclature are currently being made by both governments.
Source: US Department of Labor, and Cline et al. (1978) for import elasticities.

estimates of the employment impact in 21 US industrial sectors (Shea 1988). This is consistent with the relatively small aggregate welfare gains for the US economy from the FTA. Employment gains will be generated primarily by the trade balance effect. However, if one uses the rule of thumb that 25,000 jobs are created in the United States for each $1 billion increase in net exports, US employment should expand by only about 32,000. By contrast, the Canadian government estimates that Canadian employment should increase by 120,000 jobs by 1993 due to the welfare effects noted above (Canadian Department of Finance 1988).

Government Procurement—The FTA will also open up significant new trading *opportunities* because the threshold of the contract value for the application of competitive bidding procedures and other rules provided for in the GATT

Table 1.5 Impact of tariff cuts on US imports from Canada*

SIC	Industry	1985 US dutiable imports from Canada (million dollars)	1985 Duties paid (million dollars)	Average duty (percent)	Import elasticity	Increased imports (million dollars)
13	Oil and gas extraction	4,429	15	0.3	−1.21	16.0
35	Machinery	2,090	74	3.5	−1.02	72.1
33	Primary metals	2,012	65	3.2	−1.21	75.5
29	Petroleum refining	1,610	13	0.8	−0.96	12.3
36	Electrical machinery	1,441	78	5.4	−1.00	73.8
20	Food products	956	46	4.8	−1.13	49.5
30	Rubber	863	38	4.4	−5.26	191.3
34	Fabricated metals	793	36	4.5	−1.40	47.8
28	Chemicals	790	69	8.7	−2.53	160.0
37	Transportation equipment	779	26	3.3	−3.28	81.6
25	Furniture	437	16	3.7	−3.00	46.8
38	Instruments	437	23	5.3	−1.70	37.4
26	Paper	341	12	3.5	−0.55	6.3
24	Wood products	266	13	4.9	−0.69	8.6
32	Stone, clay, and glass	258	11	4.3	−1.60	17.0
	Subtotal	17,502	535	3.1	−1.70	896.0
	Other industries	1,554	89	5.7	−2.00	167.6
	Total	19,056	624	3.3	−1.75	1,063.6

* See note to table 1.4.
Source: US Department of Labor, and Shiells, Stern, and Deardorff (1983) for import elasticities.

Government Procurement Code will fall from $171,000 to $25,000. The governments estimate that $3 billion of US contracts and $500 million of Canadian contracts will be affected by the lower threshold. Note, however, that the FTA does not extend GATT discipline to procurement by subnational governments, or expand the scope of entities subject to the rules, or include services contracts. As such, the FTA makes only a small inroad in reforming procurement practices and offers little in the way of precedent for the Uruguay Round negotiations.

How much trade will expand depends on the types of goods subject to competitive tender and the propensity to import such goods in each country instead of sourcing from domestic companies. In a study conducted before the FTA was completed, the Economic Council of Canada concluded that the removal of barriers to federal procurement of goods would result in a net gain of C$800 million (in 1984 prices) for Canada. However, the preponderance of the gains derive from increased sales of transport equipment other than motor vehicles, which are *not* subject for the most part to the FTA revisions. Without "other transport equipment," their estimates show that Canadian exports would increase by C$690 million and US exports by C$746 million (in 1984 C$), resulting in a net gain of C$56 million for the United States (Magun et al. 1987).

Energy—The FTA bans most border restraints and minimum price requirements on bilateral energy trade, which totaled about $10 billion in 1987. Most of the trade involves Canadian exports of natural gas, electricity, uranium, and oil—indeed, Canada was the largest supplier of oil to the United States in 1987.

The FTA contains broad-based commitments not to impose restrictions on imports and exports—including quotas, taxes, or price requirements—subject to limited national security and short supply exceptions. Compared to GATT rules, however, the energy security safeguards are sharply circumscribed. For example, the national security exemption is limited to fulfillment of military-related requirements, and short supply restrictions must provide for proportional sharing of supplies with the other country.

In essence, the FTA ensures that in most cases energy trade will be based on commercial considerations, with prices set by market forces. As such, the FTA protects against a repeat of the pricing disputes and the oil export controls and export taxes that Canada imposed during the decade following the 1973 OPEC oil shock. This should give US consumers greater assurance of access to energy supplies at market prices.

For electricity, the FTA restricts the application of Canadian surplus tests that could limit US access to Canadian supplies, and "least-cost energy alternative" pricing practices that tend to increase the price of Canadian electricity exports to the United States. As a result, key obstacles to New England's purchases from hydroelectric plants in Quebec will be removed. In addition, US consumers should also benefit somewhat from FTA provisions that accord Canadian producers of electricity improved, though still somewhat limited, access to the California market over the Northwest Intertie.

For natural gas, FTA provisions should promote trade by eliminating price discrimination and by facilitating consultations on regulatory disputes.

Canadian gas exports should continue to grow, although differences in regulatory policies in each country may slow progress. Assuming the necessary transportation facilities are built, the US Energy Department estimates that growth in domestic demand for natural gas should lead to a displacement of some oil imports, particularly from the Middle East.[12] As such, the FTA should help increase gas sales in the United States. While the impact of the FTA may differ by region, overall the FTA should help US gas producers.

The situation in uranium is different. Barriers to the export of Canadian uranium and to its enrichment in the United States will be lifted, removing a source of long-standing trade friction but subjecting the US industry to increased competition. US uranium producers have been dogged in recent years by overcapacity, by the slump in the nuclear power industry, and by excess inventories. The US industry has been consolidating, and this trend will continue with or without the FTA. Given the problems faced by the US uranium industry, the US government might consider providing adjustment assistance for the industry under the appropriate trade statutes to ease the burden of adjustment.

Some US producers have complained that the FTA market access guarantees leave them vulnerable to increased competition from energy imports from Canada. While this may be true for uranium, other Canadian energy imports represent only a small share of US consumption (5.3 percent of natural gas, 1.8 percent of electricity, and 3.6 percent of oil in 1985). Thus, increased Canadian energy imports—which as noted above will displace other imports in some instances—should not pose significant competitive problems for US producers. And if US industry is concerned that such trade benefits from subsidies, the FTA still allows recourse to protection under national countervailing duty statutes.

Overall, the energy section of the FTA reinforces US energy security and benefits US consumers, especially energy-intensive industries, by removing minimum price requirements and by enhancing supply access assurances. However, the stimulus to the development of energy resources that should result from increased trade and access guarantees needs to be weighed against the restrictive impact on exploration and development resulting from the grandfathering in the FTA of Canadian ownership restrictions in the energy sector. Such investment controls could impede the development

---

12. The US Department of Energy has estimated that over time natural gas could displace as much as 1 million barrels per day of imported oil. See statement of William F. Martin, Deputy Secretary of Energy, before the Subcommittees on International Economic Policy and Trade and Western Hemisphere Affairs of the House Committee on Foreign Affairs, 25 February 1988.

of North American energy supplies and thus could have a potentially adverse impact on long-run energy security (see Verleger 1988). This problem already exists and is not remedied by the FTA. Close bilateral cooperation is needed to ensure that this risk is avoided and that remaining investment controls are liberalized over time.

Agriculture—The United States and Canada are two of the world's largest exporters of grain and are strong supporters of liberalization in the agricultural sector. However, because of extensive quotas and licensing requirements, and the complementary nature of the farm economy in the two countries, trade in agricultural goods accounts for only about 4.5 percent of total bilateral trade.

While the FTA eliminates agricultural tariffs and removes some nettlesome nontariff barriers, the major farm policies in both countries are left untouched.[13] The most significant result is the immediate elimination of Canada's discriminatory pricing system for distilled spirits and the phaseout over seven years of barriers against wine imports. Both sides knew that reforms of national farm policies could only be accomplished in a multilateral context. As a result, they kept their powder dry in the North American talks awaiting the bigger battle in the GATT, where the United States is working closely with Canada and other members of the so-called Cairns Group to develop new multilateral disciplines on subsidies and other agricultural support programs (see Hathaway 1987).

Improvements in the Investment Climate

As the barriers to bilateral trade in goods and services are reduced substantially over the next decade, the FTA provisions on investment will become increasingly important. The agreement will ensure that companies can take advantage of new opportunities by scaling production to the enlarged North American market, and by pursuing intraindustry specialization strategies.

The FTA provisions improve the investment climate in both countries in two important respects. First, they establish common rights and obligations—including a commitment in most instances to national treatment—that

---

13. Some US farmers have complained about FTA benefits provided Canadian wheat producers, which currently supply less than 6 percent of the US market for hard red spring and durum wheat. The FTA provisions could lead to increased Canadian exports, which would affect primarily producers in the northern plains states. However, the aggregate economic impact should be small.

should preclude a repetition of the fractious investment disputes and policy reversals that put a cloud over US investment in Canada during the past decade. Second, both the investment and the financial services chapters should open up broad new opportunities for US investment in Canada, particularly in financial services.

The United States entered the FTA talks seeking to preclude a return to the interventionist investment policies of the Trudeau regime, when the National Energy Policy forced US divestment of holdings in Canadian energy companies, and when screening by the Foreign Investment Review Agency (now renamed Investment Canada) prompted US firms to forgo profitable investments or to commit to costly performance requirements as an implicit condition for approval of the investment. In many respects, the FTA removes the threat of a return to Canada's interventionist investment policies of the past.

After a short transition period, the FTA eliminates screening requirements in most cases for the establishment of new businesses in Canada by US interests (greenfield investments) and indirect US acquisitions, and raises the threshold for screening of direct acquisitions so that by 1992 it will apply only to about the top 600 firms in Canada. The FTA will reduce by more than 90 percent the number of Canadian firms for which screening would be required before US investments could be made. However, screening will still apply to US investments in firms accounting for a substantial proportion of the Canadian economy because of the relatively high concentration of Canadian industry typical of smaller economies. The FTA therefore removes numerous barriers to US investment in Canada, but leaves intact some controls over takeovers of major Canadian companies.

The FTA bars the introduction of new trade-related performance requirements, which have been used in the past to discourage foreign investment in Canada, to influence the location of investments, and to impose costly conditions on the sourcing of inputs and the distribution of final products. These changes apply to foreign investment in Canada only by US interests. While nontrade related performance requirements may still be imposed, the FTA makes them more difficult to impose and enforce because of the curtailment of screening by Investment Canada. This should be a major benefit for US companies seeking to invest in Canada.

In particular, the FTA makes significant progress in opening up new investment opportunities in the Canadian financial services sector. The FTA removes many restrictions on US banks that inhibited their expansion, including the 16 percent ceiling on the total assets of foreign subsidiaries in the Canadian market. Insurance companies will likewise benefit from the relaxation of the so-called "10/25 rule," which limits both individual and aggregate foreign participation in certain Canadian companies. This rule had restricted their investment opportunities in Canada and thus undercut their competitiveness in the Canadian market. In brief, the FTA will allow US companies to participate—with a distinct advantage over other foreign firms—in the dynamic growth and integration of Canadian financial markets.

In addition, the FTA contains numerous safeguards for US investors already established in Canada. In particular, it imposes the US-preferred international law standard to deal with expropriation claims to ensure adequate compensation, and provides a "right of exit" to sell holdings to US and other foreign investors.

Despite the liberalization of important investment controls and screening requirements by the Canadian government, the FTA does not create a completely open environment for investment in either country. Significant restrictions remain in sectors such as energy and in cultural industries, and screening still applies to US investments in the major Canadian companies. The United States also maintains its existing, though more limited, controls on inward foreign direct investment. In addition, the FTA does not discipline the use of investment incentives that can distort investment flows. Because of the remaining controls, critics of the investment chapter of the FTA have raised two serious concerns:

□ the FTA legitimizes exclusions from investment obligations for other than prudential, fiduciary, or national security reasons by exempting cultural industries, thereby creating an undesirable precedent for other international investment agreements

□ the FTA explicitly accepts the continuation of an asymmetrical policy regime, in which the United States maintains its open investment policy while Canada maintains some restrictions.

The latter concern is inspired in part by the prospect of hostile foreign takeovers of US firms in the aftermath of the sharp depreciation of the US dollar. While legitimate, this concern overemphasizes the shortcomings of the FTA and undervalues the US gains in several respects.

First, the FTA contains across-the-board exclusions for the cultural industries, not just for the investment chapter. The Canadian concern about cultural sovereignty was a unique aspect of the FTA negotiations given the proximity, and the prospective degree of integration, of the two economies. The exclusion of cultural industries need not set a precedent for open-ended exceptions to treaty obligations in investment negotiations in other contexts and in other forums.

Second, the asymmetry in investment policies is not ideal—the United States would have fared better with a Canadian policy as open as its own.

However, given current political constraints, it is uncertain whether greater liberalization than that achieved in the FTA would have been sustainable in Canada. The FTA reforms make it a great deal easier for US firms to invest in Canada. The FTA requires Canada to undertake substantial reforms in its investment policies. As such, the FTA reduces, but does not eliminate, the asymmetries in bilateral investment policies.

Before attaching too much importance to the remaining asymmetry in investment policies, however, one should consider other areas of the agreement where the United States achieves asymmetrical gains. A good example is financial services, where the Glass-Steagall Act continues to impair Canadian activity in the United States while the FTA substantially opens up the Canadian market for US banks, securities firms, and insurance companies. "Symmetry" would have compelled the United States to junk Glass-Steagall, or accept a level of discrimination in the Canadian market (since Canada does not maintain comparable barriers to commercial and investment banking). "Reciprocity," on the other hand, involves balanced changes in policy from the existing situation, but not necessarily the achievement of equal levels of protection. Clearly, in a "second-best" world, the United States and Canada are better off with reciprocal and substantial liberalization in both investment and financial services, even if the *sectoral* result is not symmetrical or balanced.

Resolution of Bilateral Auto Trade Problems

Since the negotiation of the Automotive Products Trade Agreement of 1965 (the Auto Pact), which eliminated tariff barriers—subject to specific Canadian safeguards noted below—for bilateral trade for most products with the notable exception of tires, the United States and Canada have had a growing and prosperous auto trade. The Auto Pact promoted the rationalization and integration of the North American auto market. The resulting intraindustry specialization spurred a dramatic growth in bilateral trade from less than $1 billion in 1965 when the Auto Pact was signed to more than $45 billion in 1986 (see Wonnacott 1987b). The auto sector now comprises about one-third of bilateral merchandise trade, by far the largest component of bilateral trade.

Given the scope and size of bilateral trade in this sector, it is not surprising that autos have been the subject of numerous bilateral trade disputes. Indeed, a subsidy/countervail dispute prompted the negotiation of the Auto Pact almost 25 years ago. That accord again has come under pressure due to the establishment by non-North American companies of new assembly and auto parts plants, abetted in Canada by duty-remission subsidy schemes. While the FTA negotiators did not attempt to reopen the Auto Pact, they did try—

and generally succeeded—in fixing many of the problems that have beset bilateral auto trade in recent years.

In particular, Canada agreed in the FTA to eliminate immediately its export-based duty-remission scheme and to phase-out its production-based scheme by the end of 1995, to remove its embargo on used cars within five years, and not to extend the benefits of the Auto Pact to new companies that have established assembly plants in Canada—essentially limiting the pact to the Big Three (General Motors, Ford, and Chrysler). The duty remission schemes encourage firms to produce in Canada *inter alia* by rebating Canadian import duties when production is exported. The schemes allow foreign assemblers in Canada to subsidize shipments to the United States and benefit from the duty-free access accorded by the Auto Pact (see Wonnacott 1987b). The FTA will remove the subsidies—albeit over time— that threatened to provoke a bitter countervailing duty case that could have wrecked the Auto Pact.

To date, the export-based duty-remission subsidies have not been very large. Potentially, however, they could have become quite troublesome as Japanese and other foreign subsidiaries in Canada began to take more advantage of the program by using the remissions to subsidize their exports to the United States. This threat has been preempted by the FTA. Furthermore, public information is not available on the extent of the production-based subsidies. The phase-out of this program pursuant to the FTA could possibly be of much greater significance (see Wonnacott 1988).

US parts suppliers and labor unions remain unhappy with the FTA, however. Their demands for increased protection against competition from overseas suppliers, which predate the FTA talks, were not fully satisfied. In particular these groups wanted to curb multilateral sourcing by the Big Three automakers, which they claim is costing jobs in the US parts industry. By maintaining the Canadian safeguards, under which duty-free access to the Canadian market depends on Canadian production and value added requirements, the FTA does not afford greater protection for the domestic parts industry.

However, the FTA does redefine the production base from which companies calculate the level of North American content required to qualify for bilateral duty-free trade. Although this "rule-of-origin" requirement remains at 50 percent, the change in the method of calculation effectively increases the amount of US and Canadian-sourced parts needed to meet the origin requirement. In short, the FTA encourages somewhat the use of North American parts. However, both the US and Canadian parts industries would prefer a 60 percent origin rule, which would provide them greater protection against imported parts.

Furthermore, these US groups fear that if global overcapacity in the auto industry forces a rationalization of North American production, then plant closings would be more likely in the United States than in Canada because of the safeguards, Canadian investment incentives, and the differential in the external tariff (applied to third-country trade) of the two countries—Canada's tariff is higher and would afford more protection. Some rationalization in the auto sector undoubtedly will occur, but the concerns about potential job losses relate primarily to the press of global competition rather than to the FTA provisions in the auto sector.

Resolution of Subsidy/Countervail Problems

Disputes about subsidies and countervailing and antidumping duties have been a continual source of bilateral trade friction for decades. More recently, contentious antidumping (AD) and countervailing duty (CVD) cases such as those involving softwood lumber and potash have raised serious concerns in Canada about security of access to the US market.

Surprisingly, Canada has taken AD and CVD actions against bilateral trade much more frequently than the United States since the end of the Tokyo Round. The United States imposed CVDs against Canadian goods in 6 cases and ADs in 9 cases since 1980; Canada imposed 1 CVD (on corn) and 23 ADs. However, the trade affected by the US cases has been much greater (see Canadian Department of Finance 1988, p. 22).

The results of the FTA in these areas are mixed. As noted above, the subsidy problems of the Auto Pact were substantially fixed, but much less progress was made on developing new rules and discipline on subsidies and antidumping and countervailing duties in general. As a result, both countries maintain the right to resort to countervailing and antidumping duties under their national trade statutes to guard against injurious subsidies or predatory pricing practices.

Problems have occurred because many domestic subsidy programs fall into a gray area in the international trading rules where subsidies are permitted—but could trigger countervailing duties if goods benefiting from the subsidies are exported and injure the industry in the importing country. A negotiated solution involved two steps: agreeing on what types of domestic subsidy programs may be vulnerable to CVDs; and reducing or phasing out trade-distorting subsidies. Discipline on domestic subsidies and new rules on CVDs go hand in glove; progress on either is difficult without progress on both. The FTA negotiations sought to preempt future disputes by developing common policy guidelines for the treatment of specific national subsidy programs under each country's CVD law, but broke down on the inability to define domestic subsidies that could be actionable under CVD laws. The same problem plagued the Tokyo Round negotiators, and now confronts the Uruguay Round talks.

Unfortunately, most of the subsidy issues dealt with in the FTA could not be resolved in the bilateral context, because the political costs of removing the programs far outweighed the concessions that could be offered by the other country. Moreover, in some areas such as agriculture, discipline on US and Canadian subsidy practices would be ineffective in the absence of comparable reforms in Europe and Japan. Given the small size of most CVDs in bilateral cases, the FTA negotiators would have been better off to work out a *de minimus* rule for subsidies in bilateral CVD cases, as proposed last year by Paul Wonnacott (Wonnacott 1987a). Instead the FTA simply commits both countries to continue efforts to negotiate new disciplines in these areas over the next five to seven years, a time frame that can accommodate discussions in both bilateral and multilateral negotiating forums. The best hope for success, however, will be in Geneva in the Uruguay Round.

Does this mean the FTA failed in this area? Quite the contrary. While there may have been inflated expectations—as there always seem to be in subsidy negotiations—there were also some notable results. First, the FTA talks themselves should pave the way for a concerted joint effort by the United States and Canada in Geneva—while not reaching agreement for reasons noted above, the talks did bring about some convergence in the positions of both countries on prospective reforms of GATT rules. Second, the FTA did resolve the biggest sectoral subsidy problem affecting bilateral trade by phasing out auto subsidies.

Third, and perhaps most importantly, the FTA establishes an *ex post* procedure to resolve disputes about the consistency of final CVD orders with national laws and GATT obligations. Disputes on subsidy/CVD issues will be subject to binding arbitration. In theory, this should have no effect on the administration of the US CVD law because the procedure only applies as a surrogate for judicial review after the issuance of final orders. In practice, the disputes that arise under this procedure will probably occur in areas where national laws and GATT rules are vague, and need clarification.

As such, the most important impact of the bilateral subsidy/CVD dispute resolution procedure may be on the GATT negotiations. The FTA provisions relating to the resort to binding arbitration and surveillance of national trade policies could serve as models for important elements of an improved GATT dispute settlement system. Furthermore, clashes over CVD cases often lead to reforms of CVD rules, and the bilateral CVD dispute procedure could prove helpful in building a body of case law. For example, if the FTA procedures had been in place, the softwood lumber case would have been a perfect test case: the dispute revolved around differing interpretations of whether the Canadian stumpage payments constituted a "generally available" subsidy and of how to apply the "specificity" test under the GATT Subsidies Code rules. Rulings on such issues by a binational panel will help to define the gray areas of international rules on domestic subsidies that need to be clarified in the GATT talks.

Services

In services, the FTA broke new ground by establishing firm contractual obligations on services for both countries. The FTA elaborates a framework of rights and obligations regarding national treatment, establishment, and licensing and certification procedures (see Schott and Smith 1988). Bilateral services transactions had been substantially unaffected by international discipline because of the lack of coverage of services in the GATT, the absence of a bilateral treaty of friendship, commerce, and navigation, and the extensive reservations to the OECD codes on invisibles and capital movements. The FTA promotes fair trade in services by *creating* a playing field and rules of the game.

The FTA is better on rulemaking than on liberalization; almost all existing restrictions are grandfathered. This is not a problem in the bilateral context, however, given the relative openness of services trade (compared to other markets) and the low number of bilateral disputes that have arisen in the past. Moreover, the negotiation of a "standstill" obligation, under which each country commits to refrain from new laws and regulations that discriminate against services provided by the other country, should forestall new protectionism in these sectors. The greater certainty of the rules of the game and the scope of regulatory policies should help businesses to take better advantage of new trading opportunities.

The FTA does promote liberalization in some areas, however. The most notable reforms are in financial services as noted above. In addition, the liberalization of temporary entry procedures will facilitate the provision of professional labor services across the US–Canada border. Finally, some liberalization will occur as a result of annexes on architecture, tourism, and computer- and telecommunications-network-based enhanced services that elaborate how particular rights and obligations will be applied. The aggregate impact of these provisions is quite small, however, particularly in comparison to the potential liberalization that could have resulted if agreements had been reached in other service sectors, especially transportation.

Administration and Dispute Settlement

Despite the size and importance of the US–Canada economic relationship, the management of bilateral trade and investment issues usually has been accorded second-order priority by US officials. This was true even during the FTA negotiations up until the final weeks and in part explains the limited consultation with the Congress about the FTA itself. The implementation of the FTA should help remedy this neglect, for two reasons:

□ the FTA itself establishes a new framework for bilateral economic relations and extensive new rights and obligations that will have to be monitored and enforced

□ the consultative and dispute settlement procedures should help to preempt some disputes and more expeditiously resolve others.

The United States will have to devote more resources to the management of the bilateral relationship for two reasons. First, the FTA institutionalizes procedures for notification, consultation, and dispute resolution regarding measures affecting bilateral trade and investment. Second, because of the extensive rights and obligations of the FTA, the United States will have to monitor closely the implementation of the agreement to ensure that US rights under the FTA are safeguarded.

To this task, the FTA establishes a Canada–US Trade Commission, composed of the trade ministers of both countries and their representatives, to supervise the operation of the agreement and to resolve all disputes except those relating to subsidy/CVD and antidumping matters (noted above), and financial services (which will be handled through a separate consultative mechanism between the US Treasury and the Canadian Department of Finance). However, the administrative provisions of the FTA are not nearly as important as the dispute settlement procedures.

The FTA sets up two separate dispute mechanisms. One deals solely with subsidy/countervail problems as noted above; the other involves all other aspects of the FTA (see Horlick et al. 1988).

The general dispute settlement procedures serve two important functions. First, they provide a consultative forum to preempt potential disputes. When disputes do arise, the FTA sets out procedures to resolve them more expeditiously than currently available in the legal system of either country or in the GATT. The timetable for FTA dispute resolution is measured in months; by contrast, judicial appeals usually drag on for years. The GATT process is still prone to being blocked by disputants and by other delays, though some progress has been made in recent years to expedite settlements.

Second, the "early warning" consultations and the case law emerging from the decisions of binational panels should promote a convergence in national trade laws, particularly with regard to prospective changes in trade remedy laws. This should reduce the number of bilateral disputes and reinforce US and Canadian cooperation to achieve better GATT rules.

All this comes at very little cost to the United States. The FTA does not require the United States or Canada to make changes in the administration of national trade laws. It does, however, trigger consultations when trade measures or proposed changes in laws, regulations, or policies threaten to distort bilateral trade and investment flows and to impair the benefits derived under the FTA. In short, the procedures are designed to verify and secure the rights and obligations of the FTA.

Promotion of Multilateral Cooperation

The FTA should provide a boost not only for bilateral trade relations, but for the world trading system as well. The systemic benefits derive from three main areas:

□ The FTA helps to counter the protectionist drift of national trade policies and bolsters momentum for multilateral trade liberalization.

□ FTA provisions contain many useful precedents for the Uruguay Round negotiations.

□ The FTA reinforces the need for multilateral discipline in areas such as agriculture and subsidies.

If one subscribes to the bicycle theory of trade liberalization—which holds that momentum for trade reform must continually move forward else countries fall back to protectionism—then the reduction of trade barriers in the FTA should carry over and encourage trade reforms in the GATT talks as well. At a minimum, it should help to resist pressure for more protection in both countries. Indeed, the FTA is a reaffirmation of the open trade policy that underpins the GATT.

Second, the FTA provisions contain numerous innovations and useful models that could help negotiators work out multilateral agreements in the Uruguay Round (see Schott 1988). The chapters on services and investment are particularly important in this respect, as are some of the innovative approaches toward dispute settlement. The precedents set by the introduction of binding arbitration and surveillance of national trade policies could prove quite instructive for GATT negotiators grappling with the difficult task of reinforcing the GATT safeguards and dispute settlement systems. More work needs to be done in Geneva to bridge the gap between various national positions in these areas, but the FTA will help clarify the negotiating issues for the GATT as well as the negotiating objectives and positions of the United States and Canada.

Third, the FTA should redouble US and Canadian cooperative efforts to achieve a successful result in the Uruguay Round. Discipline on subsidies and agricultural programs—the biggest threats to the trade of both countries, though not necessarily to bilateral trade flows—remain unresolved and require the imposition of multilateral discipline that can only be negotiated in the GATT.

Some may argue, however, that the success of bilateralism reduces the value to both countries of the Uruguay Round negotiations. Given the lengthy duration of GATT talks, and the diluted influence of the United States over the outcome, the relative speed and success of the FTA negotiations could be seen as a reason to promote bilateralism instead of multilateralism. Indeed, Treasury Secretary James A. Baker comes close to supporting this view when he explicitly threatens to pursue trade liberalization among like-minded countries in a "market-liberalization club" if GATT talks bog down (see Baker 1988).

Such an approach might work well as a threat, but it would be a very costly policy to implement. Indeed, no one has shown how a comprehensive FTA on the model of the US–Canada agreement could be achieved with any other important trading partner.[14] Where past US efforts to open foreign markets have succeeded, they have resulted in special preferences for US suppliers to the detriment of other exporters. At times, US pressure has only resulted in a redistribution of import shares and not overall liberalization. Moreover, such efforts inevitably are imitated by other countries seeking their own special deals. In the end, such actions often result in market-sharing arrangements instead of market liberalization—an outcome that is clearly inferior to the maintenance of GATT for US trading interests.

Above all, however, both the United States and Canada need to build on the results of the FTA to support the GATT because of their weak trade and current account positions. Both countries will have to pursue export-led growth strategies in the coming years to restore their current accounts to equilibrium. To do so, they will need to expand exports beyond North America. While bilateral efforts to open markets could help if they are consistent with GATT, increased exports would be best promoted by multilateral liberalization under GATT auspices. In the end, this may be the most important reason for the United States not to turn protectionist and to pursue actively trade liberalization in the Uruguay Round.

---

14. These issues will be analyzed in more detail in my forthcoming study, *More Free Trade Areas?* Washington: Institute for International Economics.

Conclusion

Both the United States and Canada enter the FTA needing to bolster their external positions and to promote a stronger world trading system. Both will benefit from the expanded home base that the FTA provides to improve the competitiveness of their firms at home and abroad. The FTA contributes to that objective through significant trade reforms and through the establishment of a binational framework of rules that provide greater stability and predictability for trade and investment by both countries.

In each of the seven areas detailed above, the United States derives significant benefits from its participation in the FTA. Some may be disappointed that the FTA does not do more to curb subsidies; some may argue that their constituents have lost some protection and face adjustment pressures; and some may complain that many existing restrictions have been grandfathered under the agreement. But the sum of these disappointments does not outweigh the broad-based benefits that the United States will derive from the FTA.

Overall, the United States and Canada will profit significantly from the FTA, both through gains in efficiency and real income and through a strengthening of bilateral economic relations and the world trading system as a whole. The main results for the United States are summarized below.

First, the trade reforms in the FTA will spur growth in output and some minor employment gains. US exports will increase as a result of the elimination of tariffs, the opening up of additional government contracts to competitive bidding, and the liberalization of specific nontariff barriers. As importantly, the prohibition on trade-related performance requirements and other reforms in Canadian investment policy will allow US firms to take advantage of new opportunities in the Canadian market, particularly in the financial services sector. New contractual obligations on services and investment preclude the return to the more interventionist policies that sparked trade disputes in the past, and ensure that current Canadian policies evolve in the direction of nondiscrimination and liberalization.

Second, the FTA resolves many long-standing trade problems. It provides for the phase-out of subsidies in the auto sector under the Canadian duty-remission schemes, which had threatened to undermine the Auto Pact. The FTA also removes most border restraints and minimum price requirements on energy trade, and thus provides greater US security of access to Canadian energy resources whose availability and price in the past frequently were influenced by noncommercial considerations. In addition, the FTA removes important barriers to US exports of distilled spirits and wine.

Third, the FTA contains substantial systemic benefits for the United States. The FTA creates a much better framework for the conduct of bilateral economic relations in the future and for cooperative efforts to strengthen the GATT. The two-track dispute settlement procedures and the formation of the Canada–US Trade Commission should encourage closer consultations on bilateral problems, preempt the development of fractious trade disputes, and expedite the resolution of disputes that do occur. In particular, the provision for binding arbitration in CVD disputes should promote objectivity in the application of trade laws, removing a major source of discord in bilateral relations.

In addition, the FTA provides a big boost for GATT in two respects: the tariff cuts and other reforms maintain momentum for global trade liberalization; and the FTA provisions themselves contain many important implications for the negotiation of GATT accords. Aspects of the dispute settlement mechanisms—particularly recourse to binding arbitration and surveillance of national trade policies—as well as provisions of the services and investment chapters establish useful models for new GATT rules in these crucial areas in the Uruguay Round.

These systemic benefits for the United States are of utmost importance: the United States needs open access to foreign markets, as well as a more productive and competitive economy to take advantage of new trade opportunities, to help bring its current account back into balance. The FTA will support that effort by encouraging increased productivity in the US economy and by promoting a strong and effective multilateral trading system.

References

Baker, James A. III. 1987. "Remarks before a conference at the Institute for International Economics," 14 September.

Baker, James A. III. 1988. "The Geopolitical Implications of the US-Canada Trade Pact." *The International Economy,* January/February.

Bergsten, C. Fred. 1987. "Economic Imbalances and World Politics." *Foreign Affairs,* vol. 65, no. 4, 770-794.

Bergsten, C. Fred, Kimberly A. Elliott, Jeffrey J. Schott, and Wendy E. Takacs. 1987. *Auction Quotas and United States Trade Policy.* POLICY ANALYSES IN INTERNATIONAL ECONOMICS 19. Washington: Institute for International Economics, September.

Canadian Department of Finance. 1988. *The Canada-US Free Trade Agreement: An Economic Assessment.* Ottawa.

Cline, William R., Noboru Kawanabe, T.O.M. Kronsjo, and Thomas Williams. 1978. *Trade Negotiations in the Tokyo Round: A Quantitative Assessment.* Washington: Brookings Institution.

Destler, I. M. 1986. *American Trade Politics: System Under Stress.* Washington: Institute for International Economics, and New York: Twentieth Century Fund.

Hathaway, Dale E. 1987. *Agriculture and the GATT: Rewriting the Rules.* POLICY ANALYSES IN INTERNATIONAL ECONOMICS 20. Washington: Institute for International Economics, September.

Horlick, Gary N., Geoffrey D. Oliver, and Debra P. Steger. 1988. "Dispute Resolution Mechanisms." In Jeffrey J. Schott and Murray G. Smith, eds. *The Canada-United States Free Trade Agreement: The Global Impact.* Washington: Institute for International Economics.

Hufbauer, Gary Clyde, and Jeffrey J. Schott. 1985. *Trading for Growth: The Next Round of Trade Negotiations.* POLICY ANALYSES IN INTERNATIONAL ECONOMICS 11. Washington: Institute for International Economics, September.

Magun, Sunder et al. 1987. "Impact of Canada-US Free Trade on the Canadian Economy." Discussion Paper 331, Economic Council of Canada. Ottawa, August.

Schott, Jeffrey J. 1988. "Implications for the Uruguay Round." In Jeffrey J. Schott and Murray G. Smith, eds. *The Canada-United States Free Trade Agreement: The Global Impact.* Washington: Institute for International Economics.

Schott, Jeffrey J. 1983. "The GATT Ministerial: A Postmortem." *Challenge,* May/June.

Schott, Jeffrey J., and Murray G. Smith. 1988. "Services and Investment." In Jeffrey J. Schott and Murray G. Smith, eds. *The Canada-United States Free Trade Agreement: The Global Impact.* Washington: Institute for International Economics.

Shea, Brian F. 1988. *The Canada-United States Free Trade Agreement: A Summary of Empirical Studies and An Industrial Profile of the Tariff Reductions.* Economic Discussion Paper 28, US Department of Labor, March.

Shiells, Clinton R., Robert M. Stern, and Alan V. Deardorff. 1983. *Estimates of the Elasticities of Substitution Between Imports and Home Goods for the United States.* Institute of Public Policy Studies Discussion Paper 183, University of Michigan, January.

Statement by Thirty-Three Economists from Thirteen Countries. 1987. *Resolving the Global Economic Crisis: After Wall Street.* Special Report 6. Washington: Institute for International Economics, December.

Verleger, Philip K., Jr. 1988. "Implications of the Energy Provisions." In Jeffrey J. Schott and Murray G. Smith, eds. *The Canada-United States Free Trade Agreement: The Global Impact.* Washington: Institute for International Economics.

Wonnacott, Paul. 1987a. *The United States and Canada: The Quest for Free Trade.* POLICY ANALYSES IN INTERNATIONAL ECONOMICS 16. Washington: Institute for International Economics, March.

Wonnacott, Paul. 1987b. *US and Canadian Auto Policies in a Changing World Environment.* Washington: National Planning Association and Toronto: C. D. Howe Institute for the Canadian-American Committee. July.

Wonnacott, Paul. 1988. "The Auto Sector." In Jeffrey J. Schott and Murray G. Smith, eds. *The Canada-United States Free Trade Agreement: The Global Impact.* Washington: Institute for International Economics.

2

The Free Trade Agreement In Context: A Canadian Perspective

Murray G. Smith

The signing of the Canada–US Free Trade Agreement by Prime Minister Brian Mulroney and President Ronald Reagan on 2 January 1988 launches the political process of implementation and ratification in both nations. Decisions taken in 1988 by the United States and Canada on the Free Trade Agreement (FTA) and other trade policies will have enduring consequences for bilateral economic relations and broader repercussions for the global trading system as well.

This overview begins with an impressionistic history of efforts to achieve "free trade" between the United States and Canada and examines why the two countries pursued the current initiative in the mid-1980s. A comment on the architecture of the Canada–US Free Trade Agreement from the perspective of Canadian goals and objectives follows along with a discussion of the implications of the agreement for both economies and for the management of the bilateral economic relationship. It concludes with some observations on the longer term interests of the two countries and how perceptions of those may affect the prospects for implementation of the agreement.

On the US side, the threats to implementation come from specific constituency pressures and the seductive appeal of toughening the trade laws in light of the large US trade deficit. Unfortunately, the term "equal protection" resonates deeply in American political culture, although it is cloaked frequently in the guise of "a level playing field." The pressures on the Canadian side come largely from vaguer concerns about sovereignty that are rooted in Canada's political culture and perceptions of the history of Canadian–US relations and from distrust of the United States in bilateral economic relations.

Free Trade: The Elusive Goal

Past efforts to achieve free trade between Canada and the United States have been beset by one common difficulty.[1] One country or the other was always reluctant to consummate the process, either because of protectionist sentiment on the US side or nationalist sentiments on the Canadian side. In 1911, at the time of the best known initiative, the United States was enthusiastic. In the United States the draft Taft-Fielding Treaty passed with an overwhelming majority in the House of Representatives and the Senate despite an organized lobbying campaign to prevent ratification.[2]

Yet in Canada the enthusiasm of the Congress became a nationalist lightning rod in the 1911 election campaign, in part because of the rhetoric used by some of the US proponents of the treaty, which raised nationalist suspicions that the United States was seeking to annex Canada, not merely to expand trade. The mythology of the 1911 election—when a Canadian government was defeated on the slogan of "No Truck or Trade with the Yankees"—lives on in the Canadian public psyche.

This Canadian mythology is a curious phenomenon, because the Fathers of Confederation in Canada were not so inhibited about the prospects of free trade. Indeed having prospered under the Reciprocity Treaty of 1854, which was abrogated by the United States as a result of disputes with Great Britain over support for the South during the Civil War, the Fathers of Confederation made several attempts to negotiate another reciprocity treaty with the United States. Indeed the draft Elgin-Macy Treaty of 1874 was ratified by Great Britain on behalf of Canada, but it was rejected by the United States. It was only after successive efforts to negotiate expanded trade with the United States failed that Canada turned inward with its National Policy of 1879, which erected high tariffs against US exports. Few

---

1. Some of the earlier history of Canadian–US trade relations is discussed in Brecher and Reisman (1957) and Young (1957). A briefer review of the history is available in Reisman (1984, 35–50).

2. Lobbying is not a new phenomenon in Washington as Tom Velk and A. R. Riggs (1987) observe:

> Much of the opposition of farmers was genuine, especially among jittery wheat growers of the West, but too much of it was also provided for them by a lobbying organization, Allen and Graham, of New York City. In May 1911 Senate Finance Committee hearings revealed that the hundreds of articulate petitions and resolutions flooding Congress from Grange organizations, against reciprocity, were drawn up by Whidden Graham, a Canadian expatriate who turned the National Grange, with a membership of approximately 425,000, into a stalkinghorse for two other Allen and Graham clients, the International Paper Company, or Paper Trust, and the Timber Trust. With much to gain by denying Canadian competition, these businesses had promised to pay the bills for the Grange campaign.

Americans or Canadians are aware, however, that the swing toward Canadian protectionism followed a series of attempts by the first prime ministers of Canada to negotiate freer trade with the United States.

The 1930s brought the low point in Canadian–US economic relations. To start the decade, the United States enacted the Tariff Act of 1930, the Smoot-Hawley tariff, which established record heights for US tariffs. Faced with foreign trade barriers, Canada's Prime Minister, R. B. Bennett, increased Canadian tariffs in an effort "to bust into foreign markets," a cry that echoes today in the US Congress. The international spread of protectionism and massive debt defaults precipitated the Great Depression of the 1930s. Canada then, as now, was vulnerable to protectionism in world trade and suffered severely. Canadian exports plunged by 50 percent from 1929 to 1932.

Yet if the 1930s represented the nadir of Canadian–US and global economic relations, it also began a remarkable period of growth and prosperity. Neither Smoot, Hawley, nor R. B. Bennett, were re-elected. In 1935 the Liberal government of Mackenzie King negotiated a bilateral trade agreement with the United States under the aegis of US Secretary of State Cordell Hull's far-sighted Reciprocal Trade Agreements Act of 1934. The 1935 Canada–US trade agreement, which was subsequently broadened in 1938, began the process of reducing tariffs between the two countries, and helped build the underpinnings of the postwar General Agreement on Tariffs and Trade (GATT) and create the framework for the multilateral system that has fostered expanded trade and global prosperity over the last four decades.

Immediately after the Second World War, Canada and the United States again explored the possibility of a free trade zone. This time a draft protocol was developed secretly by officials from both sides, but the Liberal government of Mackenzie King demurred and adopted the more cautious tack of pursuing gradual reduction of trade barriers through the GATT negotiations.

During the 1950s and 1960s, both countries mainly focused their trade policies on GATT negotiations, with a notable exception.[3] In 1965, Canada and the United States concluded the Automotive Products Trade Agreement, otherwise known as the Auto Pact. The specific impetus for negotiating the Auto Pact was a countervailing duty suit filed in the United States against Canada's export-based duty remission program for automobiles. Faced with the probable application of countervailing duties, which would have had a disruptive impact on bilateral automotive trade and damaged the interests of the US automotive companies and the United Auto Workers' members on both sides of the border, the two federal governments negotiated a complicated set of automotive trade arrangements (see Paul Wonnacott's

---

3. Some of the obstacles to consideration of free trade in the 1950s and 1960s are discussed in Lea (1987, 11–29).

paper in this volume). Although both sides were aware that benefits were to be derived from rationalizing bilateral automotive trade and production, the motivation came from the attempt to resolve a specific bilateral problem, the countervailing duty suit.

Subsequent to the 1965 automotive agreement, there has been significant rationalization of automotive trade and production within North America, and considerable benefits have accrued to both countries as well as to the North American automotive producers and their employees. Consider the greater potential commitment of US government assistance under the 1979 Chrysler bailout package that would have been required to ensure the survival of Chrysler during the 1980–82 recession if Chrysler had not rationalized previously its Canadian and US operations. Although the Auto Pact was not conceived as a strategic response to offshore competition, the production rationalization under the Auto Pact has yielded significant benefits in this regard.

In addition to the Auto Pact, Canada and the United States concluded a series of bilateral agreements on defense procurement during the 1950s and 1960s. Known as the Defense Production Sharing Arrangements, these agreements date back to the Second World War.

During the 1970s, both countries again focused their trade initiatives on the multilateral front. Immediately after completion of the Tokyo Round, however, bilateral trade and investment issues re-emerged on the agenda. During 1980–82, the Canadian government was concerned that oil prices would continue to escalate and moved aggressively under the National Energy Program to control foreign investment, to favor the activities of Canadian oil companies, and to increase procurement from Canadian sources for megaprojects. At the same time, the Foreign Investment Review Agency became more aggressive in seeking to control the activities of foreign corporations operating in Canada.

In the aftermath of the 1982 recession and in light of the collapse of oil prices, the Canadian government pursued a more conciliatory policy toward foreign investment and began to focus on trade initiatives. In August 1983, the Trudeau government tabled its Trade Policy Review, which provided the basis for exploring sectoral negotiations with the United States aimed at achieving free trade in selected sectors.

Chief among the sectors proposed by Canada for bilateral talks were items of unfinished business from the Tokyo Round. Canada had failed to obtain some of its principal objectives, including access to the US petrochemical market and to public procurement for urban transit vehicles. Although Canada's sectoral initiative raised issues with respect to the compatibility of sectoral agreements with the GATT, the US administration responded favorably and began consultations with domestic industries to identify sectors where the United States might wish to consider negotiations.[4] Quite apart from problems in reconciling sectoral arrangements with the GATT, the sectoral initiative soon foundered because there was not much overlap in the Canadian and US lists of sectors that were candidates for sectoral agreements (Hufbauer and Samet 1985).

Why Now?

In light of the tortuous history and political perils involved in the pursuit of free trade between Canada and the United States, why did both countries undertake the current initiative? For both sides, there was a mixture of positive and negative factors that served to motivate them in this undertaking.[5]

For the United States, the disappointing results of the GATT Ministerial in 1982 illustrated the obstacles to progress on trade liberalization on a multilateral basis. It was proving difficult to solve old problems, such as distortions to agricultural trade, or to deal with new issues, such as developing rules for trade in services and investment issues. A bilateral approach to trade negotiations offered the prospect of making greater progress on some of these difficult issues, which could stimulate multilateral progress.[6]

Of course, macroeconomic developments in the 1980s have had a dramatic impact on the evolution of trade policy, particularly in the United States. The global trade imbalances of the 1980s and the resulting rise of US protectionism have created severe stresses in bilateral economic relations and stretched the fabric of the world trading system. There was greater pressure for the application of US unfair trade laws, as well as increasing resort to escape clause actions and voluntary export restraints, which were used to institute managed trade regimes in major industrial sectors.

On the Canadian side, the rise of US protectionism was an important motivating force. The strong US dollar in the mid-1980s created stresses in

---

4. The mixture of encouragement and concern of the US administration about GATT rules in responding to the Canadian sectoral proposal is reflected in Brock (1984, 65–68).

5. Several studies recommended that Canada pursue the negotiation of a free trade area with the United States. The most prominent was the *Report of the Royal Commission on Canada's Economic Union and Development Prospects,* chaired by Donald S. Macdonald (Ottawa: Supply and Services Canada, 1985). See also Lipsey and Smith (1985), and Canadian-American Committee (1985).

6. For a fuller discussion of the interaction between bilateralism and multilateralism, see Diebold (1988). On the significance of a demonstration effect for US trade policy, see Aho and Levinson (1987, 143–155). Also see Jeffrey J. Schott's "US Assessment" and "Implications for the Uruguay Round" in this volume.

resource sectors that became a source of conflict between Canada and the United States. Since US protectionism has been channeled into complaints about unfair foreign trading practices, the threat to impose penalty duties adversely affects the investment climate in Canada and unleashes political pressures on Canadian governments. Thus, countervailing duties and other remedies against unfair trade became a central Canadian concern during these negotiations.

The impulse for Canadian unilateralism often takes the form of nationalist investment policies. Particularly during 1980–82, Canada pursued interventionist investment policies under the National Energy Program as well as more activist policies by the Foreign Investment Review Agency. Thus, obtaining a more open and predictable regime for investment and trade in services became an important objective for the United States, just as Canada sought to obtain greater security of access to markets. Indeed, some of the difficulties with Canada during 1980–82 over services and investment issues may have helped stimulate US interest in dealing with these issues on a multilateral, as well as a bilateral, basis.

On both sides, the desire to avoid disputes that threaten to disrupt bilateral commerce has been an important motivating factor in pursuing the negotiations. To be sure avoiding disputes is in the mutual economic and political interests of both nations, but such negative arguments have tended to dominate in the public debate. However, the positive case for bilateral trade liberalization receives less attention than is warranted.[7]

Despite the progress achieved in the GATT in reducing tariffs on trade between Canada and the United States, significant tariff and nontariff barriers to trade between the two countries remain. Removal of these remaining barriers offers significant economic benefits to both countries. First, both countries stand to gain from greater interindustry specialization when trade barriers are removed, although these gains are relatively small. Second, the United States stands to gain improvements in its terms of trade, while Canada is likely to lose in this regard, because Canadian tariffs are significantly higher than US tariffs. In 1985, the average Canadian tariff on dutiable imports was 9.9 percent compared with 3.3 percent on dutiable US imports from Canada. Third, both countries could gain substantially in terms of increased productivity and rationalization within the manufacturing sector. All quantitative estimates indicate that the United States gains from bilateral trade liberalization. Estimates of the potential impact on Canada range from small losses under a pessimistic productivity and trade expansion scenario to substantial gains of almost 9 percent of Canadian GNP under a more optimistic productivity scenario (see Harris 1987, Morici 1987, and

---

7. The classic work is Wonnacott and Wonnacott (1967).

Brown and Stern 1987). The quantitative models do not capture well, however, the expansion of intraindustry trade, which has been the main effect of tariff elimination among industrial countries. Furthermore, the models do not incorporate measure of the gains from liberalization of trade in services or investment flows.

Clearly the most significant gains from freer trade between Canada and the United States will accrue from the potential for greater productivity and specialization within particular industries in the more integrated Canadian and US markets. Historically the potential for rationalization within industries and within multinational corporations has been a matter of indifference to the United States and a matter of great anxiety in Canada because of concerns that US-based branch plants will retrench.

Global competition appears to have altered perceptions on both sides. Offshore competitive challenges facing both economies have increased greatly, reflecting more intense competition among the developed countries in high technology industries, rapid expansion of exports by newly industrializing countries in heavy industries such as steel and shipbuilding, and ever increasing competition from developing countries in labor intensive products such as apparel and footwear. The liberalization of trade between Canada and the United States is a strategic response that will increase the competitiveness of both economies and is particularly important to multinational firms with operations on both sides of the border (Smith 1988).

Large segments of the Canadian economy, particularly manufacturing industries in Ontario and Quebec that had long resisted trade liberalization, changed their positions dramatically during the 1980s. As Canada's tariffs were reduced in accordance with the Tokyo Round agreements, many Canadian manufacturing firms and subsidiaries of foreign multinational enterprises found that they could adjust and compete successfully.

Macroeconomic developments in the 1980s also served to shift Canadian attitudes toward trade liberalization. During the 1970s the Canadian government had pursued stimulative fiscal policies resulting in an overvalued exchange rate and a persistent current account deficit. As a consequence of Canada's growing international liabilities, external debt service obligations mushroomed with the high interest rates of the early 1980s. The need to generate a trade surplus to service these mounting international liabilities placed downward pressure on the Canadian dollar. Many US industries competing with Canadian products felt that Canada was deliberately devaluing its currency in order to gain a competitive advantage. In fact, from 1982–85, Canada pursued fiscal policies that were as expansionary as US policy on a proportional basis. Although Canadian fiscal policy in the 1980s tended to make the Canadian economy less competitive, the legacy of accumulated international debt dominated current policy developments, compelling exchange rate adjustments that made the Canadian economy more competitive.[8]

For both the United States and Canada, global developments tended to make bilateral negotiations of a comprehensive free trade agreement more attractive than in previous decades. The exchange rate misalignments and resurgent US protectionism helped prod Canada into the negotiations, but the resulting hostile environment in the Congress made it difficult to negotiate the unfair trade issues of particular interest to Canada. In addition to these powerful currents in the global economy, which generated political pressures on trade policy in each country, there were a range of bilateral issues and irritants, some of longstanding duration, that required attention.

The Architecture of the Agreement

Although the agreement is shaped by the many pressures and interests impinging on the world's largest bilateral commercial linkage, it is compatible with the multilateral system. Not only are the two nations proposing a classic free trade area, consistent with Article XXIV of the GATT, but the agreement is interwoven with their respective multilateral trade obligations and interlinked with the Uruguay Round negotiations.

The Canada–US Free Trade Agreement also compares favorably with past precedents for the formation of free trade areas, such as the European Free Trade Association (EFTA), the bilateral free trade agreements between EFTA countries and the European Community (EC), the Australia–New Zealand Closer Economic Relations Agreement of 1983, and the US–Israel Free Trade Agreement of 1985. In particular the Canada–US Free Trade Agreement provides for the elimination over ten years of all tariffs, not only in the industrial sector but also in food and agricultural products.

Thus, the agreement goes further in liberalizing agricultural trade and in avoiding sectoral exclusions than do many other free trade areas that have been reviewed under Article XXIV of the GATT. True, the United States and Canada retain quotas that serve to buttress supply management regimes and price support mechanisms for agricultural products. However, such selective exceptions are permitted under Article XXIV, if the measures conform with GATT Article XI or Article XX. Similarly only limited progress was made in resolving agricultural subsidy issues—both sides will cease export subsidies on bilateral trade—because the real problems in world agricultural trade result from the interaction of European and Japanese with US and Canadian policies and can be only addressed in the Uruguay Round.

---

8. For a fuller discussion, see Lipsey and Smith (1987, 18–19).

It must be stressed that the agreement creates a free trade area, not a customs union. Thus, each country retains separate commercial policies for trade and economic relations with third countries. Maintaining this commercial policy independence while at the same time preventing undesired pass-through trade or deflections of trade and production, requires the negotiation of clear and predictable rules of origin. On a technical level, the rules of origin in this agreement are much clearer and will involve much less paper burden and uncertainty than do the rules used by EFTA–EC bilateral agreements and the internal EFTA arrangements. Of course, some of the most difficult issues in balancing conflicting sectoral interests required special rules of origin for textiles, apparel, and automotive trade.

The obligations in the Canada–US Free Trade Agreement regarding technical barriers to trade and government procurement build on the GATT codes negotiated in the Tokyo Round. The procurement and technical barriers provisions of the agreement are not sweeping and revolutionary changes, but they are further steps to liberalize trade and to make more transparent the impediments that remain. The limited scope of the procurement provisions is one area where the negotiations fell short. It is ironic that Canada did not obtain the improved access to US procurement of urban transit equipment that was sought in the earlier sectoral initiative.

Except for the European Community, there is little previous experience in regional trade arrangements in dealing with disputes over subsidies, antidumping and countervailing duties, or services and investment issues. All of these issues proved difficult in the Canada–US talks, and the issue of trade disputes threatened the collapse of the negotiations at least twice in the final two weeks.

In Canada, one of the most controversial aspects of the agreement involves the rules and dispute settlement mechanism pertaining to the application of antidumping and countervailing duties to bilateral trade. A major concern of Canadians is that the rules regarding subsidies, and the application of countervailing and antidumping duties, remain for the time being those of the national laws of both countries. While the agreement provides a five-to-seven-year window to develop new common rules for unfair trade, the outcome of this process is uncertain.

The fact that Canada did not get "a complete exemption" from, or removal of, US countervailing and antidumping duties, has been greeted with considerable disappointment by many Canadians. Before and during the negotiations, however, independent analysts proposed incremental changes to the trade laws, not exemption (see P. Wonnacott 1987; Smith, Aho, and Horlick 1987). In light of the proposals in the omnibus trade bill, however, it was difficult to develop a set of rules on subsidies that would have persuaded the Congress to agree to the removal of countervailing duties in bilateral trade. The undertakings with respect to subsidies that might have been acceptable to the Congress would have placed greater restrictions on Canadian than US subsidy policies, and caused great concern, particularly among Canadians who are concerned that Canada is ceding sovereignty in the Free Trade Agreement (Reisman 1987, 113–114).

Instead of an "exemption" from countervailing duties, I suggest that the issue has to be recast along lines suggested by John Jackson:

> What is often surprising . . . is that even nations with very similar economic systems, such as two industrial country market economies, can find that minor variations in their economic systems can create situations which have the appearance of unfairness. Those situations may have arisen almost completely by accident. That is, there may have been no intention to engage in any practice which is deemed 'unfair' . . . I have termed this problem the 'interface' problem. . . . When it is desired that two computers of different makes work together, it often takes some kind of 'interface' mechanism or program to mediate between them and to translate the language of one machine to that of the other. Likewise, when two societies with even minor economic differences desire to work together, frictions or misunderstandings can occur unless there is an interface mechanism. To a certain extent, the national trade laws and the GATT Bretton Woods System are operating today as a rather crude interface mechanism. The problem often is that policy leaders have not perceived this, but instead believe that it is necessary to characterise some practices as 'unfair' or 'illegal.' In at least some of the international trade problems which exist today, a more neutral terminology and policy approach that would avoid moral overtones may operate with greater utility for world economic welfare and harmony (Jackson 1986, 124).

Jackson's "interface problem" is an apt characterization of the issues confronting the negotiators of the Canada–US Free Trade Agreement. The agreement seeks to develop rules and procedures that will facilitate private commerce between two highly interdependent economies, while imposing the fewest possible constraints on the exercise of sovereignty by governments. To assess the achievements of the agreement, one has to examine some of the sector-specific aspects as well as the basic architecture of the agreement.

In his paper in this volume, Paul Wonnacott gives a ringing endorsement to the automotive provisions of the agreement, because they resolve a looming bilateral conflict. Specifically, Canada's export-based duty remissions are to be eliminated immediately, and domestic duty remissions are to be phased out. Companies that attain Auto Pact status by 1989, principally the big three North American producers, retain the right to import parts and automobiles duty-free from third countries as long as they continue to meet Canada's existing Auto Pact regulations. Wonnacott concludes that the agreement carefully balances Canadian and US concerns and resolves a festering conflict that has emerged between Canada and the United States over how the Auto Pact ought to apply to third country automotive companies investing in North America. One indicator of the validity of Wonnacott's judgment is that neither the state of Michigan nor the province of Ontario is enthusiastic about the outcome. Yet Wonnacott's argument that the agreement helps prevent another potential countervailing duty action that would have been very damaging to bilateral automotive trade is persuasive. If the Free Trade Agreement has foreclosed such an explosion in the largest component of bilateral trade, this alone is an important achievement and would appear to be in the mutual interest of both countries.

The automotive provisions resolve some bilateral issues involving investment and trade by third country automakers, but at the same time the provisions raise some third country concerns. By agreeing to a common rule of origin for automotive trade to replace the Auto Pact provisions, the FTA is more fully compatible with Article XXIV of the GATT. However, because the direct cost of processing standard is more restrictive than the present value-added standards and because offshore automotive manufacturers stand to lose the benefits of Canadian duty remission, these provisions raise concerns for European, Japanese, and Korean automakers. In his commentary on the automotive provisions in this volume, Lonmo argues that the content level should be raised to 60 percent from 50 percent. Although this proposal has appeal to auto parts producers and auto workers on both sides of the border, it would exacerbate the concerns of offshore automakers.

The sector-specific element of the agreement that is one of the most disappointing aspects from a Canadian perspective is the grandfathering of a special managed trade regime in softwood lumber. The threat of countervailing duties forced Canada to negotiate the 1986 Softwood Lumber Memorandum of Understanding involving a 15 percent export tax on lumber (Percy and Yoder 1987). The failure to negotiate common subsidy rules meant there was no basis in the agreement to resolve this dispute. Some of the Canadian provinces have instituted replacement measures, such as higher stumpage fees, in lieu of the export tax but with the same revenue objectives as the 15 percent level set out in the preliminary affirmative countervailing duty determination by the US Commerce Department in October 1986. These provincial measures have been acceptable to US industry and government officials.

Drafting general rules of competition to deal with subsidies, dumping, and other allegations of unfair trade practices, and rules to liberalize trade in services and investment, were the major challenges in the Canada–US talks. The two models that provide the most relevant basis for comparison are the rules of competition that are contained in the Stockholm Convention, which created the European Free Trade Association, and the Treaty of Rome, which created the European Community. Neither of these models provides a perfectly appropriate analogy for Canada and the United States. Instead, the bilateral talks have produced a hybrid, which shares elements of the

EFTA system, the EC system, and includes some unique and distinctive elements, not found in any other free trade area.

Other bilateral free trade areas, such as between Switzerland, Austria or Sweden and the European Community, or the US–Israel Agreement, do not have such formal dispute settlement processes. The principal mechanism for resolving disputes in these other bilateral agreements is a joint committee of the two governments. The proposed Canada–US Trade Commission is a similar type of joint committee, but there are some important and unique innovations in the dispute settlement process in the Canada–US Agreement.

The agreement will institute an expeditious binding binational appeal process for antidumping and countervailing duty cases and a binational review process governing changes in the trade laws. Furthermore, as Horlick-Oliver-Steger observe in their chapter in this volume, the potential recourse to judicial review should have a sobering effect on the administrative processes. Thus, the agreement seeks to stop the protectionist drift in each country's trade laws and to buffer the administration of those laws from political influences.

If we look at other agreements around the world, the only regional agreement that removes countervailing duties is that of the European Community. The European Community has a supranational mechanism, through the European Commission and the European Court, to discipline the use of subsidies. It seems doubtful that Canada and the United States will ever agree to grant a supranational agency the right to disallow subsidy programs. However, if the more "imaginative" types of subsidies, such as the rule proposed in the omnibus trade bill for determining general availability of subsidies in US countervailing duty law (for example, disproportionate use of university-trained personnel by an industry) are not incorporated into US trade law, then subsidy-countervailing duty issues are likely to become more manageable in the future.

Both Americans and Canadians believe the myth that Canadian governments subsidize more than their US counterparts. In fact, excluding a few industries such as agriculture and fisheries where there are explicit subsidies in the United States and Canada, most industries in both countries receive subsidies that amount to less than 1 percent of the value of production (Moroz 1988, Kaminow 1988). If subsidies in agriculture and fisheries are dealt with in the Uruguay Round, then incremental changes in the countervailing duty law could be sufficient to resolve most bilateral disputes over subsidies.

Antidumping duties could prove to be a more persistent problem. As tariffs are eliminated, classic dumping in the sense of price discrimination will decline in significance. Antidumping duties will remain a bilateral issue, however, because both countries have protectionist "sale below cost" and "constructed cost" provisions in their laws. Thus, antidumping duties can be invoked in cyclical downturns simply because producers are not recovering the full cost of production including an allowance for profit. If this provision of the antidumping laws of both countries is not removed, then antidumping duties will impede rationalization of production and trade in the more integrated Canadian and US markets. As trade barriers are reduced between Canada and the United States, it may become feasible to move toward a predatory pricing standard through reciprocal enforcement of US antitrust and Canadian competition laws in lieu of antidumping laws.

There are some grounds for optimism about the prospects for negotiating new bilateral rules to govern antidumping and countervailing duty laws. It is likely that US protectionism will decline in intensity as the US trade deficit begins to turn around in the years ahead. By the early 1990s, the United States will be obliged to run a trade surplus to service its mounting foreign liabilities, just as Canada must now, and for the foreseeable future, run a trade surplus to service net foreign liabilities equivalent to 40 percent of Canadian GNP.

Thus, over the next few years, the political climate could become more conducive to the two countries negotiating the removal, on a bilateral basis, of some of the more protectionist provisions of the antidumping and countervailing laws of both countries. However, because of the sovereignty concerns in both Canada and the United States, it seems unlikely that the two countries will implement the kind of supranational regulatory regimes for subsidy practices that exist in the European Community. Instead they are likely to pursue variations on the EFTA approach by focusing on practices that distort competition.

In the services and investment areas as well, the Canada–US Agreement goes further than the EFTA–EC bilateral agreements, but falls well short of the full commitment to national treatment that applies within the European Community. (One might take note of the gap between the principles enunciated in the Treaty of Rome and actual practice, although the stated goal of the Community is to narrow this gap by 1992). Many existing laws and measures that derogate from national treatment are grandfathered on both sides of the Canada–US border.

The cultural and transportation sectors were exempted from the provisions of the agreement regarding services and investment, because of Canadian concerns about the vulnerability of the cultural industries in light of heavy penetration by US media, and because of lobbying pressures from US maritime interests to permit new cargo preference legislation in addition to existing Jones Act restrictions. For Canada, the most sensitive national concerns involve issues of cultural sovereignty and identity; while, in the United States, national security goals are the rationale for special consideration.

Although public debate in Canada has tended to focus on the trade law issues, the agreement also implements a general dispute settlement mechanism that provides for binding arbitration if both countries agree. Even if there is no prior agreement for binding arbitration, the general dispute settlement process embodies some significant improvements over existing GATT procedures, at least some of which may be useful in promoting reform of GATT dispute settlement mechanisms during the Uruguay Round.

The Canadian debate has not focused on the general dispute settlement mechanism, but substantive provisions of the energy, investment, and services chapters have become controversial. The energy and investment chapters are viewed by many as imposing serious constraints on Canadian policy.

Potential Implications

Before turning to the policy debate about implementation, it is worth examining the implications of the agreement. Implementation of the FTA will have significant economic implications for both nations and create a new framework for the management of bilateral economic relations.

Economic Implications

Significant economic benefits to both countries will be realized from the implementation of the Free Trade Agreement. The agreement removes nearly all barriers to bilateral merchandise trade imposed by the two federal governments, except for the contentious quota restrictions on agricultural trade and government procurement preferences not covered under the GATT code. As a result, most of the potential efficiency gains anticipated by earlier studies will be realized.

Although the absolute economic gains to both countries may be roughly symmetrical, because of the asymmetry in the size of the economies, the proportional gains to Canada probably will be larger. The greater proportional gains in real income, estimated at 2.5 percent of Canadian GNP in a recent study, imply that there will be greater adjustment costs borne by the Canadian economy (Department of Finance 1988).

In assessing the economic adjustment implications, there are two methodologies we might employ. One approach would be to use various computer-based general equilibrium models of the Canadian and US economies. The conclusions from that analysis are that the adjustment implications are not extensive for the Canadian economy, unless one assumes very strong productivity growth concentrated in a few industries, and are modest indeed for the US economy.

These conclusions are borne out by historical analysis of two episodes of economic integration in Europe. The first episode was in the 1960s at the time when the European Community and the European Free Trade Association were formed. Contemporary observers were surprised when those regional trading arrangements started to lower tariffs and to expand trade among them, without suffering major dislocations of individual industries. Everyone expected that whole industries would expand in one country and disappear in another. However, that is not what happened. Instead, intra-industry trade expanded. Companies specialized in narrow product niches; they became more productive; and on the whole adjustment was a very benign, not a painful, experience.

One can argue that the 1960s were a period of buoyant economic growth in the world economy, and perhaps the European experience at that time is not the best guide to tell us whether opening of trade among industrial countries will require major adjustments. The second episode in Europe, however, involving the opening of trade between the EFTA countries and the European Community, was in the 1970s when economic conditions were more difficult. The EFTA–EC bilateral agreements eliminated tariffs over five years, from 1973 to 1978, against the backdrop of a severe recession in Europe accompanying the first oil shock. Furthermore, the EFTA–EC agreements opened trade between very small countries, such as Austria, Finland, Iceland, Norway, Sweden, and Switzerland, with the much larger and already integrated economies of the European Community. For example, an economy such as Austria had relatively high tariffs and a number of German branch plants. Again, the adjustment impact, particularly in terms of dislocation of jobs, was much less than anticipated. So the European experience corroborates the conclusion from the economic models that adjustment to the proposed Canada–US Free Trade Agreement is unlikely to disrupt labor markets, particularly because the phase-in period is 10 years for the sensitive sectors.

Although past experience with trade liberalization among industrial countries suggests that the adjustment pressures from the Canada–US Free Trade Agreement are not likely to be severe, even for the smaller Canadian economy, both countries need to consider whether their existing adjustment policies are appropriate (R. Wonnacott 1987, Economic Council 1988). Both countries face offshore competitive challenges, volatile interest and exchange rates, and rapid changes in technology, all of which create adjustment pressures. Special adjustment policies targeted toward specific groups of workers may help ensure that the adjustment burden of freer bilateral trade does not fall disproportionately on certain groups and can complement a broader range of policies intended to facilitate adjustment in the economy.

There appear to be cyclical influences that affect attitudes on these issues in both Canada and the United States, but the cycles are not synchronized. In the United States, protectionism tends to be most pronounced at times when dollar overvaluation has given rise to large trade deficits, such as in the 1968–72 period and the mid-1980s. Canada, however, tends to resort to nationalist investment policies when resource prices are buoyant, which fosters delusions of grandeur coupled with suspicions that foreign resource firms are reaping the spoils of the boom. Commodity prices tend to be more buoyant when the US dollar is weak such as in the late 1970s. Certainly soaring oil prices stimulated Canada's National Energy Program of 1980 and the resulting bilateral trade and investment frictions of the early 1980s (see Leyton-Brown 1985).

It might be assumed that Canada is less likely to resort to nationalist investment policies in the future, because Canadian direct investment in the United States has increased greatly over the last decade.[9] The greater stake of Canadians in the US economy may not influence significantly Canadian public policy. First, even if the stock of Canadian direct investment in the United States were to rise to a level that matched the value of US direct investment in Canada, there would still be a significant asymmetry in the share of the domestic economy owned by the other country. Second, economic interests do not necessarily translate into political influence in a straightforward and proportional fashion. For example, the interests of many US multinational enterprises risk being damaged by "process" or "contingent" protectionism under the trade law, but various domestic constituency pressures from import competing interests, including employee groups or local communities tied to particular plants, can be much more influential in the political process. Similarly in Canada, the rising stake of business interests in the US economy may not influence the evolution of investment policies in Canada, which is likely to be more responsive to domestic constituency pressures.

In the complex interplay of private and public channels of contact and interaction that characterizes Canada–US relations, Keohane and Nye (1977) argue that Canada often obtains outcomes to the advantage of Canadian interests, because Canadian governments and organizations focus more attention and effort on the bilateral relationship. Thus the asymmetry in the economies may not always work to Canada's disadvantage.

Nonetheless, Canada is more vulnerable to aggressive US trade actions. International scholars characterize economic relations as being power based

---

9. The growing stock of Canadian direct investment in the United States is documented in Rugman (1987).

when disputes are resolved on an ad hoc basis by negotiation, and rules-based when disputes are subject to formal adjudication based on previously agreed rules and norms. Logic would suggest that the smaller economic partner would have the greater interest in a rules-based system of dispute settlement as contrasted with a more discretionary power-based system (Jackson 1979).

Despite the asymmetries in the economies, however, the symmetry of US and Canadian interests in a rules-based system of dispute resolution may be greater than is often supposed. If a narrow factional interest in either country gains a special advantage through an action prejudicial to interests in the other country, it may rebound in a cycle of reaction and retaliation that is ultimately damaging to the public interest in both nations. The real test for the Canada–US Free Trade Agreement is whether the provisions of the agreement, and the dispute settlement mechanisms contained in it, will moderate the mood swings and tensions that have become endemic to the highly interdependent and complex relationship between the two economies.

Will the Agreement Be Implemented?

There is a strong presumption that, having come this far, the agreement will be implemented. But there are obstacles to implementation on both sides and the simultaneity of the processes complicates the situation considerably.

The US Process

On the US side, consultations by the administration with the Congress and domestic lobbies subsequent to the Elements of Agreement signed on 4 October 1987 led to some modifications of the final agreement. For example, transportation industries were exempted from the services and investment chapters in response to pressure from US maritime interests. Canada acceded to this US request in the preparation of the final text, but in return Canada obtained a number of US concessions, including duty-free quotas for apparel incorporating third country fabrics, the right to introduce new duty remission schemes up until 30 June 1988, and export controls on fish from Atlantic Canada. Additional efforts to "tune" the agreement to meet particular constituency pressures are likely to be counterproductive as the risk of unraveling the agreement becomes greater.

For Canada, the key questions with respect to US implementation involve the interplay between the Congress and the administration over the drafting of the implementing legislation for the Free Trade Agreement and the omnibus trade bill. Although the fast track mechanism provides useful disciplines on the legislative process, there is still some latitude for interpretation in the implementing legislation. More importantly, there are some key questions about how the agreement may interact with legislative changes that would result from passage of the omnibus trade bill when it emerges from the House–Senate conference.

The US Debate

Thus, the implementation of the Canada–US Free Trade Agreement is linked to the debate about how to respond to the large US trade deficit (Lipsey and Smith 1987). The persistence of the nominal US trade deficit, despite the significant realignment of exchange rates since 1985, has produced great pressure to rewrite the trade laws to make it easier for US producers to obtain import relief under the guise of redress against unfair foreign practices.

Destler and Odell (1987) argue that the Congress has a blind spot with respect to generic "process protectionism" or what Canadians such as Rodney Grey (1981) have called "contingent protection." Yet changes in the trade laws can be much more protectionist in effect than sector specific quotas which are recognized as protectionist. As Lipsey and I have argued:

> US policymakers, perhaps recalling the effects of the Smoot-Hawley Tariff Act of 1930, have shied away from passing explicitly protectionist legislation that would impose tariffs or quotas on foreign goods. For example, Congress did not pass the Burke-Hartke bill in the early 1970s and it is unlikely to pass the Gephardt proposal in 1987. Instead, it has tended to make US import relief laws more responsive to domestic interests and, in particular, to strengthen the laws directed against unfair foreign trade practices. These changes have so far followed a ratchet principle; with rare and modest exceptions, the changes in the trade laws have all been in the direction of toughening them. Thus, postwar US protectionist episodes have tended to make it progressively easier for domestic producers to obtain import relief in the form of duties or quotas imposed under trade laws (Lipsey and Smith 1987).

The delayed response of the US trade deficit to the decline in the US dollar against the currencies of some of the major industrial countries since March 1985 was to be expected for several reasons. First, the pattern of relatively weak economic growth in Europe and Japan has persisted, in part because of the cautious monetary and fiscal policies of those countries. Second, the adverse effects of the appreciation of the US dollar through the first half of the decade had not been reflected fully in the US trade position. Therefore, the traditional J-curve effect, which leads to a short-term deterioration of the trade balance in response to a depreciation in the currency, was exacerbated by the lag in the response to the previous appreciation. Third, the US dollar has declined dramatically relative to the currencies of Japan and Germany, but the movement has been much less dramatic against other currencies.

Trade policy factors also have influenced the response of the US trade account to the depreciation of the US dollar. The voluntary export restraint arrangements in key industrial sectors reduced the impact of exchange rate movements on trade volumes in the short term. Under the export restraints, foreign producers were limiting their export volumes and taking higher profit margins from their sales in the United States. As their costs rise, because of appreciation of their domestic currencies, foreign producers tend initially to absorb the impact by lowering their profit margins. It is only when the exchange rate has moved a sufficient amount—to where their domestic costs necessitate a price increase in the US market to a level that makes the export restraint arrangements no longer binding—that the exchange rate movement begins to have a significant effect on trade volumes.

Finally, the prolonged period of dollar overvaluation in the mid-1980s distorted investment decisions. It appeared more attractive to invest offshore instead of investing in the United States. It will take years of new investment to catch up, but the slow response of the US trade balance to exchange rate movements does not provide a basis for pessimism about the long-term competitiveness of the US economy. Many believe that the movement in the exchange rate will not restore external balance in the US economy. Similar views were expressed during the early 1980s when Canadian government officials and others thought that energy prices would rise exponentially and that energy demand and supply would not respond to those price increases.

As the J-curve predicts, there was a sharp discrepancy between the change in the real and nominal US trade balance that resulted from the dollar depreciation. During 1987 real US exports grew by 11.5 percent compared to real import growth of 2.5 percent. Similarly real import growth was strong in Japan and West Germany, while their real exports stagnated.[10]

There was a remarkable tension in the US economic policy during 1987, which may have echoes in 1988. Through much of 1987 the Federal Reserve Board was pursuing cautious monetary policy because of concern that the US economy was approaching full employment and was experiencing export-led growth (due to the improvement in the real trade balance) that required some dampening influence to prevent a resurgence of inflation. At the same time, monthly records in the nominal trade deficit, which is perceived as a threat to US jobs, goaded the Congress to reinforce the arsenal of US trade laws.

---

10. GATT Press Release 1432, 29 February 1988, 9.

Apparently, the October 1987 stock market crash temporarily cooled congressional ardor for a protectionist trade bill, but with the large and persistent US nominal trade deficit, unilateral measures to buttress the arsenal of US trade laws remain highly seductive. Even a "responsible" trade bill could change the trade laws in ways that are highly undesirable from a Canadian point of view. In particular, if changes in the definition of subsidy in US countervailing duty law and many other proposed changes that would make it easier for US petitioners to obtain relief from import competition contained in the bills passed by the House of Representatives and the Senate become law and are applied to Canada, then support in Canada for implementation of the Free Trade Agreement will be eroded substantially (Horlick 1987, Schott 1987, Smith 1987).

The Canadian Implementing Process

The process of implementation of the FTA is quite different in Canada from the United States. In a parliamentary system, the Conservative government of Brian Mulroney can implement major components of the agreement by orders-in-council, and since the government has a substantial majority in the House of Commons, it can draft the implementing legislation to give effect to the FTA without engaging in the kind of negotiation that occurs between the US administration and the Congress.

There are, however, two complications to the implementing process in Canada. The first complication is that legislation in the federal sphere must pass the Senate as well as the House of Commons. The Conservative Party does not have a majority in the Senate and implementing legislation could be delayed by the Liberal majority in the Senate.

The role of the provinces adds another complication in Canada. There are few areas in the agreement that require positive action by the provinces to implement provisions in the agreement. The most obvious example where provincial action is required is with respect to provincial policies giving preferential markups on local wines. On this issue, the GATT complaint by the European Community with respect to provincial practices regarding distribution of alcoholic beverages is an additional pressure on the provincial governments regarding wine markups.

In areas such as services, investment, and possibly energy, the provisions of the agreement may impinge on provincial jurisdiction in the sense of precluding provinces from undertaking certain types of discriminatory actions in the future. In these areas the issue of provincial compliance arises in the longer term. Thus, the issue is not so much whether provinces implement the agreement, but whether they might introduce measures in the future that derogate from the agreement.

There is a legal case that the federal government of Canada has authority under the Trade and Commerce Power of the Constitution Act to enact general legislation that would be binding on the provinces of the type contemplated in the services and investment chapters of the Free Trade Agreement.[11] In this context then, it is argued that such federal legislation would have constitutional validity and could in fact preclude discriminatory policy actions by the provinces that conflict with the agreement. This case is the subject of legal debate. Beyond the legal issues, the specific strategy of the federal government—in drafting implementing legislation that impinges on provincial areas of jurisdiction—will have significant constitutional and political implications. If the federal government takes an aggressive approach to staking out its jurisdiction, then provinces that might otherwise support the agreement may feel obliged to challenge the constitutional dimensions of the implementing legislation (see J. H. Warren's comments in this volume).

The provinces play a political role in Canada that goes beyond their specific constitutional authority and responsibilities to implement the agreement. In Canada, the provinces can be important in creating, or failing to create, a nonpartisan consensus on an issue, in the same way that brokering in the key committees of Congress produces—at least sometimes—a bipartisan consensus on an issue. Thus, it is politically significant that not only seven premiers out of ten support the agreement, but also that two of the four Liberal premiers, the premier of Quebec and the newly elected premier of New Brunswick, support implementation of the deal. Furthermore, the premier of Manitoba, who opposed the agreement, has been plunged into a sudden election and has resigned. As long as a majority exists in Canadian public opinion that favors implementation of the agreement, then the formal obstacles to implementation on the Canadian side are likely to be manageable.

The Canadian Debate

Of course, attitudes in Canada might shift as the year unfolds. Events in the United States—or perceptions of those events—can have a powerful influence on attitudes in Canada with respect to bilateral trade relations. Polling done in Canada after the softwood lumber case illustrates this general point. The softwood lumber case had a dramatic affect on public perceptions of the desirability of negotiating a free trade agreement with the United

---

11. Background on the Canadian constitutional issues is available in Steger (1987). The specific debate about the constitutional dimension of the Canada–US Free Trade Agreement is contained in presentations by H. Scott Fairley and Patrick Monahan at a conference co-sponsored by the University of Ottawa, Faculty of Law and the Institute for Research on Public Policy, Ottawa, 22 January 1988 (forthcoming).

States. In particular, the softwood lumber dispute shifted the public opinion of about 69 percent of the respondents in one poll, but the net decline in total support for the free trade negotiations was only 21 percent because of offsetting reactions (Waddell 1987). Some Canadians became more apprehensive about the risks arising from US protectionist sentiment and the evolution of US contingent protection systems. Thus, they attached greater significance to negotiating new trade rules and dispute settlement processes. Others, however, became more skeptical about the desirability of pursuing negotiations or reaching an agreement, on the grounds that the United States might amend or fail to abide by a trade agreement once negotiated.

In large part, the Canadian debate about the Free Trade Agreement involves either real or imagined constraints on Canadian public policies that flow from commitments under the agreement. In addition, there is concern about increased economic and political pressures to harmonize domestic economic policies because of the greater integration of the two economies.

One of the key areas of concern to many Canadians involves the energy chapter of the agreement. The prohibition on export taxes is conventional under free trade areas, such as between Norway and the European Community. But this is not the perception of some Canadians who are disturbed that Canada no longer will be able to introduce the two-price energy regime that existed under the National Energy Program of 1980. Even more controversial in Canada are the provisions to assure US purchasers of Canadian oil, natural gas, and electricity that they will be guaranteed a stable proportion of Canadian energy supplies in the event of government-imposed rationing, regardless of whether that rationing is for reasons of short-term supply crisis or longer term efforts to conserve exhaustible resources. Of course, the obligations on energy are symmetric, but because Canada has proportionally more abundant energy supplies and is a net exporter of energy, the implications for each country are different.

The investment provisions of the agreement are controversial in Canada as well. Canadians remain concerned about the conduct of US multinational firms who control a substantial portion of the Canadian economy. Americans perceive the investment provisions as consolidating recent trends toward liberalization of Canadian investment policies, but these provisions are perceived in Canada as permanently entrenching highly controversial policy measures. Services issues raise some similar concerns. For example, some Canadians are concerned that the inclusion of health care management services in the agreement will be the thin edge of the wedge in a US assault on Canada's health care system.

In this regard the perspective expressed by Philip K. Verleger in this volume, about what was not achieved in the energy and investment chapters, resonates with the fears of many Canadians. Free trade is imagined as requiring a laissez-faire world where all government regulations are forbidden and market forces are allowed to prevail untrammeled. This model conforms with US mythology but not US practice in many sectors of the economy. Only Hong Kong among modern economies comes close to this laissez-faire ideal, and we might anticipate that even Hong Kong may undergo some changes in this regard before the Canada–US Free Trade Agreement is scheduled to be implemented fully.

The policy commitments in the agreement on investment and energy represent as great a commitment as most Canadians are prepared to accept. Like Edmund Burke, Canadians are less inclined than many Americans to trust the stewardship of natural resources to the dictates of the market. Other aspects of the agreement, notably the exclusion of cultural industries, represent strongly held views by many Canadians as well.

Many Canadians fear that liberalization of trade between Canada and the United States will increase economic pressures to harmonize domestic policies, even if there are no explicit commitments to do so in the agreement itself (Caplan 1987). It is true that economic interdependence on a global basis constrains the exercise of sovereignty by nation states. It is a mistake, however, to conclude that the removal of the remaining tariff and nontariff barriers to trade between Canada and the United States will increase substantially economic pressures that constrain the policy choices of Canadian governments (Lipsey and Smith 1985, chapter 7; Lipsey and Smith 1986).

Even within nations, economic pressures for policy harmonization are not overwhelming. Significant divergence in taxes, regulatory policies, labor legislation and environmental standards exist within the United States and Canada. Despite the openness of markets for goods and services and the mobility of labor and capital within the countries, states and provinces differ substantially in their tax, regulatory, and social policies. Thus, even within federal systems, subnational jurisdictions pursue very different policies, and are not subject to crushing economic pressures that would force them to harmonize their policies.

In an international context, the economic pressures for policy harmonization, which operate internally within a federal country, are greatly reduced by two factors. First, exchange rate adjustments over time offset the effects on location and trade that are associated with differences in broad-based tax or social policies. Second, the mobility of factors across international boundaries may exert greater pressures for policy harmonization than does expanded trade in goods and services. For example, emigration by highly skilled workers puts pressure on governments to harmonize marginal income tax rates. Indeed, expanded trade may reduce international pressures for policy harmonization because the economic benefits from trade can be used to finance public expenditures or to permit higher standards of environmental regulation. Furthermore, increased profit and employment opportunities in high technology industries may serve to reduce incentives to the highly skilled to emigrate that might be associated with differing marginal income tax rates. Although this basic set of arguments was articulated clearly by Harry Johnson and Paul Wonnacott many years ago, it is not understood by noneconomists and is often forgotten or neglected by economists (Johnson, Wonnacott, and Shibata 1968). Although the economic reasoning may be flawed, perceptions of potential economic pressures to harmonize tax and social policies emanating from a free trade agreement are deep-rooted concerns of many Canadians.

Beyond economic pressures, there is concern in Canada about the political and institutional pressures that might be associated with the ongoing conduct of economic relations within the context of the Free Trade Agreement. There is a fear that the United States will use its greater economic influence to put pressure on Canadian governments to conform with US policy objectives. The softwood lumber case provides some basis for this concern where Canadians perceive that the United States unilaterally reinterpreted the definition of subsidies in its countervailing duty legislation in response to political pressure from the US lumber lobby. Certainly, the threat of countervailing duties in the amount of 15 percent, and the negotiated settlement involving an export tax, put great pressure on Canadian governments to alter their stumpage policies in line with the objectives of US lumber interests, whatever the merits of their complaints. From a Canadian perspective, one main purpose of the agreement is to develop agreed rules and procedures to govern trade disputes that help reduce political conflicts in bilateral economic relations. Critics of the agreement in Canada argue that the threat of the trade bill and continuing negotiation of the rules on antidumping and countervailing duties make Canada more vulnerable to US political pressures on Canadian public policies (Surich 1987, Rotstein 1987).

The Joint Decision

Two points need to be made about the decision that each country, acting separately, must make about ratification of the Free Trade Agreement. The first point to stress is the simultaneity of the processes. Delay on the US side could impede timely action for implementation in Canada and increase the possibility that implementation of the agreement would be deferred until after an election whose outcome remains uncertain. If the United States enacts into law measures in a trade bill that are prejudicial to Canadian interests, or are perceived as being contrary to the agreement, such action will undermine the consensus that exists in Canada about the merits of the deal. Canadian public attitudes toward the agreement are critical because of the influence on provincial government positions and because implementation of the agreement could be a central issue in the next federal election.

Second, it is worth reflecting upon the longer term interests of both countries. The United States has become, like Canada, a debtor nation and in the 1990s both nations will be obliged to run trade surpluses with the rest of the world. The necessary realignment of trade patterns on a global basis may facilitate efforts to roll back bilaterally some of the protectionist provisions in each country's trade laws. Furthermore, each country's national interest will impel them to offer negotiated reductions in trade barriers to third countries during the Uruguay Round. Whether each nation will resist political pressures for unilateralism in 1988 and whether other countries will respond to US and Canadian negotiating efforts are different questions. But the answers are closely linked. Implementation of the agreement will strengthen the negotiating position of both countries, while failure to implement the agreement will undermine their respective international interests.

The Canada–US Free Trade Agreement will increase modestly the leverage of both countries in the Uruguay Round negotiations. This additional negotiating leverage will be very useful in efforts to achieve a positive result in the Uruguay Round. With the exchange rate alignments that we now observe and that are likely to prevail in the years ahead, the enthusiasm of the Europeans and Japanese for liberalization of trade is likely to wane, not increase. Already, one can hear protests from producers of Airbus to Bordeaux wines to semiconductors that the prevailing exchange rates are unfair. Since Canada experienced similar complaints from the United States over the last few years, these offshore complaints suggest that trade liberalization will be difficult to achieve with Europe and Japan in the near future, particularly in highly protected sectors such as agriculture.

Conclusion

In considering the agreement, the two countries have differing primary concerns. For Canada, the dominant concern is whether the agreement provides the appropriate basis for managing economic relations with its large neighbor. For the United States, the consideration of the Free Trade Agreement itself, and of how the agreement might mesh with the provisions of the trade bill, is part of a larger debate on how the United States will conduct its global economic relations in the 1990s and beyond when—like Canada—the United States will have to service its growing international liabilities.

The key question for Canadians will be whether the proposed agreement, and the dispute settlement mechanisms contained in it, provide a better "interface" mechanism for managing economic relations with the United States without imposing undesirable constraints upon Canadian policy choices. Answering this question requires a judgment about the policy constraints that will be imposed on Canadian energy and investment policies and a judgment about the effectiveness of the dispute settlement mechanisms. The domestic Canadian debate addresses these policy constraints, but the prospects for Canadian implementation hinge on events in the United States.

Apart from the deferral of the negotiation of substantive changes to the trade laws and the uncertainties that are associated with the outcome of that process, the negotiated provisions of the agreement represent a remarkable achievement. The failure to reconcile differences over the trade laws—a crucial aspect of the "interface" problem—ties the fate of the agreement to the outcome of the maneuvering between Congress and the Reagan administration over the trade bill. If provisions of the US trade bill redefining subsidies in the countervailing duty statute and making it easier to obtain import relief become law, and if these provisions apply to Canada, then support in Canada for implementation of the agreement will be seriously eroded.

Implementation of the agreement is in the mutual interest of the United States and Canada, despite and also because of, the asymmetries in their economies and economic interests. The agreement offers substantial economic benefits to both countries and could facilitate management of the world's largest bilateral commercial relationship. Beyond bilateral trade and investment, implementation of the agreement could serve to stimulate progress in negotiations in the Uruguay Round. It appears to be in the longer term interests of both countries to resist their impulses to unilateralism in the year ahead and to proceed with implementation of the Free Trade Agreement.

References

Aho, C. Michael, and Marc Levinson. 1987. "A Canadian Opportunity." *Foreign Policy*, no. 66, Spring, 143–155.

Brecher, Irving, and Simon Reisman. 1957. *Canada–United States Economic Relations*. Ottawa: Queen's Printer.

Brock, William E. 1984. "Canadian–U.S. Trade Negotiations: A Status Report." In *U.S.–Canadian Economic Relations: Next Steps*. Edward R. Fried and Philip H. Trezise, eds. Washington: Brookings Institution, 65–68.

Brown, Drusilla K., and Robert M. Stern. 1987. "A Modeling Perspective," with comments by Richard Harris and Peter Petri. In *Perspectives on a U.S.–Canadian Free Trade Agreement*. Robert M. Stern, Philip H. Trezise, and John Whalley, eds.

Washington: Brookings Institution and Institute for Research on Public Policy, 155–190.

Canadian–American Committee. 1985. *Canadian–U.S. Trade Options*. Toronto and Washington.

Caplan, Gerald. 1987. "The Effect of the Proposed Free Trade Agreement on Sovereignty Issues." In *Assessing the Canada–U.S. Free Trade Agreement*, Murray G. Smith and Frank Stone, eds. Halifax: Institute for Research on Public Policy, 229–233.

Department of Finance. 1988. *The Canadian–U.S. Free Trade Agreement: An Economic Assessment*. Ottawa.

Destler, I. M., and John S. Odell. 1987. *Anti-Protection: Changing Forces in United States Trade Policy*. POLICY ANALYSES IN INTERNATIONAL ECONOMICS 21. Washington: Institute for International Economics, September.

Diebold, William, Jr., ed. 1988. *Bilateralism, Multilateralism and Canada in U.S. Trade Policy*. Cambridge, Mass.: Ballinger for Council on Foreign Relations.

Economic Council of Canada. 1988. *Managing Adjustment*. Ottawa.

Grey, Rodney. 1981. *Trade Policy in the 1980s: An Agenda for Canadian–U.S. Relations*. Montreal: C. D. Howe Institute.

Harris, Richard. 1987. "Economic Impact on Canada." In *Building a Canadian–American Free Trade Area*. Edward R. Fried, Frank Stone, and Philip H. Trezise, eds. Washington: Brookings Institution and Institute for Research on Public Policy.

Horlick, Gary N. 1987. "Proposed U.S. Trade Legislation: A Brief Guide to the Lobbyrinth." In *International Economic Issues*. Ottawa: Institute for Research on Public Policy, September.

Hufbauer, Gary C., and Andrew Samet. 1985. "United States Response to Canadian Initiatives for Sectoral Trade Liberalization: 1983–84." In *The Politics of Canada's Economic Relationship with the United States*. Denis Stairs and Gilbert Winham, eds. Toronto: University of Toronto Press for the Royal Commission on the Economic Union and Development Process for Canada.

Jackson, John H. 1979. "Government Disputes in International Trade Relations: A Proposal in the Context of GATT." *Journal of World Trade Law*, 13:1.

Jackson, John H. 1986. "Achieving a Balance in International Trade." *International Business Lawyer*, April, 124.

Johnson, Harry G., Paul Wonnacott, and Hirofumi Shibata. 1968. *Harmonization of National Economic Policies Under Free Trade*. Toronto: University of Toronto Press for the Private Planning Association of Canada.

Kaminow, Ira. 1988. "Current Subsidy Estimates of Selected U.S. Production Subsidies." Discussion Paper, Institute for Research on Public Policy, Halifax.

Keohane, Robert, and Joseph Nye. 1977. *Power and Interdependence*. Boston: Little, Brown.

Lea, Sperry. 1987. "An Historical Perspective." In *Perspectives on a U.S.–Canadian Free Trade Agreement*. Robert M. Stern, Philip H. Trezise, and John Whalley, eds. Washington: Brookings Institution and Institute for Research on Public Policy, 11–29.

Leyton-Brown, David. 1985. *Weathering the Storm: Canadian–U.S. Relations, 1980–1983*. Toronto and Washington: Canadian–American Committee.

Lipsey, Richard G., and Murray G. Smith. 1985. *Taking the Initiative: Canada's Trade Options in a Difficult World*. Toronto: C. D. Howe Institute.

———, eds. 1986. *Policy Harmonization*. Toronto: C. D. Howe Institute.

———. 1987. *Global Imbalances and U.S. Policy Responses*. Toronto and Washington: Canadian–American Committee.

Morici, Peter. 1987. "Impact on the United States." In *Building a Canadian–American*

Free Trade Area. Edward R. Fried, Frank Stone, and Philip H. Trezise, eds. Washington: Brookings Institution and Institute for Research on Public Policy.

Moroz, Andrew. 1988. "Grant Support and Trade Protection for Canadian Industries." Discussion Paper, Institute for Research on Public Policy, Halifax.

Percy, Michael, and Christian Yoder. 1987. *The Softwood Lumber Dispute and Canada–US Trade in Natural Resources.* Halifax: Institute for Research on Public Policy.

Reisman, Simon. 1984. "The Issue of Free Trade." In *U.S.–Canadian Economic Relations: Next Steps.* Edward R. Fried and Philip H. Trezise, eds. Washington: Brookings Institution, 35–50.

————. 1987. "Comments." In *Assessing the Canada–U.S. Free Trade Agreement.* Murray G. Smith and Frank Stone, eds. Halifax: Institute for Research on Public Policy, 113–114.

Rotstein, Abraham. 1987. "A Balance Sheet on the Free Trade Agreement." In *Assessing the Canada–U.S. Free Trade Agreement.* Murray G. Smith and Frank Stone, eds. Halifax: Institute for Research on Public Policy, 246–247.

Rugman, Alan M. 1987. *Outward Bound: Canadian Direct Investment in the United States.* Toronto and Washington: Canadian–American Committee.

Schott, Jeffrey J. 1987. "U.S. Trade Legislation: Vintage 1987." In *International Economic Issues.* Ottawa: Institute for Research on Public Policy, September.

Smith, Murray G. 1987. "New Hazards for Canada." In *International Economic Issues.* Ottawa: Institute for Research on Public Policy, September.

————. 1988. "What is at Stake." In *Bilateralism, Multilateralism and Canada in U.S. Trade Policy.* William Diebold, Jr., ed. Cambridge, Mass.: Ballinger for Council on Foreign Relations.

Smith, Murray G., with C. Michael Aho and Gary N. Horlick. 1987. *Bridging the Gap: Trade Laws in the Canadian–U.S. Negotiations.* Toronto and Washington: Canadian–American Committee.

Steger, Debra P. 1987. "Constitutional Implications of the Implementation in Canada of a Trade-In-Services Agreement." Discussion Paper in Series on Trade and Services, Institute for Research on Public Policy, Victoria, June.

Surich, Jo. 1987. "Labour Concerns About Free Trade." In *Assessing the Canada–U.S. Free Trade Agreement.* Murray G. Smith and Frank Stone, eds. Halifax: Institute for Research on Public Policy, 198–199.

Velk, Tom, and A. R. Riggs. 1987. "Reciprocity 1911: Through American Eyes." In *Canadian–American Free Trade: Historical, Political and Economic Dimensions.* Tom Velk and A.R. Riggs, eds. Halifax: Institute for Research on Public Policy.

Waddell, Christopher. 1987. "Poll Finds Discontent Over Foreign Policy." *Globe and Mail.* August 18, A5

Wonnacott, Paul. 1987. *The United States and Canada: The Quest for Free Trade.* POLICY ANALYSES IN INTERNATIONAL ECONOMICS 16. Washington: Institute for International Economics, March.

Wonnacott, Ronald J. 1987. *Canadian and U.S. Adjustment Policies in a Bilateral Trade Agreement.* Toronto and Washington: Canadian–American Committee.

Wonnacott, Ronald J., and Paul Wonnacott. 1967. *Free Trade Between the United States and Canada: The Potential Economic Effects.* Cambridge, Mass.: Harvard University Press.

Young, J. H. 1957. *Canadian Commercial Policy.* Ottawa: Queen's Printer.

3

Dispute Resolution Mechanisms

Gary N. Horlick, Geoffrey D. Oliver, and Debra P. Steger

The governments of Canada and the United States have reached an agreement known as the Canada–United States Free Trade Agreement (FTA), intended to remove obstacles that keep Canadians and Americans from doing business in one another's country. An integral part of the FTA is the provisions for resolving disputes that arise between the two countries in the area of trade. The FTA will provide for an impartial binational dispute resolution system. It will also greatly shorten the deadlines for resolving these disputes; one problem for both countries has been the potentially chilling effect on trade while cases drag through the courts or the dispute resolution mechanisms of the General Agreement on Tariffs and Trade (GATT). In addition, the FTA changes US and Canadian substantive law in the escape clause area by limiting its application in cases involving exports from the other party and by improving dispute resolution procedures.

These provisions take the form of two separate mechanisms for dispute resolution, one applying to disputes arising out of the other country's enforcement of its antidumping (AD) and countervailing duty (CVD) laws, and one applying to all other disputes arising under the FTA. The FTA provides for "binding" decisions with respect to all escape clause or GATT Article XIX disputes, all binational antidumping or countervailing panel

Gary N. Horlick, of the Washington office of the law firm O'Melveny & Myers, was formerly Deputy Assistant Secretary for Import Administration, US Department of Commerce, 1981–83; and International Trade Counsel, US Senate Committee on Finance, 1981. Geoffrey D. Oliver is also at O'Melveny & Myers. He was the Robert Bosch Foundation Fellow in the Federal Republic of Germany, 1986–87. Debra P. Steger is with the Ottawa, Ontario, law firm of Fraser & Beatty and teaches international trade law at the University of Ottawa.

Because of their length and complexity, the notes for this chapter follow the text instead of appearing at the foot of each page.—Ed.

reviews, and any other matter affecting the FTA where both parties agree. Finally, the FTA provides that the two governments will negotiate common rules in the AD/CVD area to replace rules that are increasingly perceived as being outmoded or barriers to economically desirable trade between businesses in the two countries.

Elements of the Dispute Resolution Mechanisms

The FTA provides two separate mechanisms for settlement of trade disputes between the United States and Canada. The "Institutional Provisions" chapter of the FTA (Chapter 18) establishes the general procedures to be followed in avoiding or resolving a dispute arising under the agreement. The procedures set forth in Chapter 18 apply to all disputes arising under the FTA with the exception of disputes dealt with under Chapter 19,[1] "Binational Panel Dispute Settlement in Antidumping and Countervailing Duty Cases," and disputes relating to the provision of financial services. Disputes involving escape clause cases are subject to the binding arbitration procedures set forth in the Institutional Provisions chapter of the FTA.[2]

Under the Institutional Provisions, each country is obligated to provide written notice to the other country of "any proposed or actual measure" that it considers might materially affect the operation of the agreement.[3] Each country is also required to respond promptly to questions or requests for information from the other country. The next step is consultation; either country may request consultations regarding "any actual or proposed measure or any other matter" that it considers affects the operation of the FTA.[4] This opportunity for consultation exists whether or not the measure or matter was previously notified.

If the parties fail to resolve a matter through consultations within 30 days, either country may refer the matter to the Canada–US Trade Commission.[5] The commission will be established under the FTA to supervise the proper implementation of the agreement, to resolve disputes concerning its interpretation or application, to oversee its further elaboration, and to consider any other matter that affects its operation. The commission will be composed of representatives of both countries, with the principal representative being the cabinet-level officers or ministers primarily responsible for international trade matters or their designees.[6] If the commission is unable to resolve the dispute within 30 days, it may refer the dispute to a binding arbitration panel, or it is required to establish a panel of experts to consider the matter.

Disputes involving escape clause actions must always be sent to a binding arbitration panel.[7] The Canada–US Trade Commission may refer any other dispute to binding arbitration. The commission is to establish the terms under which a binding arbitration panel will operate. It will function differently from a panel of experts in one important respect: Its findings will be final and binding on both member governments with no further report back or action by the commission. Where one country fails to comply with a panel finding in a timely fashion, and the two countries are unable to agree on appropriate compensation or remedial action, then the other country may retaliate by suspending the application of equivalent benefits of the FTA to the offending country.[8]

Where the commission decides not to refer a matter to binding arbitration, it will establish a panel of experts to investigate. Such a panel is required to present to the member countries, within three months after its chairman is appointed, an initial report with its findings of fact, a determination as to whether the matter complained of is inconsistent with (or would cause nullification or impairment of) the FTA, and its recommendations for resolution of the dispute. Both countries will be given an opportunity to present any reasons for disagreement with the panel report. After making any further examination that it considers appropriate, the panel must issue a final report within 30 days after presenting the initial report. The final report and any separate opinions will be published. The commission is to receive the final report of the panel and make a decision on how to resolve the dispute. In the normal case, its decision should accord with the panel's recommendation. However, the commission may decide on a different remedy. Decisions of the commission must be made by consensus.[9] Therefore, both parties must agree on any resolution recommended. If the commission is unable to reach a consensus resolution within 30 days after receiving the final panel report, the complainant country may suspend the application of equivalent benefits under the FTA where it considers that its fundamental rights or benefits are or would be impaired by the continuation of the measure on which the complaint was brought.[10]

The binational panel system for dispute settlement in antidumping and countervailing duty cases will operate independently from the general dispute settlement mechanism, with a different roster of panelists and unique procedures. However, a permanent secretariat will be established to facilitate the operation of binational antidumping and countervailing duty panels and provide support for the commission.

Upon the request of either country, a binational panel will be established to review final agency orders in antidumping or countervailing duty cases or to review legislative amendments to either country's antidumping or countervailing duty laws. In a specific AD/CVD case, if requested by either member country, a binational panel will be established to take the place of judicial review of final AD or CVD orders in the United States and Canada. A binational panel will be required to apply the standard of judicial review applicable under the domestic law of the investigating country to determine whether the agency decision in question complied with domestic law.[11] A panel may either uphold the agency decision or remand the decision to the relevant agency for specific action.[12] A panel decision is binding on both parties and on the relevant agencies in the United States and Canada.[13] A panel will be required to follow a strict timetable for hearing a dispute and must issue its final decision within 300 to 315 days from the time that the request for the panel is made.[14]

If either country considers that the integrity of the binational panel review process has been threatened by gross misconduct, bias, or serious conflict of interest of a panel member; a departure by the panel from a fundamental rule of procedure; or a panel manifestly exceeding its jurisdiction, an extraordinary challenge committee may be established to review the binational panel's decision. Consisting of three federal court or superior court judges from both countries, the extraordinary challenge committee must render its decision within 30 days and cannot be appealed. Its decisions are binding on both member countries.[15]

The binational review mechanism for dispute settlement in AD/CVD cases will be in place for a period of five years, with the possibility of extension for an additional two years.[16] During this period, the two countries are to cooperate to develop a "substitute system" of AD/CVD laws applicable in both countries.[17] Failure to reach agreement on a common system of AD/CVD laws within seven years is grounds for either party, upon six month's notice, to terminate the agreement.

Improvements in Judicial Review Procedures for AD/CVD Cases

At present, Canadians who are dissatisfied with a final determination in a US antidumping or countervailing duty investigation or, to a limited extent, a Section 201 escape clause proceeding,[18] may seek review of that determination by the Court of International Trade (CIT) in the first instance, followed if necessary by a subsequent appeal to the Court of Appeals for the Federal Circuit (CAFC).[19] The standard of review applied by the CIT is that the agency determination should be held unlawful if it is "arbitrary, capricious, [or] an abuse of discretion"; "unsupported by substantial evidence on the record"; or "otherwise not in accordance with law" (19 USC §1516a[b][1]).

In Canada, the relevant agency investigations are conducted by the Department of National Revenue, Customs and Excise (DNR) and the Canadian Import Tribunal (Tribunal). Currently, private parties (including a US exporter or an importer of US products under investigation) who are dissatisfied with a final order of the Tribunal, relating to injury caused or threatened to Canadian producers by products found to be dumped or subsidized by DNR, may seek judicial review of that order in the Federal

Court of Appeals (FCA).[20] Under the Federal Court Act, the FCA may review and uphold, reverse, or remand a final decision of the Tribunal upon the grounds that the Tribunal:

☐ failed to observe a principle of natural justice or otherwise acted beyond, or refused to exercise, its jurisdiction

☐ erred in law in making its decision or order

☐ based its decision or order on an erroneous finding of fact that it made in a perverse or capricious manner or without regard for the material before it.[21]

Customs officials enforce final AD or CVD orders by the Tribunal by applying duties in the amount of the margin of dumping in an AD case, or in the amount of the subsidy in a CVD case, on imported goods. A determination by a customs official as to whether imported goods are the same as goods to which the AD or CVD order applies or a determination assessing the amount of the duty payable may be appealed to a Dominion customs appraiser and subsequently to the Deputy Minister of DNR. A redetermination by the Deputy Minister may be appealed to the Tariff Board and subsequently to the FCA on a question of law only.

The FTA would make a final injury finding by the Tribunal or a redetermination by the Deputy Minister subject to review by a binational panel. In addition, certain decisions made by DNR and the Tribunal that are not currently subject to appeal or review in the courts would become reviewable by a binational panel. These include final determinations by DNR of dumping or subsidization and reviews by the Deputy Minister of undertakings.

Under the Special Import Measures Act, the Tribunal may review its own orders or findings as they relate to imported goods that have not been released for entry, to imported goods that were released during the provisional period after a DNR preliminary determination, and in any case where an undertaking has been violated. Decisions by the Tribunal as to whether to initiate such reviews and orders made as a result of such reviews are often highly discretionary. To initiate such a review, the Tribunal must be convinced that circumstances have changed such that initiation of a review is warranted. Under the FTA, a decision by the Tribunal on whether to initiate a review, as well as an order or finding made as a result of a review, may be submitted to a binational panel for reconsideration.

A significant practical advantage for US exporters or importers of US products involved in an antidumping or countervailing duty case, or caught by existing AD or CVD orders, is that they will be able to seek binational panel review of certain DNR and Tribunal decisions that could not be previously reviewed by the courts. Thus, the FTA has improved the transparency of, and opportunities for, challenging certain agency decisions in the Canadian system.

It is difficult to predict whether these increased opportunities will be utilized by US exporters or importers of US products. The standard of judicial review to be applied by a binational panel in such a case is onerous. However, because a US exporter will be able to rely on the US government to initiate and plead its case before a binational panel, the costs of losing will be reduced. Given the greater opportunity for challenge of agency decisions and the reduced risk in doing so, US exporters and importers of US products may be encouraged to make more effective use of the binational AD/CVD panels than they ever have of the Canadian courts.

The AD/CVD and escape clause dispute settlement mechanisms contained in the FTA considerably change existing methods of appeal and judicial review. Many of these changes are very practical ones. They may seem mundane compared with theories of international trade, but they could be of great significance to US and Canadian petitioners and respondents involved in AD or CVD cases.

A significant improvement with respect to US and Canadian AD and CVD determinations is the lessening of the time period for the review process. The binational panel review process contemplated by the FTA would operate much faster than the current US and Canadian judicial review procedure. The FTA dispute resolution mechanism for AD/CVD cases would be subject to a deadline of 300 to 315 days, measured from the end of the administrative proceeding being reviewed.[22] This would provide for final review of US and Canadian AD/CVD determinations in less time than it usually takes to obtain a decision from the CIT alone. Furthermore, the maximum time limit would eliminate the opportunity for open-ended delays under US and Canadian law.[23] It also would provide private parties with greater certainty and security than is available under the current system.[24]

A second major practical change in the binational dispute resolution mechanism is the use of five binational panelists (rather than a single judge in the US system). The US Court of International Trade is made up of nine judges as well as six judges of senior status, each of whom sit, hear cases, and issue decisions individually.[25] Interpretations of the law can vary significantly from judge to judge even though they all apply the same laws and same standard of review.[26] While the Court of Appeals for the Federal Circuit ensures eventual uniformity, this is not a satisfactory solution; the CAFC will only operate to correct a split among the CIT judges after it has already occurred, and the delay involved in the additional appeal adds to the burdens of the parties.[27]

In Canada, three judges generally sit and hear cases in the FCA involving judicial review of a final order of the Tribunal. However, as discussed earlier, certain determinations, such as a final determination by DNR on subsidization or dumping, are not reviewable in the courts. Obviously, in these cases review by five impartial binational panelists will be better than no review at all.

The binational composition of the AD/CVD review panels should encourage a full airing of different interpretations of US and Canadian law in a particular case. The make-up of the panels should prevent extreme positions from being adopted and becoming precedent.[28] Moderate decisions would be necessary to achieve panel consensus. Although the membership of each panel will vary from case to case, the possibility of recourse to previous panel decisions in future cases will help to encourage continuity and consistency in decision making.

This represents a major advantage in comparison with existing judicial review procedures. Currently, each country's views on the application of the other's AD/CVD laws in specific cases are relevant only to the extent that the judge or judges hearing a case choose to accept the arguments of the parties from the other country. In Canada, in particular, the standard for judicial review is so onerous that foreign exporters are often disinclined to apply for judicial review. Under the dispute resolution mechanism, representatives from both the United States and Canada will take part in the process, and the views of all parties will be assured a full hearing.

Not only will the binational character of the panels create more equitable application of each country's AD/CVD laws to industries in the other country, but it will also increase the perception of fairness and impartiality among business people in the application of those laws. An improved business climate and confidence in the fair application of each country's trade laws should result in more willingness to export to the other country and a corresponding removal of investment distortions between the two countries.

The FTA binational AD/CVD panel system also significantly helps small businesses in each country. At present, businesses and trade associations must take an appeal or an application for judicial review to the CIT, CAFC, Tariff Board, or FCA themselves. (Sovereign governments rarely appear in the domestic courts of a foreign government.) Under the FTA, each government may request the establishment of a binational review panel. As a result, a small business or trade association that previously could not afford the expense of challenging an agency ruling before the CIT or FCA now can have its viewpoint presented by its government before a binational review panel. Indeed, if a private party involved in an AD/CVD case requests that its government initiate a binational panel review, its government must comply.

The AD/CVD binational panel review mechanism contained in the FTA has been criticized for failing to correct alleged defects in the content or application of US and Canadian antidumping and countervailing duty laws.

Others have criticized the mechanism because it would apply the same standard of judicial review currently applied under US and Canadian law. The implication is that the standard of review used by the courts is not sufficiently rigorous.

In numerous cases the CIT has reversed final affirmative findings by the US Department of Commerce.[29] But the criticism that the Canadian standard of review is not sufficiently rigorous carries more weight. The FCA has remanded only four out of seventeen cases to the Tribunal since 1979.[30] It has not remanded a single case since 1983. By reducing the cost and the inherent risks of seeking review of Canadian authorities' decisions, however, the number of cases submitted to the binational panels should be greater than the number of cases previously reviewed in the courts. Because the sample of AD/CVD cases reviewed by the FCA is so small, it remains to be seen whether the availability of review by binational panels in more cases will lead to a softening of the Canadian standard of review.

A second criticism voiced by some Canadians is that the critical problem for Canadian exporters has not been adverse US Department of Commerce or USITC final determinations, but rather adverse preliminary determinations, which would remain outside the scope of the binational panel review mechanism. First, it is worth noting that the USITC is no rubber stamp; it has made negative preliminary determinations in many cases, thus terminating the investigations within 45 days after the petition was filed.[31] Furthermore, it is not true that affirmative preliminary findings become "cast in stone." In a number of cases, the USITC has ruled in the final determination that the domestic industry was not suffering injury caused by the imports at issue.[32] Likewise, in a number of cases a preliminary affirmative determination by Commerce has been substantially modified in the final determination.[33] If a final determination does repeat the mistakes of an erroneous preliminary determination, however, the binational panel review mechanism in the FTA will provide a faster, cheaper, and more impartial method of review and redress than that which currently exists.

The critics have not advanced any evidence to support the claim that Canadian or US exports are seriously affected by the imposition of provisional (preliminary) AD or CVD duties in cases in which the Canadian or US exporters are successful at the final determination stage. In such cases, in either the United States or Canada, any provisional (preliminary) duties collected are promptly refunded. The FTA does not change the administrative and judicial procedures that provide recourse for return of such duties.

Improvements in Application of the Escape Clause

In addition to the new dispute resolution mechanism in AD/CVD cases, the FTA significantly changes the application and review of action taken by either the United States or Canada in accordance with GATT Article XIX under their countries' respective escape clause provisions. Section 201 of the US Trade Act of 1974[34] provides that the United States can take measures, including imposing duties and quantitative restrictions, against imports of certain products from all countries if increased imports are found to be a substantial cause of serious injury or threat thereof to a domestic industry.[35] Canada has similar measures available under Section 8 of the Customs Tariff[36] and Section 5 of the Export and Import Permits Act.[37] Because action under an escape clause is taken against imports from all countries, US or Canadian products can be caught in such an action initiated by the other country, even if the increase in imports and injury to the domestic industry are caused largely by products imported from third countries.[38]

In the event of an escape clause action, the FTA provides that imports from the other country would be excluded from such a proceeding unless they were "substantial" and "contributing importantly" to the "serious injury or threat thereof caused by imports." Imports from the United States or Canada in the range of 5 to 10 percent or less of the other country's total imports of the good or goods in question "would normally not be considered substantial."[39] Furthermore, even if the other country's imports exceed the 5 to 10 percent range, the FTA requires that they be excluded unless they are found to be "contributing significantly" to the injury.[40]

In a US or Canadian escape clause action involving a product from the other country, the initiating government would be required to notify the other government (and, if so requested, to enter into consultations) prior to taking action.[41] If a country considers that an escape clause measure imposed by the other country is contrary to, or impairs benefits anticipated under, the FTA or the GATT, that country may ask the Canada–US Trade Commission to refer the matter to a binding arbitration panel.

Improvements in Dispute Resolution Under GATT

Designed to emphasize consensus among the parties,[42] GATT panel procedures have not proven to be an entirely satisfactory way to resolve trade disputes. Moreover, panel decisions are not binding in their own right. The dispute resolution mechanisms under the FTA are a clear improvement over the GATT procedures because they provide a faster and more effective forum for resolving disputes and because panel decisions are final in many cases.

The collection of agreements contained within the framework of the GATT do not provide for a single dispute settlement procedure, but rather a number of distinct although similar procedures applicable in specific types of cases. The most relevant procedures for purposes of the FTA are those found in Articles 17 and 18 of the Agreement on Interpretation and

Application of Articles VI, XVI, and XXIII of the General Agreement on Tariffs and Trade (the Subsidies Code), Article 15 of the Agreement on Implementation of Article VI of the General Agreement on Tariffs and Trade (the Antidumping Code), and Articles XXII and XXIII of the GATT.[43]

The first advantage of the FTA over these various GATT procedures is that it requires notice and consultation between the parties prior to any future change in AD/CVD law and an express statement in any amending legislation that the changes are to apply to the other country.[44] The FTA procedure for early notice of challenge sends a useful "warning shot" *before* an objectionable action is taken, while also expediting the dispute resolution process if it becomes necessary.

A second advantage lies in the membership of the panels. A large majority of GATT panelists come from the official delegations in Geneva of the GATT member countries.[45] The members of each panel are expected to act independently of their countries' individual interests in reaching a determination.[46] As civil servants employed by their countries, however, they cannot help but appear to be influenced by national interests. Under the FTA, the ad hoc panelists who would be appointed to AD/CVD panels will be free from such constraints. In fact, government officials are prohibited from acting as panelists. No one will make a career out of service on such panels, and it is unlikely that the remuneration will permanently lure people from the private sector. Consequently, panel members will be more independent and less subject to national interests than government officials can be.

A major advantage of the FTA dispute resolution mechanisms is the much faster time frame within which they will operate. For example, of the relevant GATT procedures, Article XXIII of GATT and the GATT Antidumping Code do not provide specific time frames for establishing a panel and obtaining a final decision or ruling.[47] By contrast, the FTA clearly sets out the time limits for each stage of the panel review process.[48] The FTA dispute resolution mechanisms also permit institution of a panel prior to the final determination in an AD/CVD investigation, in readiness for the filing of a formal complaint following the final agency decision.[49] With respect to changes in legislation, the FTA does not wait for the injurious effects of a new law to be felt before requiring the parties to consult with each other. A panel may be brought into play after notification of, and consultation concerning, proposed legislation.[50] Although the GATT panel procedures have been improved, there are still often considerable delays in starting up the GATT "motor."

Decisions made under the FTA will be more direct and effective than rulings made by GATT panels, which have to be approved by the consensus of the GATT Council. In addition, under the GATT third countries can intervene in a dispute between the United States and Canada, either before a panel or at the time of adoption of a panel ruling, significantly complicating and delaying any resolution.[51] Furthermore, the offending country can itself block adoption of an objectionable panel report (as the United States has done in several agricultural cases).[52] Under the FTA, by contrast, the panel rulings in AD/CVD cases and escape clause actions will be final and binding on both countries and their investigating agencies.[53]

In the event of a failure to resolve a dispute involving proposed changes to AD/CVD laws, comparable legislation or equivalent executive action or withdrawal from the FTA may occur. Retaliation under this provision of the FTA is expressly limited to comparable legislative or executive action. This will be clearly preferable to the practice that has developed under the GATT whereby parties have the leeway to retaliate in ways that escalate or widen the dispute into areas not originally involved. If the dispute concerns an escape clause measure or other matter affecting the operation of the FTA, and if no resolution is achieved within a specified period of time, the injured country has the right to suspend the application of equivalent benefits under the FTA. These measures are an improvement over the GATT, which does not provide for an automatic right of retaliation. Such direct, prompt retaliation should help to encourage mutual avoidance and resolution of disputes and to limit retaliatory action to the particular matter on which the complaint was brought.

Unparalleled Protection Against Future Changes in Trade Laws

Both the AD/CVD and general dispute resolution mechanisms apply not only to specific cases, but also to changes in Canadian or US legislation that the other country believes might materially affect the operation of the FTA. The two processes differ in their operation, but the ultimate result is a binding dispute resolution mechanism for all changes in AD/CVD legislation and the opportunity for the Canada–US Trade Commission to invoke binding arbitration or establish a panel of experts in all other instances.[54]

The AD/CVD dispute resolution mechanism applies to proposed changes in either country's AD/CVD laws.[55] Thus, neither the United States nor Canada would be allowed to apply changes in its AD/CVD laws to the other country unless there had been prior notification and consultations (if requested) with the other country; the amending legislation stated specifically that it would apply to the other country (something that the US Congress and the Canadian Parliament have sought to avoid in the past); and the changes were consistent with the GATT, the Antidumping Code and the Subsidies Code, and with the object and purpose of the FTA, including the object and purpose of the dispute settlement provisions.[56]

If a dispute involving proposed amendments to the AD/CVD laws is not resolved by consultations, either member country may refer the matter to a binational panel. This panel would have the authority to issue a declaratory opinion with respect to the proposed amendments, to determine their consistency with the GATT, the Antidumping Code and the Subsidies Code, and with the object and purpose of the FTA, and also to determine whether such amendments would have the function and effect of overturning a prior decision of a binational AD/CVD panel.[57] If a panel recommends modifications to the proposed changes in antidumping or countervailing duty laws, the government seeking to make the changes must consult with the other government for a period of 90 days. In the event that no mutual resolution is reached and enacted upon within nine months, the complainant government is empowered either to take comparable legislative or executive action, or to terminate the FTA with 60 days' notice.[58]

The general dispute resolution mechanisms in the FTA require each country to provide written notice to the other country of any actual or proposed change in its legislation, regulations, or government practice (other than AD/CVD legislation) that might materially affect the operation of the FTA. That country must also provide information requested by the other country and respond to questions of the other country concerning any such change. The other country may request consultations regarding any actual or proposed measure, whether or not notified, that it considers might materially affect the operation of the FTA.[59] This new formal channel for communications represents an improvement over existing practice in which the US and Canadian governments are not notified of changes in the other's legislation, regulations, or government practices affecting trade, much less have rights to request consultations with the other government concerning those changes.[60]

If consultations between the two governments fail to resolve a matter, the next step is to bring the dispute before the Canada–US Trade Commission.[61] If the commission is unable to reach a decision by consensus within 30 days, arbitration follows. The commission may order that any dispute under any chapter of the FTA (except financial services or binational review of AD/CVD cases and disputes) be submitted to a binding arbitration panel.

If either government fails to implement the decisions of a binding arbitration panel within a reasonable time, the offending government is obliged to provide compensation to the other government. If the two governments cannot agree on appropriate compensation, then the injured government has the right to suspend the application of "equivalent benefits" of the FTA to the noncomplying government.[62]

These remedies—the right of compensation and the sanction of withdrawal of equivalent benefits under the FTA—make the dispute settlement mechanisms binding in international law. They are as binding as either country was ever likely to agree to, and they include more effective sanctions than the vast majority of international agreements.[63] This is particularly true in the context of AD/CVD practices, where parties to free trade agreements have rarely agreed to binding binational dispute resolution mechanisms.[64] More than most comparable international agreements, the FTA protects each country against changes in the other government's legislation and other practices affecting trade (AD/CVD legislation and practices in particular). Most importantly, the FTA mechanisms provide for prompt, effective resolution of disputes with no significant diminution of sovereignty by either government, its agencies or its courts.

Toward a Common Body of Canadian–US Trade Law

The dispute settlement mechanisms embodied in the FTA may prove exceptionally useful in the development of a Canadian–US system of trade laws. These mechanisms should help provide a period of stability in the development and application of Canadian and US trade laws while a common system of trade laws is being developed. The dispute resolution panels also may lead to the creation of a body of experts in each country with experience actually applying the laws of the other country to resolve disputes concerning specific cases. Such expertise would be helpful in the development or negotiation of common principles of trade law.[65]

Although the binational AD/CVD panels will be charged with reviewing the results of antidumping and countervailing duty investigations under the applicable Canadian or US law, over time they should be able to develop a body of cases for use in interpreting the FTA, and they might also develop certain common approaches to specific areas of trade law. These common principles and elements of law should form the foundation of future efforts to harmonize conflicting areas of Canadian and US trade law. Finally, the five-year limitation on the life of the dispute resolution mechanisms (with the possibility of a two-year extension) will give Canada and the United States the time to develop a common approach to trade law, while at the same time establishing a deadline to compel concrete action.[66]

Notes

1. Canada–United States Free Trade Agreement, Article 1801.1, 9 December 1987 (hereafter FTA).

2. FTA, Article 1806.1(a).

3. FTA, Article 1803.1.

4. FTA, Article 1804.1.

5. FTA, Article 1805.1.

6. FTA, Article 1802.2.

7. The arbitration panels will be composed of five members. The commission will maintain a roster of potential panelists; whenever possible, members of each panel should be chosen from the list of panelists. Each country in consultation with the other country will choose two members of the panel. The fifth member will be chosen by the commission. If the commission is unable to agree, the four appointed panelists shall decide upon the fifth panelist. If the four panelists are unable to agree, the fifth panelist will be selected at random from the prepared roster. FTA, Article 1807.3.

8. FTA, Article 1807.5.

9. FTA, Article 1807.6, 1807.8.

10. FTA, Article 1807.

11. FTA, Article 1911.

12. FTA, Article 1904.8.

13. Panels have the authority to issue declaratory opinions on whether proposed changes in a country's AD/CVD laws are consistent with the GATT Antidumping and Subsidies Codes and with the object and purpose of the free trade agreement, as well as whether it "has the function and effect of overturning a prior decision of a panel" FTA, Article 1903.1(b). If a panel recommends modifications to the proposed changes, the parties are obligated to consult to reach a solution. If the dispute is not resolved within nine months, the injured party may "take comparable legislative or equivalent executive action" or, after 60 days' notice, terminate the agreement. FTA, Article 1903.3(b).

14. FTA, Article 1904.14.

15. FTA, Article 1904.13; Annex 1904.13.

16. FTA, Article 1906.

17. Ibid.

18. Parties to a Section 201 proceeding may sue regarding procedural irregularities, but not on the merits of a case. See *Maple Leaf Fish Co. v. United States,* 762 F.2d 86 (Fed. Cir. 1985). No reference is made in the FTA to US Section 337 of the Tariff Act of 1930 (19 USC § 1337), which is applied mainly to imports that violate patent or trademark laws. The United States refused to agree to changes to Section 337 without Canadian commitments on patent and trademark law.

19. The following agency determinations may be appealed to the CIT: decisions not to initiate an antidumping or countervailing duty proceeding; decisions not to review agreements to eliminate less-than-fair-value (LTFV) sales, eliminate or offset subsidies, cease exports, or eliminate injurious effect; decisions not to review a determination on the basis of changed circumstances; negative preliminary injury determinations by the US International Trade Commission; determinations by the Department of Commerce that a case is "extraordinarily complicated"; negative preliminary LTFV sales determinations by Commerce; negative subsidy determinations by Commerce; final injury determinations by the USITC; final LTFV sales determinations by Commerce; final subsidy determinations by Commerce; determinations under administrative review of antidumping or countervailing duty orders; determinations by Commerce to suspend an antidumping or countervailing duty investigation; and injury determinations by the USITC during a review of a suspended investigation. See 19 USC § 1516a(a)(2)(B).

20. Federal Court Act, R.S.C. 1970, c.10 (2d Supp.), S. 28.

21. The FCA usually will not interfere with a finding by a statutory tribunal having the legal authority and expertise necessary to evaluate the evidence unless there was a complete absence of evidence to support the finding or a wrong principle of law was applied in making the decision. *Sarco Canada, Ltd. v. Antidumping Tribunal et al.*

(1979) 1 F.C. 247 (C.A.). To establish an error of fact necessary for review under Section 28(1)(c), the FCA must find that the tribunal made an "erroneous" finding of fact *and* that the erroneous finding was made in a perverse or capricious manner or without regard to the material before the tribunal. *Rohm & Haas Canada Limited v. Antidumping Tribunal* (1978), 91 D.L.R. (3d) 212 (F.C.A.).

Thus, the Canadian standard of judicial review based upon errors of fact requires proof that the Tribunal *willfully* decided either to ignore the evidence before it or to act contrary to that evidence. Errors of law might include misconstruing or misinterpreting statutory or common law, applying an incorrect onus of proof, or wrongfully admitting or refusing to admit evidence. However, where a tribunal properly admits evidence, it cannot be reversed for giving the wrong weight to particular evidence. *PPG Industries Ltd. v. Antidumping Tribunal* (1978), 22 N.R. 263 (F.C.A.); *Merkuria Foreign Trade Corporation v. Antidumping Tribunal* (1980), 2 C.E.R. 142 (F.C.A.).

Courts very rarely overturn decisions of tribunals for jurisdictional error. Such errors generally relate to mistakes concerning the composition or character of the tribunal, the nature or conduct of the inquiry, or failure to meet mandatory procedural requirements. Whether or not a tribunal could have made a more thorough inquiry is not a refusal to exercise its jurisdiction. See *Sarco Canada Ltd. v. Antidumping Tribunal,* supra; *Brunswick International (Canada) Ltd. v. Antidumping Tribunal* (1979), 35 N.R. 71 (F.C.A.).

22. A request for a panel must be made within 30 days following publication or notification of the AD/CVD decision. FTA, Article 1904.4. Thereafter, the deadlines for the panel in hearing appeals of AD/CVD cases are as follows: 30 days for the complaining party to file its complaint, 30 days for designation of the administrative record and its filing with the panel, 60 days for complainant to file its brief, 60 days for respondent to file its brief, 15 days for each party to file reply briefs, 15 to 30 days for the panel to convene to hear oral argument by each party, and 90 days for the panel to issue its decision.

The investigating authority concerned would then take action consistent with the decision of the panel and within time limits set by the panel, taking into account the complexity and difficulty of such action (for example, whether the investigating authority needs to obtain new factual information). FTA, Articles 1904.14, 1904.8.

23. Following are examples of the length of time that has been required for a final US decision (CIT or CAFC) where judicial review has been sought by Canadians: pork (CVD), two years and two months; sugar and syrups (AD), four years and five months; methyl alcohol (AD), two years and two months; and iron construction castings (AD), one year and four months.

24. A 300 to 315 day deadline for an appeal would have been very helpful in the recent US–Canadian potash AD investigation, had that investigation not been terminated by a suspension agreement. See *Potassium Chloride from Canada,* 52 Fed. Reg. 32,151 (1987) (Affirm. prelim.). In this investigation the Commerce Department allowed the US petitioners standing to sue without following the rules provided in both US law and the GATT Antidumping Code (Article 4.1). If the FTA dispute resolution mechanism had been available, Canada would have been able to obtain much faster review of this issue than is generally available from the GATT or the US courts.

25. Three judges may be requested to hear a case, but this is done only in extraordinary circumstances. See 28 USC § 255 (1982).

26. The use of panels rather than individual judges could have a major impact by eliminating the disparate results that can occur when a series of individual judges make decisions. For example, individual judges of the CIT imposed differing treatment of generally available subsidies. Compare *Carlisle Tire & Rubber Co. v. United States,* 564 F. Supp. 834 (Ct. Int'l Trade, 1983) (generally available subsidies are not countervailable) with *Bethlehem Steel Corp. v. United States,* 590 F. Supp. 1237 (Ct. Int'l Trade, 1984) (generally available subsidies are countervailable, except for tax deductions).

In *Cabot Corp. v. United States*, 620 F. Supp. 722 (Ct. Int'l Trade, 1985), one CIT judge rejected the established specificity test of the Commerce Department, which was used to differentiate countervailable subsidies from "generally available," noncountervailable government assistance. At issue was a Commerce Department ruling that the Mexican government's two-tier pricing scheme for petroleum products (one set price for all domestic consumers and a second, higher price for foreign consumers) was not a countervailable subsidy. The opinion stated that the programs at issue "are apparently available to all Mexican enterprises, but in their actual implementation may result in special bestowals upon specific enterprises." Ibid. at 732.

The language of *Cabot* was subject to three possible interpretations. First, if individual recipients of a government program could be identified, any benefits they received would be countervailable. Second, even if the individual recipients could be identified, the Commerce Department would have to analyze the operation of the program to determine whether certain recipients benefited more than others. Finally, Commerce merely had to confirm that, in addition to being generally available the program was also widely used. See Hunter and Kubach, "Subsidies and Countervailing Duties: Highlights Since 1984" in D. Riggs (Chairman), *The Commerce Department Speaks 1987*, 491 at 514–15 (1987).

This issue remained unresolved for two years. Recently, however, three judges of the CIT issued three parallel opinions dealing with this issue. In *PPG Industries, Inc. v. United States*, 662 F. Supp. 258 (Ct. Int'l Trade, 1987), the court upheld a Commerce Department determination that the Mexican government's pricing system for natural gas was noncountervailable because it was generally available and in fact widely used even though the export price was much higher than the home market price. In two subsequent cases two other CIT judges adopted the same standard. See *Al Tech Specialty Steel Corp. v. United States*, 661 F. Supp. 1206 (Ct. Int'l Trade, 1987); *Can-Am Corp. v. United States*, 664 F. Supp. 1444 (Ct. Int'l Trade, 1987).

Although the three 1987 CIT decisions substantially clarified *Cabot*, they were not in time to spare the Canadian lumber industry. The petitioners in the 1983 lumber case filed a second petition in May 1986 claiming changed circumstances, based in large part on the *Cabot* decision. 51 Fed. Reg. 19422 (1986) (ITC prelim. institution); 51 Fed. Reg. 21205 (1986) (Initiation). The Commerce Department then relied upon *Cabot* to issue a preliminary determination that the government assistance at issue ("stumpage") was not nonspecific and thus countervailable. 51 Fed. Reg. 37453 (1986) (Affirm. prelim.). The petition was eventually withdrawn, but only after Canada agreed to impose an export tax or alter its stumpage pricing systems. Problems of this sort could be avoided by the use of a five-member panel.

27. The *Cabot* case is an example of a CIT decision that could not be corrected on appeal. See *Cabot Corp. v. United States*, 620 F. Supp. 722 (Ct. Int'l Trade, 1985). The Commerce Department attempted to appeal the 1985 *Cabot* decision to the CAFC, but the CAFC ruled that the order remanding the case to Commerce was not yet a final determination and thus not subject to appeal. *Cabot Corp. v. United States*, 788 F.2d 1539 (Fed. Cir. 1986); see also Concannon & Browne, *What Ever Happened to the Right to Appeal*, 2 *The Commerce Department Speaks 1987* at 511 (1987).

28. The procedure for assignment of panelists to any one AD/CVD case is designed to provide impartial panels. Prior to the entry into force of the FTA, Canada and the United States will each name 25 candidates to a roster of possible panelists. Canada and the United States would each appoint two members of each panel from the agreed roster of eligible panelists, subject to the requirement that a majority of the members of each panel be lawyers. The fifth panelist would be selected by agreement of both Canada and the United States or, if they were unable to agree, by agreement among the other four panelists. If no agreement is possible, the fifth panelist would be chosen by lot from the roster. Canada and the United States would each be permitted to exercise four peremptory challenges to eliminate otherwise eligible candidates from the panel. FTA, Annex 1901.2. (This procedure is similar to that used in the institutional dispute mechanism. See footnote 7.)

29. See, for example, *Canadian Meat Council v. United States*, 661 F. Supp. 622 (Ct. Int'l Trade, 1987) (unlawful for Commerce to assume that subsidies provided to swine producers also benefited pork producers); *Alberta Pork Producers' Marketing Board v. United States*, 668 F. Supp. 445 (Ct. Int'l Trade, 1987) (Commerce's determination regarding Ontario Farm Tax Reduction remanded because method of estimation not reasonably accurate); *Washington Red Raspberry Commission v. United States*, 657 F. Supp. 537 (Ct. Int'l Trade, 1987) (proceedings remanded to Commerce due to errors in prices used to calculate dumping margins and other adjustments); No. 87-104, slip. op. (Ct. Int'l Trade, 1987) (affirmed Commerce decision that changed affirmative finding to negative for major exporter); *Toho Titanium Co., Ltd. v. United States*, 657 F. Supp. 1280 (Ct. Int'l Trade, 1987) (Commerce determination to use constructed value remanded because of inability to recoup costs of production over reasonable period of time not supported by substantial evidence).

30. The FCA remanded agency determinations to the Antidumping Tribunal (precursor to the current Canadian Import Tribunal) in the following cases: *Brunswick International (Canada) Limited v. Antidumping Tribunal* (1979), 1 C.E.R. 327, *Taiwan Footwear Manufacturers Assoc. v. Antidumping Tribunal* (1980), 2 C.E.R. 251; *Noury Chemical Corporation and Minerals & Chemicals Ltd. v. Antidumping Tribunal et al.* (1982), 2. C.F.R. 816; *De Vilbis (Canada) Ltd. et al. v. Antidumping Tribunal* (1983), 1 F.C. 706.

31. From 1980 to 1986, the ITC terminated 58 AD investigations at the preliminary stage; of these, 5 involved Canadian imports (line pipes and tubes, asphalt shingles, clams, chlorine, and frozen french fried potatoes). See *Certain Line Pipes and Tubes from Canada*, Inv. No. 731-TA-375, USITC Pub. 1965 (1987); *Asphalt Roofing Shingles from Canada*, Inv. No. 731-TA-29, USITC Pub. 1100 (1980); *Frozen French Fried Potatoes from Canada*, Inv. No. 731-TA-93, USITC Pub. 1259 (1982); *Chlorine from Canada*, Inv. No. 731-TA-90, USITC Pub. 1249 (1982); and *Clams in Airtight Containers from Canada*, Inv. No. 732-TA-17, USITC Pub. 1060 (1980).

32. In a preliminary determination, the USITC is only required to find that there is a "reasonable indication" of material injury or threat. In a final investigation, it must find actual evidence of material injury or threat, not merely a "reasonable indication." Most of the USITC's preliminary determinations are affirmative, and these findings in no way prejudice the finding that the commission will make in a final determination. Of the twelve AD investigations involving Canadian imports that went to the final determination stage since 1980, five were terminated (fresh potatoes, egg filler flats, rock salt, heavy walled rectangular pipes, and miniature carnations). See *Heavy-walled Rectangular Welded Carbon Steel Pipes and Tubes from Canada*, Inv. No. 731-TA-254, USITC Pub. 1691 (1985); *Rock Salt from Canada*, Inv. No. 731-TA-239, USITC Pub. 1798 (1986); *Egg Filler Flats of Pulp from Canada*, Inv. No. 731-TA-201, USITC Pub. 1577 (1984); *Fall Harvested Round White Potatoes from Canada*, Inv. No. 732-TA-93, USITC Pub. 1259 (1986); *Certain Fresh Cut Flowers from Canada*, Inv. No. 731-TA-327, USITC Pub. 1956 (1987) (miniature carnations).
Similarly, of the eight CVD investigations that went to the final determination stage, the ITC made three negative determinations (pork, fresh groundfish fillets, and miniature carnations). See *Live Swine and Pork from Canada*, Inv. No. 701-TA-224, USITC Pub. 1733 (1985); *Certain Fresh Atlantic Groundfish from Canada*, Inv. No. 701-TA-257, USITC Pub. 1844 (1986); and *Certain Fresh Cut Flowers from Canada*, Inv. No. 731-TA-327, USITC Pub. 1956 (1987).

33. For example, the weighted average AD duty was reduced from 17.65 percent to 6.35 percent in *Rock Salt from Canada*, 50 Fed. Reg. 49741 (1985) (Final affirm.); from 11.3 percent to 6.8 percent in *Certain Fresh Cut Flowers from Canada*, 52 Fed. Reg. 2126 (1987) (Final affirm.); from 16.47 percent to 9.73 percent in *Choline Chloride from Canada and the United Kingdom*, 49 Fed. Reg. 36532 (1984) (Final affirm.); and from 24.30 percent to 16.22 percent in *Certain Dried Heavy Salted Codfish from Canada*, 50 Fed. Reg. 20819 (1985) (Final affirm.).

34. 19 USC § 2251 et seq. (1982 & Supp. 1985).

35. 19 USC § 2251(b)(1) (1982).

36. R.S. 1970, c. C-41, as amended.

37. R.S. 1970, c. E-17, as amended.

38. For example, in the 1983 stainless steel case, Canada accounted for less than 4 percent of total US imports; Japan, the Federal Republic of Germany and France accounted for more than 50 percent of all imports. *Stainless Steel and Alloy Tool Steel*, Inv. No. TA-201-48, USITC Pub. 1377 (1983) at table 13 (based on 1982 data). The US trade was important to Canada: Canadian exports of stainless steel and alloy tool steel to the United States totaled about $11.3 million in 1982. Nevertheless, the Canadian industry was simply lumped together with the others for purposes of the investigation.

The ludicrous case of frozen breaded mushrooms from Canada caught in a Section 201 action aimed at canned mushrooms from Taiwan, Korea, and China—which went through the CIT and CAFC unsuccessfully—would never have occurred under the FTA. See *Maple Leaf Fish Co. v. United States*, 596 F. Supp 1076 (Ct. Int'l Trade, 1984), aff'd 762 F.2d 86 (Fed. Cir., 1985). In that case the US ITC focused on canned mushrooms, the product that accounted for the overwhelming volume of the subject imports. It never paid any attention, however, to the issue of whether the Canadian imports of frozen breaded mushrooms, which were minuscule and arguably a totally different product, should be excluded. See *Mushrooms*, Inv. No. TA-201-43, USITC Pub. 1089 (1980). This would not occur under the FTA because Canadian imports that account for less than 5 to 10 percent of total imports would be excluded.

The USITC has held itself legally prohibited from excluding from investigations imports from Canada exported pursuant to the Agreement Concerning Automotive Products Between the Government of the United States of America and the Government of Canada (the Auto Pact). See *Certain Motor Vehicles and Certain Chassis and Bodies Therefor*, Inv. No. TA-201-44, USITC Pub. 1110 (1980) at 13, 43–48 and 101–03.

39. Thus, in the stainless steel case, the Canadian industry would have been excluded. Similarly, Canadian exports that were subject to the following investigations presumably would have been exempted from the Section 201 action had the FTA been in effect at the time: *Certain Metal Castings*, Inv. No. TA-201-58, USITC Pub. 1849 (1986) (although specific data are often confidential, Canada is believed to account for less than 10 percent of imports of many categories on an aggregate basis); *Nonrubber Footwear*, Inv. No. TA-201-55, USITC Pub. 1717 (1985) at A-83 (Canada as part of "all other" category, accounted for less than 4.4 percent of latest year's imports); *Mushrooms*, Inv. No. TA-201-43, USITC Pub. 1089 (1980) at Tables 9 and 12 (Canada as part of "all other" category accounted for less than 2 percent and 3 percent of total imports); *Television Receivers, Color and Monochrome, Assembled and Non-Assembled, Finished or Not Finished, and Subassemblies thereof*, Inv. No. TA-201-19, USITC Pub. 808 (1977) at Table 12 (Canada less than 1 percent); *Sugar*, Inv. No. TA-201-16, USITC Pub. 807 (1977) at A-17 (Canada as part of "all other" category accounted for only 9 percent); *Apple Juice*, Inv. No. TA-201-59, USITC Pub. 1861 (1986) at Table 10 (Canada accounted for 1 percent of total imports); *Certain Canned Tuna Fish*, Inv. No. TA-201-53, USITC Pub. 1558 (1984) at Table 6 (Canada accounted for less than 2 percent of total imports).

40. This would have been of enormous significance to Canada in the US Section 201 case on *Automobiles* in 1980 if the vote in that case had been affirmative. (The vote was 3-2 negative, but could easily have been decided the other way.) An affirmative decision would have been based on the injury caused by imports of small Japanese cars. Thus, under the standard provided in the FTA, Canada could have made a persuasive argument that the large "Big Three" cars from Canada were not "contributing importantly" to the serious injury.

Another example of how one country's exports may be excluded because they do not "contribute importantly" to the other industry's import problems was posed by the 1986 US case on foundry products, which was targeted at imports from low-cost less-developed countries. By contrast, the costs of Canadian exporters generally were equal to their US counterparts; accordingly, their prices did not affect US prices the way that the lower cost imports had, but imposition of the large tariffs requested (which could have been absorbed by the low-cost exporters) would have completely excluded Canadian exports from the US market. Had the USITC made an affirmative determination, the issue of whether it should have excluded the Canadian imports would have been entirely discretionary, and the USITC probably would not have focused on it. Under the FTA, it would be required to do so. Since one can assume that many future escape clause cases in the United States and Canada will be targeted at imports from low-cost countries, this exception from escape clause action for US and Canadian imports that do not "contribute importantly" could prove to be quite valuable.

41. The United States failed to do this in the 1986 case on shakes and shingles. *Western Red Cedar Shakes and Shingles;* Import Relief Determination, 51 Fed. Reg. 19157 (1986).

42. See generally, "Understanding Regarding Notification, Consultation, Dispute Settlement and Surveillance," adopted 28 November 1979, 26th Supp. BISD 210 (1980). Since that time, the role of GATT dispute settlement procedures has shifted somewhat; GATT panels convened under Article XXIII have been authorized to reach a "clear finding" with respect to any alleged contravention of GATT provisions or nullification or impairment of benefits. Dispute Settlement Procedures, Ministerial Declaration adopted 29 November 1982, 29th Supp. BISD 13 at 14, para. 5 (1983). At the same time, the Contracting Parties reaffirmed that "consensus will continue to be the traditional method of resolving disputes." Ibid. at 16, para. 10. Furthermore, the requirement that a panel report be adopted by the Contracting Parties before becoming effective has been retained, and the parties to the dispute participate fully in the consideration of the matter by the Contracting Parties. Ibid. at 15, para. 7; 16, para. 10. Thus, the elements of conciliation and consensus still permeate the dispute settlement process under Article XXIII of GATT.

43. Article 3 of the GATT Subsidies Code provides that each signatory shall be afforded a reasonable opportunity for consultations prior to another signatory's initiating a countervailing duty investigation, as well as during the investigation itself. If this fails, the dispute may be referred to the committee (consisting of representatives from each of the signatories) for conciliation. Article 17 further provides that should the matter remain unresolved, either party may request that the committee refer the matter to a three- or five-member panel. The panel finding is not binding, however; rather, the panel submits a written report to the committee, which in turn considers the report and makes recommendations to the parties. The sole enforcement provision, should a party refuse to follow the committee's recommendations, is that the committee may authorize appropriate countermeasures.

Article 15 of the GATT Antidumping Code establishes a similar procedure that involves consultations, followed by conciliation procedures by the committee and reference to a panel if necessary. Although the effects of a panel determination are not already established in Article 15, practice has made clear that panel determinations under the GATT Antidumping Code must also be adopted by the committee. Articles XXII and XXIII of GATT also provide for consultations, followed by reference to the Contracting Parties for a recommendation or a ruling. Article XXIII:2 also provides that the Contracting Parties may authorize countermeasures if "the circumstances are serious enough to justify such action."

See also Agreement on Technical Barriers to Trade, Article 13a; Agreement on Government Procurement, Part VII.

44. Ibid. at 23.

45. In the past, almost all GATT panelists were members of official delegations to GATT. For example, the GATT panel that ruled against Canada in its 1981 case against the United States on spring assemblies was made up of members of the official delegations of Malaysia and Hong Kong, along with a British adviser to the GATT Secretariat. *United States—Imports of Certain Automotive Spring Assemblies,* Report of the Panel adopted on 26 May 1983, GATT, 30th Supp. BISD 107 (1984). Although there has been a recent trend toward appointing more independent experts to GATT panels (see Dispute Settlement Procedures, Proposal adopted 30 November 1984, GATT, 31st Supp. BISD 9 (1985)), the majority of GATT panelists continue to be government officials.

46. See, for example, Article 18.5, GATT Subsidies Code.

47. See Article XXIII, GATT (if no agreement is reached by the parties in a "reasonable" time, the contracting parties shall "promptly" investigate); Article 15, Agreement on Implementation of Article VI of the General Agreement on Tariffs and Trade (GATT Antidumping Code), GATT, 26th Supp. BISD 171 (1980) (if the committee fails to resolve the dispute within three months, it shall establish a panel, with no further time constraints or guidance provided). Compare Article 18.2, (GATT Subsidies Code), GATT, 26th Supp. BISD 56 (1980) (a panel is to be established within 30 days of a request and should deliver its findings to the commission within 60 days of its establishment). See also Article VII.10, Agreement on Government Procurement, GATT, 26th Supp. BISD 33 (1980) (if the committee is unable to resolve the dispute within three months, a panel is to be formed; panels should "aim to deliver their findings . . . to the Committee without undue delay . . . normally within a period of 4 months from the date the panel was established"); Article 14.18, Agreement on Technical Barriers to Trade, GATT, 26th Supp. BISD 8 at 25 (1980) (same).

The Contracting Parties agreed upon guidelines of 30 days for the establishment of a panel and three to nine months for the completion of the panel's work in an attempt to set standards for the Article XXIII dispute resolution procedure. However, prior to 1984, these targets were "seldom met." Dispute Settlement Procedures, Proposal adopted 30 November 1984, 31st Supp. BISD 9 (1985). Since then, GATT panels have generally become faster, although the time guidelines are not binding.

48. The FTA sets a limit of 300 to 315 days for review of an AD/CVD decision, and a limit of approximately 245 days for resolution of all other disputes. See footnote 22; FTA, Article 1807. As a result, the FTA would avoid the lengthy procedures often inherent in GATT dispute resolution. In a case involving the Canadian Foreign Investment Review Act, for example, more than two years passed between the United States invocation of the GATT dispute resolution process and the adoption of a panel report. See *Canada—Administration of the Foreign Investment Review Act,* Report of the Panel adopted 7 February 1984, GATT, 30th Supp. BISD 140 (1984).

49. FTA, Article 1904.4. Under GATT, by contrast, a party must wait for the final determination before beginning the dispute settlement process. Thus, in the spring assemblies case the USITC issued an order on 10 August 1981, banning imports of Canadian spring assemblies; a panel was not established until four months later, and the final report of the panel was not adopted until 26 May 1983. *United States—Imports of Certain Automotive Spring Assemblies,* Report of the Panel adopted 26 May 1983, GATT, 30th Supp. BISD 107 (1984).

50. FTA, Article 1903. This provision also allows the FTA (unlike GATT) to act as an effective forum for resolving disputes concerning the implementation of harmful but temporary measures by the other party. The FTA would avoid the result of the tuna and tuna products case in which the United States prohibited all imports of tuna and tuna products from Canada from August 1979 to September 1980, and a GATT panel report was first adopted in February 1982. *United States—Prohibition of Tuna and Tuna Products from Canada,* Report of the Panel adopted 22 February 1982, GATT, 29th Supp. BISD 91 (1983).

51. For example, Argentina intervened before the GATT panel in the United States' complaint concerning Canada's Foreign Investment Review Act. See *Canada—Administration of the Foreign Investment Review Act,* Report of the Panel adopted 7 February 1984, GATT, 30th Supp. BISD 140 (1984).

52. In an extreme case involving a complaint against a US export subsidy (the Domestic International Sales Corporation [DISC] tax system), a GATT panel was first established in 1973, but the dispute was first heard by the panel in February 1976, decided against the United States by the panel in November 1976, blocked until 1981, and not finally remedied by the United States until 1984. *United States Tax Legislation (DISC),* Report of the Panel presented to the Council of Representatives on 12 November 1976, GATT, 23d Supp. BISD 98 (1977).

53. FTA, Article 1904.9. Professor John H. Jackson has written about the difference between "power-oriented" and "rule-oriented" diplomacy. He maintains that a rule-oriented approach allows citizens greater opportunity to affect the decision-making processes and corporations the ability to "plan and base action on more predictable and stable" government policies. Jackson, *Perspectives on the Jurisprudence of International Trade: Costs and Benefits of Legal Procedures in the United States,* 82 Mich. L. Rev. 1570, 1572 (1984). Because GATT panel determinations must be adopted by the Contracting Parties, the GATT dispute resolution procedures involve a significant measure of power-oriented relations. The influence that a country can wield in this process depends in large part upon its size, power, and wealth.

The FTA would replace this with a purely rule-oriented system; AD/CVD panel determinations would be automatically binding and would not be subject to political manipulation. As Professor Jackson points out, this benefits not only the smaller government, but also the citizens and corporations of both countries that are subject to the process.

54. FTA, Articles 1903; 1806.1.

55. FTA, Article 1903.

56. FTA, Article 1902.2(d). The broad nature of the language in the FTA—the "object and purpose of Agreement"—gives a potentially very broad grant of authority to the panels to review changes in US and Canadian AD/CVD law.

57. FTA, Article 1903.1. For example, these provisions would be applicable if the United States were to change its statute law to classify unemployment insurance as a countervailable subsidy (and specify that the amendment would apply to Canada). See, for example, *Certain Fresh Atlantic Groundfish from Canada,* 51 Fed. Reg. 10041 (1986) (Final affirm.) (Unemployment insurance was not a countervailable subsidy.) Because this provision could be applied against imports from Canada and because this would alter the implementation of the FTA, the Canadian government would have the rights to prior notification and to invoke the dispute settlement mechanism, leading to a binding determination of the panel.

58. FTA, Article 1903.3(b).

59. FTA, Article 1804.1.

60. The dispute resolution mechanism would apply to changes in US law occurring after the FTA went into effect on 1 January 1989. However, the FTA contains a standstill agreement applying to the calendar year 1988, which effectively requires the United States not to change its trade laws during that year or to compensate the Government of Canada for any changes, or else Canada may withdraw from the FTA.

61. FTA, Article 1805.1.

62. FTA, Article 1806.3.

63. See the dispute settlement mechanism contained in the Israel–United States Free Trade Agreement (22 April 1985, United States–Israel, XXIV International Legal

Materials No. 3 at 653). That dispute settlement mechanism is similar in its structure. The parties are obliged to consult regarding disputes; unresolved disputes are referred to a joint committee; disputes that are still unresolved are then sent to a conciliation panel. Ibid., Article 19.1. This panel's finding is, however, expressly *nonbinding;* the extent of its powers is to issue a report. Article 19.1(e). Furthermore, the imposition of AD/CVD duties or review of AD/CVD determinations is expressly excluded from the dispute settlement mechanism.

The general dispute resolution mechanism in the FTA also compares favorably with that in the Gulf of Maine treaty (Treaty to Submit to Binding Dispute Settlement the Delimitation of the Maritime Boundary in the Gulf of Maine Area, 29 March 1979, Canada–United States, T.I.A.S. 10204). Although that treaty provides for binding dispute resolution by the International Court of Justice, it contains no explicit sanctions. The same is true of many of the United States' treaties of friendship, commerce, and navigation. See, for example, Convention of Establishment, Protocol, and Declaration, 25 November 1959, United States–France, 11 UST. 2398, T.I.A.S. 4625.

64. Neither the European Free Trade Association nor the United Kingdom–Ireland Free Trade Area Agreement provided any mechanism to review the parties' application of AD/CVD law. See Article 17, Convention Establishing the European Free Trade Association, signed 7 January 1960; Article XI, United Kingdom–Ireland Free Trade Area Agreement. The United States–Israeli Free Trade Agreement specifically excludes AD/CVD cases from its general dispute settlement provisions, even though the dispute settlement provisions are not binding. Article 19, Israel–United States Free Trade Agreement (22 April 1985, United States–Israel, XXIV International Legal Materials No. 3 at 653).

The trade agreement between Australia and New Zealand provides for notification and opportunity for consultation between the countries in AD cases, and notification, consultation, and the expeditious resolution of disputes in CVD cases. Articles 15, 16, Australia–New Zealand Closer Economic Relations Trade Agreement (1983). It does not, however, establish any binational body to review disputes; resolution of disputes is expected to occur through consultations. By way of contrast, Article 23 of the agreement between the European Communities and the Kingdom of Sweden provided that disputes concerning subsidies would be submitted to a joint committee that, if appropriate, could order elimination of the practice in question. If the offending party fails to comply, the other party is entitled to adopt whatever measure is necessary to counteract the difficulties caused by the practice.

65. The GATT Code Committees, working on a far more theoretical basis, have been able to develop a number of useful common or administrative principles. See, *Report to the Committee on Antidumping Practices and to the Committee on Subsidies and Countervailing Measures by a Joint Group of Experts on the Definition of the Word "Related,"* GATT, 28th Supp. BISD 33 (1982); Committee on Antidumping Practices, Understanding of Article 8.4 of the Agreement on Implementation of Article VI of the GATT, 28th Supp. BISD 52 (1982); Committee on Subsidies and Countervailing Measures, Guidelines in the Determination of Substitution Drawback Systems as Export Subsidies, GATT, 31st Supp. BISD 257 (1985). They have been unable to agree, however, on such substantive matters as the definition and valuation of subsidies.

66. In the past round of negotiations, negotiators from both countries discovered that 16 months was simply not enough time to allow for the resolution of all areas of conflict between the two bodies of law. The five-year life span of the AD/CVD dispute resolution mechanism, with the possibility of an extension of an additional two years, provides the time necessary to resolve the conflicts between the two bodies of law and to create a political consensus within each country in support of the proposed changes.

Comments

Robert E. Hudec

The provisions of the Canada–United States Free Trade Agreement (FTA) on dispute settlement are complex, and the paper by Gary Horlick, Geoffrey Oliver, and Debra Steger provides a comprehensive roadmap through this difficult terrain. The authors concisely describe the main structural elements of the various procedures and then offer a coherent evaluation of their potential advantages. My comments address the three major areas of FTA dispute settlement covered in the paper:

☐ review of antidumping and countervailing duty (AD/CVD) orders (Chapter 19)

☐ the general dispute settlement procedures (Chapter 18)

☐ the rules and dispute settlement procedures on global safeguards measures (Chapters 11 and 18).

Review of AD/CVD Orders

The main point of the paper on the AD/CVD review procedures is that the FTA provisions are an improvement over existing review procedures in the courts of the two countries. The paper focuses on the advantages for Canada, and this is understandable, for it is usually the smaller and weaker partner in any deal that wants and needs the protection of effective legal remedies against violations by the other. I shall consider the United States interests later, but for the present let us look at the advantages through the eyes of Canada.

I agree with the paper's assessment that the FTA procedures are better for Canada than are the present review procedures, but my enthusiasm for the likely quality of their output is more qualified. The FTA procedures will be speedier, which is very important to the practical effectiveness of both the review proceedings themselves and their impact on the agencies being reviewed. They are potentially cheaper, which reduces another large barrier to their availability. I do not find any reason to think the FTA procedures will be any fairer than the US courts they replace, but I would concede that, if politically biased administrative decisions are a danger, speedier and cheaper review will do more to discourage such biased decisions than will

Robert E. Hudec is the Melvin C. Steen Professor of Law at the University of Minnesota.

slower and costlier review procedures. Even if there is no real problem of fairness, the perception by Canadian businesses that there is a problem is one that has to be met, and if the procedures do that, they will be an improvement.

My concern is that the quality of the decisions rendered under the FTA review process in AD/CVD cases may not be very good. Ad hoc panels of experts have been a viable mechanism for GATT dispute settlement, but I do not think that efficacy can be assumed here. GATT panels are made up of GATT delegates from countries neutral to the dispute and occasionally other persons who have had extensive experience with GATT in the past. Their homogeneous quality is sometimes described by saying, "Once you've seen one Swedish delegate you've seen them all." More important than the panelists themselves is the fact that GATT panels are aided by a Secretariat of full-time international civil servants, including a four-person legal staff, who supply technical expertise on the detail and history of GATT law and who maintain the continuity from one panel to another and from one year to another. As far as I can see, the FTA ad hoc panels will have none of this continuity, none of this assistance, and, to top it off, they will have a technically much more complex job to do.

Antidumping and countervailing duty law, at least in the United States, has become terribly complex. How the FTA mechanism will try to deal with that complexity is not yet clear. The only kind of panelist who can expertly review conformity with US law, without an enormous start-up cost, will be a lawyer actively practicing in the AD/CVD field. It seems that the FTA was written with an eye to such lawyers serving, for Annex 1901.2(11) states that a panelist may not, while serving on the panel, represent a client before another panel. The problem with lawyers, of course, is that they have clients who care about AD/CVD law. In addition, they are likely to have a "paper trail" of positions taken on behalf of such clients. Maybe the senior statespersons in the field will be viewed as capable of rising above all this, but most of them are ex-officials of the very agencies whose alleged political bias is the reason for the new panel procedure. About the only pool of AD/CVD experts I can think of would be retired officials, judges and lawyers who did AD/CVD law not too long ago but are now detached from any active involvement, plus, possibly, the few law professors who know AD/CVD well enough to do this. [1]

Setting aside the few experts who may be genuinely independent, the choice will be between experts whose neutrality is questionable and neutrals whose expertise is questionable. Most lawyers, judges, and professors

---

1. The FTA also mentions sitting judges as candidates, saying their government paycheck does not put them in the excluded class of government officials. It seems unlikely that sitting judges from the Court of International Trade or Court of Appeals for the Federal Circuit would be selected, or would agree to serve if they were.

outside the AD/CVD field will fall into the latter category. To repeat, the start-up costs for the latter group will be very heavy, and, since there probably will be little repeat business (the paper predicts a level of compensation designed to discourage careerism), those costs are likely to be a wasted investment. The potential for weak decisions from this quarter has to be rated quite high. (Perhaps this is why the procedures give governments the right to see an initial draft conclusion before it becomes final.)

The quality of the legal output as a whole cannot be expected to be much better. Ad hoc panels are unlikely to work very hard to integrate their work with what has gone before or to think much about what comes next. Moreover, while I agree with the authors that binational, multimember panels will incline toward middle-of-the-road opinions, I fear the middle will be a compromise between yes and no that gives no guidance.

The ad hoc character is also going to dilute the prestige of whatever decisions are rendered. GATT panels are part of GATT, and when they rule, GATT rules. Subject to some really creative public relations work (of which there is precious little evidence so far) panels under the FTA will stand naked to the winds. The impact of what they say will depend pretty much on who the five individuals are. There will be no carryover from the decisions of other panelists in the past.

A vital secretariat could do a lot to rescue this operation from mediocrity. That may eventually come to pass, but the opening moves are all in the opposite direction. According to the FTA, the secretariat for AD/CVD review will be a government official in Ottawa and another in Washington, each of whom will collect review petitions and assemble and file the administrative records on which review proceedings will be conducted. Given the low level of cases that is likely, these functions probably will not to amount to a full-time job. The two secretaries could be made full-time, and thus a more important force, by being assigned other tasks by the Canada–US Trade Commission, but as noted below, that does not seem likely to happen either.

The quality problem has to be seen in perspective, of course. National administrations, even with their greater resources and exceptionally talented administrators, have not exactly had a glowing record on substantive coherence. The main source of these quality problems is a very serious substantive problem with AD/CVD law itself. Neither "dumping" nor "subsidy" is a coherent legal concept. "Dumping" has no coherence at all according to most economists, making it difficult to reason from one arbitrary premise to another. "Subsidy" is a coherent economic concept, but that is not the "subsidy" that most politicians and businesses want to countervail, for they are involved in so much subsidizing of their own that, even with a generous dose of double standards, they cannot afford to punish all the things they do themselves. As a result, the only accurate *legal* definition of "subsidy" in most countries is "something your government does for you that my government does not do for me." It is small wonder that economists and business leaders view their product as more akin to witchcraft than to economic policy.

On top of the incoherence rests a problem of excess. To satisfy one set of constituents, most legislatures write AD and CVD laws much more rigorously than is good for the country's own export interests, counting on administrators to narrow them down with "creative" practical interpretations. Unfortunately, courts trained to read laws as they are written sometimes miss the point and so read words like "subsidy" to mean what they say, saddling everyone with unwanted rigor. The use of manipulative legal theories and the sometimes sharp changes of direction that result from this process quite naturally make traders unhappy with the way AD/CVD laws are administered.

Two points emerge from this final observation as to the underlying substantive problems of AD/CVD law. The first is that there are unlikely to be satisfactory decisions by any institution until a better law is written, one which at least cuts down on political excess and goes further to find other ways of dealing with some of these political goblins, such as leaving dumping to competition in an integrated market and regulating subsidies at the source. The five-to-seven-year review process for AD/CVD cases can be only an interim solution. To put it a bit more strongly, the real solution (a better law) had better be worked out in five to seven years because it is doubtful that the interim solution will satisfy its audience even that long.

Second, as for the review process itself, recognizing that it is only an interim solution is perhaps the most important part of any evaluation. Viewed from that perspective, one can see it as an improvement of some importance. With all its faults, it is still faster, and cheaper, and substantively not much worse than the alternative. And most of all, it will be viewed by businesses and politicians as fairer and more objective.

The General Dispute Settlement Procedure

In contrast to the meticulous care with which the AD/CVD review procedures are set forth, the general disputes procedure is quite skeletal. One difference that catches the eye immediately, for example, is the difference between the qualifications required of panelists. Both procedures require that panelists know what they are doing. The AD/CVD panelists must also be "of good character, high standing and repute." That requirement is not included for panelists for the general disputes procedure. Why the difference? It seems the explanation is simply that the governments did not spend as much time on Chapter 18. The evidence for that hypothesis is rather overwhelming.

The first gap in the drafting is the definition of the Canada–US Trade Commission that is supposed to administer the general dispute settlement procedure. The commission receives only one short article in this lengthy document. Article 1802 creates the commission, gives it the function of supervising things, specifies that each government's "principal representative" will be the Cabinet minister for trade, says the commission may seek advice from nongovernmental individuals, and ends by telling the commission to meet at least once a year and to decide things by consensus. What is this commission supposed to be? Who will its members be? What powers will it have? What staff will it have? None of these questions is answered directly, and the indirect answers give no consistent picture.

Given the low level of aspiration in the rest of the FTA, one would expect to find a pretty "nothing" commission, probably just a joint committee consisting of trade policy officials of the two governments that meets on a regular basis—no office space of its own, no staff, at most maybe a box of letterhead stationery. The appointment of ministers as each government's "principal representative" supports such a view, as does the suggestion that no one from outside the government will be a member.

A different image is presented by the procedural provisions of Chapter 18. Does it make sense to provide that the governments shall consult for 30 days (under the direction of ministers, one supposes), and then require the governments to refer the matter to the commission so that the same people can talk some more? Likewise, why provide that the commission rather than the governments will decide on the kind of arbitration to be held, or that, after a nonbinding arbitral ruling is made, the commission will "agree on the resolution of the dispute"? Why not say directly that the two governments will have to decide these issues by consensus?

On balance, I would suspect that the minimalist interpretation is the correct one, and that location of certain procedures and decisions within "the commission" is just a fig leaf for a disputes procedure in which, except for safeguards disputes, the governments have really done nothing more than commit themselves to nonbinding arbitration, with the option of binding arbitration if and when, but only if and when, they agree to it. The provision in Article 1807.8 stating that the commission shall agree on the resolution of disputes following nonbinding arbitration tends to confirm this suspicion, for it does not seem very likely that the United States would ever have agreed to turn over the power to impose a result to any really independent body.

Perhaps the most optimistic thing one can say about the commission at this point is that, like the secretariat, it is at least an empty bottle into which the parties could one day pour some wine. Until then, it adds nothing to the force of the FTA.

What the agreement really does, therefore, is simply to provide for automatic nonbinding arbitration of legal disputes. To be sure, this alone is still quite significant. I would agree with Horlick, Oliver, and Steger, that compared with present GATT remedies the FTA procedure provides a stronger dispute settlement mechanism—not overpoweringly so, but stronger nonetheless. The FTA gets the panel into existence automatically, without the pushing and punching sometimes needed to obtain a defendant's consent in GATT; the roster mechanism looks like it should work pretty well, once rosters are formed. The time requirements will also help to make things move faster, though they are not as solid a guarantee of rapid decision making as the paper suggests. GATT's experience with mandatory time limits in some of the code procedures, and with rather firm time guidelines elsewhere, is that they both slip a lot. Government representatives usually do not have completely open schedules, and neither will the five panelists who are working full time in various parts of North America. (GATT has only three panelists to schedule, but it has other ways of losing time.)

The quality of the decisions will probably not be much better than GATT, given that these panels, like the AD/CVD panels, will lack both the common base of experience that GATT diplomats share and, above all, the critically important assistance given by the GATT Secretariat. FTA panels will have more than their share of obscure norms and concepts to be applied. One that deserves mention in particular is the GATT concept of "nonviolation nullification and impairment," which Article 2011 of the FTA borrows from GATT. The concept permits legal complaints against actions that are not necessarily in violation of the agreement, authorizing a type of equitable remedy for actions by the other party that, while not prohibited, nonetheless do serious damage to the balance of benefits in the agreement. This is a pretty tricky provision. It should provide an interesting test of the decision-making capacity of FTA panels.

To the extent FTA procedures produce binding arbitration, of course, they will be achieving a quite significant advantage over what is presently available in GATT. Whether they will do so is an open question, however. The FTA could have a surprisingly positive effect here. Even though the agreement merely states the possibility that governments can agree to binding arbitration, having this possibility written out means that, when Congress accepts the agreement, it will be accepting the legitimacy of the executive branch agreeing to do so.

The paper addresses the question of whether the FTA definition of "binding" is as strong as it should be. The strongest kind of binding would have been the ruling that becomes effective as a matter of national law, binding on the domestic courts. The Treaty of Rome has legally binding decisions of this kind, but the two parties to the FTA have never for a moment been willing to consider the kind of political and institutional integration needed to support such a transfer of law-making power. Without such a genuine integrationist purpose, domestic legal effect is, and always was, a chimera.

I agree with the authors that the only kind of binding that was ever possible in this type of pure trade agreement was the kind that is provided for in the FTA. It's existence is usually advertised by a power to retaliate against the other part if it fails to comply. To be honest, retaliation itself is not a very powerful, or usable, sanction. The real sanction behind legally binding decisions is national tradition against violating international legal obligations. It guarantees nothing, of course. But one measure of its normal effect on governments is the effort they make to avoid being bound by it. In a political relationship as close as the Canada–United States relationship, it should be even more effective than usual. I would agree with the authors that, where binding decisions are possible, they do create an important force behind the FTA obligations.

Once again, the paper's assessment of the general disputes procedure is made largely from the Canadian perspective, which is, once again, the side on which stronger remedies matter most. Looking at the dispute settlement provisions from the United States' perspective, one becomes aware of an interesting discontinuity in US policy. Throughout the negotiation of the FTA, one of the chief US interests was the impact of FTA provisions on the GATT's Uruguay Round multilateral trade negotiations. The standard refrain was, "If two good neighbors like the United States and Canada cannot liberalize trade and reduce restrictions on services and investment, what hope will there be for the Uruguay Round?" The United States pressed quite hard, across the board, to set a good example—except, come to think of it, for dispute settlement, where it was Canada that wanted (it seemed) to promulgate a how-to-do-it-right example that would have burned a hole in the EC and Japanese earphones. Here the roles got reversed, and it was the United States that put on the brakes.

This turn of events is particularly interesting when one considers that it is the United States that has been taking the leading role so far in the Uruguay Round negotiating group charged with strengthening GATT dispute settlement procedures. Measured by GATT's rather cautious approach to dispute settlement, the United States appears to be beating down the walls in that forum; it has made proposals for improving the roster mechanism—speeding up decisions some more, providing for means to agree to binding arbitration in advance, and, once again, attacking the consensus principle that allows parties to block an adverse ruling. When compared with Canada's FTA demands, however, the US positions can be seen for the rather timid thing that they really are. "It's fine to make GATT adjudication work better at producing legal decisions, but let's not get too carried away with enforcing them, OK?"

What, then, will be the impact of the FTA on these somewhat limited GATT dispute settlement negotiations? First, the signal achievement of the FTA is its mechanism for getting the panel procedure moving automatically, by means of the agreed roster of panelists. GATT also needs to improve its starting motor, and would welcome being able to create such a roster, but seems unlikely to achieve any roster that all GATT countries can agree to. There may be a somewhat greater chance of success among the smaller memberships of the Codes, but even that is not very likely. At most, the precedent of the automatic FTA roster may help focus more attention in that direction. Second, imposing more rigorous time limits is already on the GATT agenda; the FTA adds nothing here, except possibly to reinforce the misguided faith in them. Third, the possibility of establishing a procedure under which parties can give advance agreement to binding arbitration is also on the Uruguay Round agenda already, but here the FTA precedent should help to establish the plausibility of the idea, especially the FTA provisions making binding arbitration mandatory.

Dispute Settlement on Safeguards Measures

The paper is quite correct in stressing that binding adjudication of safeguards measures is a major accomplishment. It is perhaps the most significant legal achievement of the entire agreement. It is also one of the most poorly defined. It would add much-needed certainty to these matters if governments were to confirm what the text appears to say—namely, that *any* legal dispute, even a disagreement over a finding of "serious injury," can be litigated and that the panel ruling on that issue will be binding.

My only further comment on this part of the dispute settlement process concerns the substance of the safeguards rules themselves. I refer to the provision that grants each country an exemption from the other's global safeguards restrictions when imports from the partner do not form an important part of the injury-causing trade. Technically, the provision violates Article XXIV because that provision requires that free trade area countries remove *all* safeguards measures against the other. The text of Article XXIV exempts certain kinds of restrictions, but no provision is made for retaining Article XIX measures.

My own position is to the contrary of Article XXIV. I have frankly never understood why free trade area partners are supposed to be exempted from such emergency measures. The exemption makes the effect of the safeguards restrictions worse for others, and it reduces the deterrent effect which the most-favored-nation (MFN) requirement is intended to have on the government imposing the measure. A much better rule would be to require full MFN application of Article XIX measures, thereby maintaining full deterrence in the first place and full pressure to get them removed as quickly as possible. The only case, in my view, when it is proper to excuse partners from safeguards measures is when there is a single safeguards law treating both countries as a single market, requiring injury to their combined "industry."

The FTA position straddles both Article XXIV requirements and my contrary position, offending both. Worse, the theory of this selective yes-and-no position—that it's OK to excuse the trading partner when its exports aren't really hurting anyone—is a classic restatement of the theory supporting the demand for "selective" application of GATT Article XIX safeguards generally. "Selectivity" will be a major issue again in the Uruguay Round. It is unfortunate that the FTA weighs in on the wrong side.

Frank Stone

The provisions of the Canada–US Free Trade Agreement (FTA) that deal with dispute resolution were subject to a good deal of discussion within the legal community of the two countries and among trade policy specialists, government officials, and others while the FTA was under negotiation.[1] The outcome of the negotiations, as set out in Chapters 18, 19, and elsewhere, are not as far-reaching or elaborate as many had advocated, but they should provide a workable set of arrangements for dealing with disputes arising from the operations of the agreement. As such, I agree with the conclusions of the Horlick-Oliver-Steger paper that the dispute resolution processes created by the FTA represent a significant advance over the processes that

---

Frank Stone is a Senior Research Associate at The Institute for Research in Public Policy and a former Canadian Representative to the GATT.

1. See, for example, Proceedings of the Canada-United States Law Institute Conference, *Competition and Dispute Resolution in the North American Context,* Cleveland, Ohio, April 3–5, 1987; the paper presented by Louis B. Sohn, "Dispute Resolution Under a North American Free Trade Agreement" is of special interest. The institutional and dispute resolution arrangements under the agreement were discussed in the *Report of the Royal Commission on the Economic Union and Development Prospects for Canada* (The Macdonald Commission Report), Ottawa: Supply and Services Canada, 1985; vol. 1, pp. 320-322. An analysis of the institutional issues involved is contained in Frank Stone, *Institutional Provisions and Form of the Proposed Canada-United States Trade Agreement,* Institute for Research on Public Policy, Ottawa, 1986, Discussion Paper 8604; and the trade law issues are discussed in Murray G. Smith, C. Michael Aho, and Gary N. Horlick, *Bridging the Gap: Trade Laws in the Canadian-U.S. Negotiations.* Toronto: Canadian-American Committee, 1987.

are now available either on a bilateral basis or under the General Agreement on Tariffs and Trade (GATT).

The Horlick-Oliver-Steger paper contains a good analysis of the dispute resolution provisions of the agreement and brings out the positive aspects of these provisions. It seems useful, however, to look more critically at certain aspects of these arrangements, to speculate on how the dispute resolution process will operate in practice and on how it may evolve in the future, as experience is gained with its use and as the agreement is progressively implemented by the parties. In this regard, it is instructive to recall that the elaborate dispute resolution processes of the GATT, and the institutional arrangements that underpin them, have evolved from the most slender and tentative legal provisions set out in GATT Articles XXII, XXIII, and XXV. It may be expected that a similar evolutionary process will take place over time as the legal texts of Chapters 18 and 19 of the bilateral agreement are translated into practice.

The dispute resolution elements of the agreement are, of course, intertwined with the institutional arrangements created by it, which are largely but not entirely set out in Chapters 18 and 19. They are also intertwined with the provisions of the agreement that will govern the trade remedy laws and practices of the two countries in the future, as these apply to cross-border trade.

The Canada-US Trade Commission

The Commission is given a central role in the operation of the provisions of the agreement for dealing with disputes other than those arising from the use of antidumping and countervailing duty systems. This body consists essentially of two Cabinet-level representatives of the parties—the Canadian Minister for International Trade and the US Trade Representative. It will thus not have any kind of independent, third-party functions such as those given to the International Joint Commission under the 1909 Boundary Waters Treaty, or those performed by the Director General and Secretariat of the GATT. The bilateral agreement does not create any new independent, permanent, binational organization, and it may be supposed that the US negotiators in particular were opposed to the creation of such a body.

Of potential significance is the Commission's authority to establish and delegate responsibility to ad hoc or standing committees or working groups, and to seek the advice of nongovernmental individuals or groups. This provision could play a useful role in the avoidance of disputes by providing opportunities for the input of informed, objective outside advice into the process of consultations between the parties, which is a precondition for establishing panels under Chapter 18 to help resolve disputes. Moreover, this provision could provide opportunities for involving provincial and state governments, as well as private sector people, in the operation of the agreement. It is possible that the two federal governments will see the need in the future for some kind of standing advisory boards with mixed federal, provincial and state, and private sector representation, analogous to the advisory boards that have been often used quite successfully to assist the International Joint Commission in its work under the 1909 Boundary Waters Treaty.

The Secretariat

The agreement does not give the Commission any staff or resources of its own, underlining its role as a contact point between the two federal governments. However, Article 1909 will establish a permanent Secretariat to service panels and committees established under Chapter 19 to deal with antidumping and countervailing duty issues, and it is expressly provided that "The Secretariat may provide support for the Commission . . . if so directed by the Commission." It is possible that, over time, this Secretariat could evolve to play a quasi-independent and prominent role in the broader operation of the agreement. No such role, however, is suggested by the text of the agreement as it stands, which places the Secretariat firmly under the control of the two governments and divides it into separate offices in Ottawa and Washington.

Changes in Trade Rules

As noted earlier, the dispute resolution processes of the FTA are intertwined with the trade remedy systems of the two countries. The rules governing the use of safeguards (escape clause) measures, as set out in Chapter 11, apply to cross-border trade only in limited circumstances. When applied on a global basis, they exempt imports from the other country if the trade involved accounts for a small share of total imports. These rules should reduce the scope for future disputes in this area by, among other things, limiting the "sideswipe" effect of safeguard measures aimed principally at imports from third countries. Where disputes arise over safeguards measures, whether applied globally or on a bilateral basis, it is mandatory under Chapter 18 that these be referred to the "binding arbitration" panel process if they cannot be settled through bilateral consultations.

No parallel changes are made in the rules governing the use of other trade remedy laws and practices of the two countries, including the countervailing and antidumping duty systems. However, the agreement will initiate a further process of negotiations over a five- to seven-year period aimed at designing new binational rules to govern the use of countervailing and antidumping laws as they apply to bilateral trade. Meanwhile, provision is made under Chapter 19 for independent, third-party panels to carry out judicial reviews of final decisions about the use of such measures. The Horlick-Oliver-Steger paper correctly emphasizes the value of the provisions for judicial review, which can be triggered by the private sector parties concerned. These provisions should not only exercise needed discipline on the use of countervailing and antidumping duty remedies in both countries, but should also increase the confidence of business people in the fairness of these systems. If, and when, new bilateral rules are agreed upon to govern the use of countervailing and antidumping systems as applied to bilateral trade, it may be expected that new processes would also be created to deal with disputes over their use.

The Dispute Panel Process

The Commission, however narrowly structured, will play a central role in the establishment of independent, third-party panels to help resolve disputes arising from the operation of the agreement other than disputes over the use of antidumping and countervailing duty measures. If both commissioners agree, "binding arbitration" panels will be established to deal with a particular dispute. As noted earlier, binding arbitration panels are required to be used, as well, to deal with disputes over the use of safeguards measures. If the commissioners disagree, either side can oblige the creation of an independent third-party panel whose findings and recommendations will be advisory. The ability of any one party alone to trigger this advisory panel process is an important feature of the FTA and differs from the GATT panel process, which requires the agreement of both parties.

As is the case with the GATT process, the dispute panel process set out in Chapter 18 can only be initiated by the federal governments. Also, like the GATT process, a dispute panel will only receive the views of the two governments; and Article 1807.4 also states that "unless otherwise agreed by the Parties, a panel shall base its decision on the arguments and submissions of the Parties." There is thus little or no scope in the process for input by the private sector or by provincial and state governments, in contrast to the opportunity for private sector parties to trigger and participate in the joint judicial review of countervailing and antidumping duty cases. Moreover, panels will not carry out any independent research or analysis of their own concerning issues under dispute. In this respect, the process appears to be more limited than the GATT process, which allows the panelists to draw on the advice and analytical resources of the GATT

Secretariat. This absence of research and analytical support could weaken the panel process under the agreement, unless the two governments find some way of providing such support. Use could possibly be made of the Secretariat which is to be established under Article 1909 and which is mandated to support the panels that will deal with countervailing and antidumping issues.

Using panels of independent experts to help resolve trade disputes is not new and has been used with increasing frequency within GATT over the past decade. The GATT dispute resolution process has operated better than suggested in the Horlick-Oliver-Steger paper and has been used successfully to deal with a number of disputes between Canada and the United States as well as disputes each country has had with other GATT members. The GATT dispute resolution facilities will remain available to deal with bilateral Canada-US trade disputes, although it may be expected that these will be engaged mainly to deal with disputes over GATT rights and obligations, not those arising from the operation of the new bilateral agreement.

Both Canada and the United States have relatively good records, so far, of complying with the outcome of the GATT panel dispute process and withdrawing or changing trade practices in response to GATT panel findings and recommendations. There is thus reason to expect that the dispute panel processes under the bilateral agreement will also operate successfully.

Binding Arbitration versus Advisory Panels

The distinction between "binding arbitration" panels and advisory panels is not entirely clear. In neither case do the parties actually commit themselves to abide by the decisions or recommendations of a panel. However, the binding arbitration route requires the consent of both parties, and inherent in this process from the outset will be the resolve of both sides to reach a mutually satisfactory solution to their differences. At the same time, the opportunity under the FTA for one side alone to trigger the advisory panel process is a valuable one; the very existence of this right should pressure the two sides to join together in the pursuit of solutions, rather than have the process forced by one side. Furthermore, neither country can delay or block adoption of the panel reports, as they can in the GATT.

Nevertheless, as noted above, the agreement does not compel the parties to abide by the findings and recommendations of panels. Article 1806.3 states that if the offending country fails to implement the findings of a binding arbitration panel, and the parties are unable to agree on compensation or remedial action, "then the other Party shall have the right to suspend the application of equivalent benefits of this agreement to the non-complying Party."

Reports of advisory panels are to be submitted to the Commission; and Article 1807.8 states that "the Commission shall agree on the resolution of the dispute, which normally shall conform with the recommendations of the panel. Wherever possible, the resolution shall be non-implementation or the removal (of the offending measure) or, failing such a resolution, compensation." If none of these solutions are agreed, again, the injured party "shall be free to suspend the application to the other Party of benefits of equivalent effect. . . ."

These provisions represent, in effect, the right to retaliate. They are quite similar to those enjoyed in parallel circumstances by GATT contracting parties under Articles XIX and XXIII of the General Agreement. In practical terms, the right to retaliate is often difficult to exercise, especially between countries of unequal size. It is hoped, therefore, that efforts to resolve disputes under the bilateral agreement will rarely lead to this outcome; and the experience with dispute resolution processes under GATT offers grounds to expect that the use of independent panels will lead to the resolution of most disputes under the FTA on terms that are satisfactory to both sides.

The Future of the System

The provisions for dispute resolution, as well as other institutional elements of the agreement, should be regarded as representing more than the legal text of the relevant articles. Experience with their use in the context of the actual operation of the agreement will inevitably lead to the evolution of its dispute resolution and institutional elements, as has been the experience under GATT. Meanwhile, it will be useful for public debate to continue on the actual operation of these arrangements under the bilateral agreement, and this discussion can proceed in parallel with the discussion that has begun in the Uruguay Round on the reform and strengthening of the dispute process and other institutional elements of GATT. Public debate should also focus on the negotiations that will take place over the next five to seven years on new rules for countervailing and antidumping duties as applied to cross-border trade. Again, these bilateral negotiations will occur in parallel with discussions in Geneva that might lead to changes in the GATT rules governing countervailing and antidumping duties and other trade remedy practices.

4

The Auto Sector

Paul Wonnacott

Two major objectives of the Canada–United States Free Trade Agreement (FTA) are to make economic relations between the United States and Canada:

☐ more open, with fewer barriers; and

☐ more stable, predictable, and secure.

The Automotive Products Trade Agreement of 1965 between the United States of America and the Government of Canada (the Auto Pact) provided duty-free passage of most automotive products between the two nations. For auto products, therefore, relatively little needed to be done on the first point. The most important new step in the free trade agreement is the phased elimination of remaining auto duties over the next ten years, including duties on replacement parts. In addition, Canada is to end its embargo on used cars within five years.

Because automotive trade is already so open, the second objective is by far the more important: a more secure and predictable trading relationship. This is a particularly significant issue since changes in the auto industry during the 1980s have raised questions regarding the stability of the pact. The major assumption behind the pact—that the US auto industry would continue its world preeminence—is clearly no longer the case. The rise of overseas challengers, and the responses of the two North American nations, have added to strains on the existing relationship, especially in three specific areas.

The first is the long-lasting disagreement over Canadian safeguards that accompanied the Auto Pact. In order to qualify for the right to import automotive products duty free under the pact, Canadian auto firms have to

---

Paul Wonnacott is Professor of Economics at the University of Maryland.

meet production targets. In simple terms, they have to produce approximately as many cars in Canada as they sell in Canada and achieve a Canadian value added in excess of 60 percent of the value of the cars sold in Canada. These safeguards meant that Canada maintained a degree of protection under the Auto Pact. Second, Canadian moves to extend the safeguards to overseas automobile producers selling in Canada have heightened US concerns in that area. Finally, competition for overseas plants has intensified, including incentives provided in both countries aimed at attracting new plants, Canadian duty-remissions programs, and US foreign trade zones.

The FTA reduces or eliminates each of these three sources of strain. Although the Canadian safeguards remain, their coverage has been limited. Canada has agreed not to extend pact status to any new members, in contrast to the previous policy of moving toward a requirement that all significant sellers of automobiles in Canada become members.[1] Canada has agreed to eliminate export-based duty-remission programs at the beginning of 1989 and production-based duty remissions by the end of 1995. Finally, disagreements over US foreign trade zones are dealt with as part of the general drawback issue.

Automotive products constitute about one-third of total US–Canadian trade, with automotive exports to the United States accounting for 7 percent of Canadian GNP. Thus, the defusing of conflicts in this area is very important. Indeed, one might look at the recent negotiations as involving two sets of topics—one applying to economic relations between the two nations in general and one intended to deal with the growing threat of a conflict in the automotive sector.

The major purpose of this paper will be to look in detail at three major sources of conflict and the ways in which they were dealt with in the free trade agreement:

☐ the Canadian export-based duty-remission program

☐ the Canadian move toward requiring overseas firms to participate in the Auto Pact, under which they would receive duty-free treatment as a reward for meeting the production levels specified in the safeguards

☐ the Canadian safeguards themselves.

Finally, I will look at reasons why the parts producers on both sides of the border are less satisfied with the outcome than are auto manufacturers.

---

1. "Membership" is used loosely to mean qualification as eligible manufacturers under provisions similar to those in the Auto Pact.

Export-Based Duty Remissions

Under the duty-remission program, Japanese and other overseas producers operating in Canada have an incentive to export from Canada; they are rewarded in the form of a rebate or waiver of duties on their imports into Canada. For example, a Japanese firm can get back the duty paid on imports of cars from Japan by exporting automotive parts to the United States or elsewhere. This program creates three problems.

First, it represents a rather clear subsidy to exports. For example, a Japanese firm may receive a reward of over $9 in duties remitted for every $100 in parts exported;[2] the $9 is in effect a subsidy to the export and thus creates problems both under US law and under the GATT Subsidies Code. In this regard, it is important to recognize the distinction between a duty remission and a duty drawback. A duty drawback, which is legal under GATT, involves the refund of a duty paid on a product when that same product is reexported.[3] The Canadian duty remissions provide a rebate when a quite different item is exported; the exported item might have been produced 100 percent in Canada. In recent years, some allegations of subsidy have raised complex questions with unclear answers. It is quite understandable, for example, that Canadians feel that the US government unilaterally and arbitrarily broadened the definition of subsidies in the softwood lumber case. But there is little doubt that export-based duty remissions constitute an export subsidy.

Second, the duty-remission program has raised the old question, associated with the Canadian refusal to phase out the safeguards, as to whether Canada is acting in good faith. One of the concessions that the United States got

---

2. The maximum subsidy is equal to the Canadian tariff of 9.2 percent, but it may be less. Details are provided in my study, *The United States and Canada: The Quest for Free Trade*, POLICY ANALYSES IN INTERNATIONAL ECONOMICS 16 (Washington: Institute for International Economics, 1987), 79–82. The text of a remission agreement is given in Annex 4A, 109–13.

3. To be precise, there may be some departure from the "same" product rule. For example, if a manufacturer imports inputs—bolts say—it may put those bolts in the same bin with domestically produced bolts and still get a drawback of the duty on bolt imports when the bolt-containing product is exported. The manufacturer does not have to prove that the actual bolts contained in the exports were precisely the ones imported, although drawbacks are limited to the duties paid on the number of bolts actually imported. This modification is designed to avoid ridiculously complex control and accounting problems.

Although drawbacks generally do not distort trade, they do so within a free trade agreement for reasons explained in Wonnacott, *The United States and Canada*, 136–38. Accordingly, duty drawbacks are not permitted for trade within the European Free Trade Association, and they will end for US–Canadian trade as part of the recent free trade agreement.

out of the Auto Pact of 1965 was the de facto termination of the old duty-remission program of 1962–63. Indeed, the problems associated with that program had been the precipitating cause of the negotiations that led to the Auto Pact. A US radiator manufacturer had sued to force the US Treasury to impose a countervailing duty (CVD), as required by US law. Most observers thought the manufacturer would win. To prevent a trade conflict, the Auto Pact was hurriedly negotiated.

The recent history of duty remissions has not been reassuring to the United States. When Canada introduced a duty-remission program for Volkswagen in 1978, the United States objected vigorously. Canada seemed to understand these objections; when duty-remission programs were offered to Japanese firms in 1980, remissions were to be granted only in reward for exports to countries other than the United States. But in 1984 the US exclusion was dropped.

Finally, the current duty-remission program is more objectionable to the United States than was the old program of 1962–63. The old program was associated with two-way trade between Canada and the United States; an export subsidy was provided when firms earned the remission of duties paid on Canadian imports from the United States. Under the current remissions, Japanese firms operating in Canada can use exports to the United States (which are duty free under the Auto Pact) as a way of earning the remission of duties on imports from Japan. In other words, the current duty-remission program tends to suck in more imports from Japan and push subsidized exports to the United States.

Thus far, export-based duty remissions have not been very large; they have mainly benefited European firms operating in Canada. However, with the expected large rise in production by Japanese firms in Canada, the duty-remission program might have become significant in dollar terms as well as symbolically. With the elimination of the export-based duty remissions at the beginning of 1989, this source of conflict will be removed. If nothing had been done, it is likely that there would have been a US countervailing duty action against the remissions.

Overseas Producers: Should They Qualify for the Pact?

In the FTA, Canada also agreed to limit the pact's membership to present participants, thus reversing the move toward requiring all firms selling significant numbers of automobiles in Canada to meet the safeguards. A set of production-based duty-remission agreements between the Canadian government and Japanese auto firms was apparently intended as a transitional step toward a full meeting of the safeguards, with its related duty-free privileges.

Participation in the pact by overseas firms raises some of the same issues as the export-based duty-remission program, although in a more complicated way. To highlight the similarity: if a Japanese auto firm were to achieve pact membership by meeting Canadian production targets, then it would not have to pay duties on its imports from Japan. But, of course, to meet the production targets, it would be encouraged to export from Canada. The most obvious place to send exports would be to the duty-free US market. Again, as in the case of the export-based duty remissions, Canada would be using the carrot of duty-free imports from Japan as a way of pushing exports into the duty-free US market.

The economic and political reasons for Canada wanting to keep the pact open to non-American participants are relatively straightforward. Most obviously, additional overseas trade can provide diversification and a balance to the overwhelming US presence. But the reasons why the United States should object to an arrangement that sucks imports from Japan and pushes exports out to the United States are also easy to understand. From the US side, an obvious point arises: if Canadians and Japanese want an arrangement for duty-free imports into Canada to be balanced with exports from Canada, then maybe Japan, not the United States, should take the Canadian exports. Or, to put it another way, if Canada and Japan want to arrange an Auto Pact of their own, with duty-free exports in *both* directions, then that would be one thing. But it is unreasonable for Japan to freeload on the US–Canadian pact, exporting duty-free to Canada and expecting the United States to absorb the duty-free exports of Canadian-based Japanese firms, while Japan at the same time maintains tariff and other barriers to a flow of auto products from Canada back to Japan.

From the US side, one way out of the problem would have been to request that Canada bilateralize the Auto Pact. Under the pact, the United States provides preferential duty-free entry to Canadian products; it would not be unreasonable to expect Canada in return to provide preferential duty-free entry only to US products. But such a bilateralization would create problems for US auto firms operating in Canada. Although the overwhelming majority of their imports into Canada come from the United States, these firms also benefit from duty-free imports from overseas. They are now importing about C$3 billion yearly from such non-US sources. With the Canadian tariff on autos and parts at 9.2 percent, this means that they save about C$300 million annually from the multilateral provisions on the Canadian side of the Auto Pact. Last summer, when the US government was considering whether to request that Canada bilateralize the pact, the US Motor Vehicle Manufacturers Association reacted strongly; they were "extremely alarmed."[4]

---

4. Letter of 22 June 1987 to Ambassador Peter Murphy from Thomas Hanna, President of the MVMA.

The outcome of the negotiations was reassuring to present participants in the Auto Pact: they will continue to enjoy duty-free imports into Canada from any country. But the door has been shut to new participants. And the production-based duty remissions, which represent a half-way station to pact membership, will be terminated by 1 January 1996.

In combination with the end of the export-based duty remissions, these steps mean that the United States will no longer face the prospect of Canadian-based Japanese firms receiving an incentive, in the form of duty remissions or duty waivers, as a reward for exporting to the United States. Of course, if they meet the 50 percent North American content rule, the firms will still have duty-free access to the US market; they simply will not receive special incentives for exporting.

This does not mean that we are completely out of the woods. The production-based remissions may still be a source of trouble, as they will remain in force until the end of 1995. One difficulty is that the US Congress is being asked to acquiesce in the continuation of these remissions for the next eight years without knowing the details; US government requests for copies of the remission agreements have been rebuffed.

The Canadian Safeguards

With the phasing out of automotive tariffs between Canada and the United States, one of the incentives for auto firms to meet the safeguards will be eliminated. They will no longer face the possibility of huge Canadian duty payments on their imports from the United States if they fail to comply. Consequently, the free trade agreement is sometimes interpreted on both sides of the border as the effective end to the Canadian safeguards.

However, this is not an accurate conclusion. The big three still have an incentive to comply—namely, the C$300 million saved annually on duties that would otherwise have to be paid on imports into Canada from overseas sources. Questions may be asked on both sides of the border regarding the safeguards. On the Canadian side, the question arises: have the safeguards been fatally weakened? On the US side, the question is the opposite: did the US negotiators make a mistake in tacitly accepting the continuation of the safeguards and not insisting on their elimination?

First, consider the Canadian question. It is true that an extremely strong incentive to comply with the safeguards was eliminated—namely, the threat of huge duty payments on imports from the United States. But the question may at least be asked whether this threat could be carried out in practice. Like an atomic weapon, it may be too powerful and dangerous to use. Before Canada presented auto firms with huge duty bills on imports from the United States, serious thought presumably would have to be given to the possibility of US retaliation. The more modest weapon—duties on imports from overseas—is more usable, both because of its size and because it does not apply to exports from the United States. Note Japan would be much less likely to retaliate against the collection of such duties because Japan has no duty-free agreement with Canada and because Japanese manufacturers operating in Canada will already be paying duties. A C$300 million incentive should be sufficient to ensure compliance in the foreseeable future. This is particularly true since Chrysler, which previously was in the weakest position to comply, now has much more elbowroom with the recent acquisition of American Motors and its up-to-date Canadian facilities.

This leads to the US question: did not the United States make a mistake in allowing the safeguards to persist into a general free trade regime? The problem, from the American side, is that there is no clear national interest; the interests of the big three are quite different from the interests of parts producers. The safeguards are inextricably tied up with duty-free imports from third countries into Canada by the big three. Without the safeguards, the pact would have been bilateralized, and such duty-free imports would have ended at a cost of C$300 million annually to the big three. On the other hand, US parts producers wanted the pact bilateralized, and the safeguards eliminated. The safeguards mean that US (and Canadian) parts producers face duty-free competition from overseas firms in getting contracts to supply the big three in Canada; they also prevent US parts producers from competing freely with Canadian producers in the Canadian parts market. Julian Morris, president of the Automotive Parts and Accessories Association, has criticized the Canada–United States Free Trade Agreement as "unfair" because it "fails to eliminate Canadian protection of its auto/auto parts sectors. It would subject one-third of bilateral trade to a pro-Canadian managed, not free, trade regime."[5]

Parts Manufacturers: The Rule of Origin

Residual duty-free competition from overseas parts producers was only one reason why parts manufacturers on both sides of the border are less satisfied with the outcome than are assemblers of automobiles. They were only partly successful in pushing for a stricter "rule of origin" for duty-free Canadian–US automotive trade. The method of calculating the 50 percent required North American content was changed; this had the effect of raising the requirement. But the parts producers did not get the increase to 60 percent or more that they wanted. The Automotive Parts Manufacturers' Association of Canada (APMAC) has recently declared that the automotive elements of

---

5. Press release, 8 October 1987.

the FTA are unacceptable if the content requirement is not raised to 60 percent.[6]

The content requirement, a standard provision in a free trade agreement, is quite different from the Canadian value-added requirement of the safeguards, which protects the Canadian parts industry from competition from all nations including the United States. In contrast, the North American content requirement protects both US and Canadian parts producers from outside competition. Therefore, parts producers on both sides of the border have a common interest in a high North American content requirement (whereas US parts producers are opposed to the Canadian safeguards). On the other hand, the auto assemblers with limited North American operations (that is, the subsidiaries of overseas firms) might have difficulty meeting a high requirement, and therefore it is contrary to their interest. Thus, the main difference of opinion regarding the North American content requirement was within each country rather than between the two countries. This is so even if we confine our attention to the interests of producers and ignore consumers.

Nonetheless, there was some difference in emphasis between the two countries. The US government was somewhat more favorably disposed to a higher content requirement than was the Canadian government (although the principal differences had to do with timing and coverage rather than the percentage). The obvious explanation for Canada's relative lack of enthusiasm for a high content requirement is that it would be more likely to act as a barrier to Canadian exports and imports since overseas firms based in Canada might find it somewhat more difficult to reach than those firms based in the United States.

Conclusion

The automotive clauses in the FTA were about as good as could be expected. The negotiators picked their way through a complex set of issues. In the end, they eliminated duty remissions, and they partially bilateralized the Auto Pact from the Canadian side, by limiting its privileges to present members.

I find it very difficult to imagine a substantially better outcome under the circumstances. The auto clauses of the FTA are a bit untidy, but they grew out of the same dynamic process as the Auto Pact itself: unilateral Canadian action, the threat of a US countervailing duty, and an international agreement to avoid an explosion.

---

6. APMAC, press release, 9 December 1987.

What would the consequences be if the FTA were rejected? For the auto industry, a rejection of the FTA would leave unfinished business on the table. The preexisting situation is quite unstable, particularly with the Canadian duty-remission programs. There would be two possible outcomes. Specific negotiations could be undertaken to deal with the outstanding problems. In this case, something like the auto clauses of the FTA would represent about as good an outcome as I can envisage. The other alternative would be to do nothing, but this would risk a major confrontation within the next few years over Canadian subsidies on automotive exports to the United States. We can address our auto problems now, or we can address them later, when they will have become much more intractable. Fortunately, the problems were addressed in the recent free trade negotiations.

Comments

Mustafa Mohatarem

I was very impressed with the comprehensiveness of Paul Wonnacott's paper. It covers some very complicated issues related to auto trade between the United States and Canada, issues that may not have been understood fully by the auto industry or for that matter, by the negotiators. The author has done a superb job of identifying the major sources of trade frictions in the industry and how the Canada–United States Free Trade Agreement (FTA) addresses these frictions.

Given the comprehensive nature of the paper, I am not sure how much anyone could add, but let me say something about the accomplishments of the agreement, which might be overly optimistic.

I agree that the agreement should resolve most of the outstanding auto trade-related disputes between the United States and Canada. However, two major sources of friction remain that could upset the author's optimistic assessment. The first is related to the Canadian safeguards. In my view, the Canadian safeguards are totally harmless since Canada has a huge surplus in auto trade with the United States. Thus, the safeguards are not influencing either production or investment decisions. Indeed, as an aside, one must ask why a country with a trade surplus wants such safeguards.

The problem is that while the safeguards serve no economic function, they provide a ready argument for opponents of the agreement who can claim that the safeguards protect Canadian auto production at the expense of US auto production. Since this is essentially a political argument, it is hard to refute logically.

We have been trying to refute this argument by pointing out that all the safeguards do is assure Canada that 60 percent of the value of vehicles sold in Canada by Auto Pact members will be produced in Canada. Thus, for the safeguards to be binding, Canada would have to have a substantial deficit in auto trade with the United States—the case through much of the 1960s and 1970s. As we moved into the 1980s, however, the depreciation of the Canadian dollar, changing management practices, and the changing quality of labor made Canada a much more cost-effective production location. This resulted in a large Canadian auto trade surplus with the United States.

In short, this surplus is not related to the Canadian safeguards but will no doubt be associated with them. Unfortunately, this means that as long as the safeguards remain, they will be criticized in the United States and will continue to be a source of trade friction between the two countries.

Mustafa Mohatarem is Director of Trade Analysis on the economics staff at the General Motors Corporation.

One would think, therefore, that Canada would not object to eliminating the safeguards. However, this is not the case. As Paul Wonnacott has pointed out, Auto Pact members, including General Motors, have a large interest in maintaining the safeguards; in return for complying with them, Auto Pact members receive multilateral duty-free import privileges. By eliminating the safeguards, Canada would not be able to enforce or justify providing multilateral duty-free benefits to the Auto Pact members. Given the interest in maintaining these duty-free benefits, I suspect the safeguards will remain.

This brings me to the second source of potential friction between Canada and the United States that is not addressed adequately in the paper—the lack of common external tariffs or barriers. To an outsider, it would appear from the rhetoric, at least in the United States, that the primary concern of the negotiators was inequities in auto trade between the United States and Canada. However, this was not the case. The major Canadian producers are also the major US producers (General Motors, Ford, and Chrysler). Therefore, they had little to gain and much to lose from new barriers between the two countries.

The real difficulties arose because of attempts to protect these North American producers from producers located in Japan and the Asian newly industrializing countries (NICs). This does not come through in the paper.

As the author recognizes, when the Auto Pact was negotiated, the US auto industry was the dominant auto industry in the world. The safeguards were put in place because there was a real fear in Canada that auto production in Canada would cease in a totally free trade environment. Furthermore, the safeguards were acceptable to the United States since Canada agreed to remove its very high (approximately 30 percent) tariffs on auto imports from the United States in return for the safeguards.

Quite a few things have changed since the Auto Pact was negotiated. Most are discussed in the paper. The one major omission is the significant reduction in Canadian auto tariffs. The US tariff has also declined, but it was never very large. Given the cost differences among the major auto-producing nations, neither the US nor the Canadian tariffs are now sufficient to keep out imports from third countries.

The improved competitive position of third country auto producers, especially the Japanese, and declining external tariffs have resulted in a sharp increase in imports into both Canada and the United States. Both have responded by imposing quantity restraints on imports from Japan. Not surprisingly, the quantity restraints on imports from Japan have invited imports from other countries. (If the experience of the textiles, steel, and television industries is any guide, there will be attempts to expand those restraints to other countries.)

Let us just focus on Japan, which is going to be an ongoing problem because Japanese producers are responding to the import restraints by establishing assembly plants in both countries. This is where the external tariffs come into play. The US tariff on auto parts averages approximately 4 percent, whereas the Canadian tariff averages over 9 percent. Therefore, everything else being equal, a firm planning to assemble vehicles in North America with a high level of imported components would choose to locate in the United States rather than Canada. And the United States has other advantages. In particular, the market is much larger, and importers generally have large enough sales to justify economically sized plants. It is thus not surprising that Canada finds it necessary to offer incentives to offset the tariff disadvantage faced by third-country producers locating in Canada.

We wish the two sides had at least considered the implications of not having common external tariffs and quantitative restraints. For example, the debate over the rule of origin would not have been as acrimonious if producers in both countries had been assured that third-country producers would not be able to circumvent quantitative restraints by establishing "screwdriver" assembly plants. It would have also avoided future conflicts between the two countries.

I would not be surprised to see Canada reduce its tariffs on auto parts to the US level. This would have some interesting consequences, both negative and positive. It should, in a sense, result in the de facto elimination of the Canadian safeguards. In addition, it would reduce the benefits Auto Pact members receive from having multilateral duty-free import privileges. Both of these results should please some of the US critics of the agreement.

No doubt, such a move also would result in accusations in the United States that Canada had changed its external tariffs in order to attract foreign-owned auto assembly plants. Interestingly, the groups making the accusations are likely to be the same as those wanting an end to the Canadian safeguards and the multilateral duty-free privileges of the Auto Pact members.

In sum, I am not as optimistic as Paul Wonnacott about what the FTA will accomplish because I believe that the Canadian safeguards for Auto Pact members and the lack of common external barriers will continue to be a source of potential conflict. These concerns notwithstanding, I want to emphasize that our negotiators did an excellent job. They succeeded in removing many of the sources of trade friction involving autos. This was somewhat surprising given the entrenched interests and given the strong perception that the Auto Pact was functioning as it was intended to do; that is, the Auto Pact was contributing to the integration of the two industries and to free trade between the two countries. Indeed, a lot of consideration was given to leaving autos out of the negotiations.

The perception that the Auto Pact was working well was not too far from the truth. It has resulted in virtually free trade in autos between the United States and Canada. It has also contributed to the development of perhaps the two most integrated auto industries among any two countries. But the paper is right that tensions were growing because of the challenge from Japanese and other Asian producers. The FTA goes a long way toward reducing some of these tensions.

From our perspective, the greatest accomplishment of the FTA is that it ensures that our integrated industry will remain so. We were extremely concerned that political pressures in both countries would result in such a high rule of origin as to create two separate industries. This concern was reflected in the letters to our negotiators cited in the paper. These letters make it clear that the industry's fundamental objective was to ensure that auto trade between the two countries would remain at least as free under the FTA as it is under the Auto Pact. Now that we have reviewed the agreement, we have no doubt that it will remain as free. Therefore, we rate the agreement very highly and have every intention of supporting it strongly.

O. Victor Lonmo

The Canada–United States Free Trade Agreement (FTA) that President Reagan and Prime Minister Mulroney signed on 2 January 1988 is a bold and unique undertaking. It is all the more important in this period of confused and worrisome economic signals—the currency fluctuations that have followed the G-5 meeting of September 1985, the stock market jolt of October 1987, and the potential for draconian trade policy initiatives as governments address trade and current account deficits.

I would like to focus primarily on the FTA's automotive provisions. It is not necessary to provide background data on the importance of bilateral automotive trade; suffice it to say that automotive trade represents 37 percent of US–Canada bilateral trade. In 1986, Canadian imports of automotive products from the United States were C$29.1 billion. While there are major automotive industry problems at our doorstep, America is not Canada's problem, and Canada is not America's problem.

Let us look first at the realities facing the North American automotive industry:

☐ *Overcapacity.* In the world today there are an estimated 6.0 million to 7.0 million units of excess automotive capacity.

O. Victor Lonmo is President of the Automotive Parts Manufacturers' Association of Canada.

□ *New production.* Nontraditional motor vehicle producers will be adding up to 2.5 million units of new capacity in North America by 1992–94 as compared with 1985.

□ *Offshore sourcing.* The number and value of third-country sourced vehicles continue to rise almost exponentially. During the month of September 1987 in Canada, complete built-up units had 40 percent of the new car registrations. The value of automotive parts imports is also rising at a rapid rate.

□ *Internationalization of industry.* The only part of the automotive industry that is internationalized is that of production, as imports into other large, high-income markets are limited in one way or another. Take a look at the market share that non-nationals enjoy in the European Common Market or Japan compared with comparable market shares in North America. North America is the *only* open automotive market in the world.

□ *Competitiveness.* North American industry can compete if a general rule of "fairness" is applied to all players. While I cannot speak for the United States, government-imposed costs affect pricing in Canada. Our competitors in the Pacific Rim or elsewhere do not have the same costs of government to shoulder that apply here in North America. Surely the question is not, "Are we competitive?" but rather "How are we able to be competitive?"

With that general background, let us look at the agreement and see if we have the kind of deal that some call a "win-win" situation. When the agreement is implemented, we will have the traditional "Big Three" operating under the Automotive Products Trade Agreement between the United States of America and the Government of Canada (Auto Pact) rules that have been in place since January 1965. The major difference between then and now is that in 1964–65 North American producers enjoyed approximately 96 percent of the North American market. Those days have gone, and the US Department of Commerce has estimated that 52 percent of the North American market will be supplied from offshore by 1992.

The other motor vehicle producers in North America who wish to trade their products duty free across our borders need to achieve 50 percent or more of the direct cost of processing in order to meet the new rules of origin. This is a step in the right direction—that is, for Canada and the United States to adopt a common, clear, and reasonably easy to enforce set of rules of origin. However, the 50 percent number, I suggest, is *not* acceptable and is one issue that the Canadian and American automotive parts industry has not and will not accept.

Some have argued that we will not support the agreement because in holding out for the 60 percent rather than the 50 percent number, we want to exclude Pacific Rim producers from the market. That is nonsense. The 60 percent number is necessary, indeed mandatory, if the North American automotive industry is to have long-term strength. At 60 percent, a producer would not only be required to assemble the vehicle to achieve duty-free entry into each of our markets, but also would have to produce (in North America) the engine, trans-axle, transmission, and/or electronics of that vehicle. Only one or possibly two of those components would be required, not all of them.

If those components are produced here in North America, it will maintain the sourcing here of the high-value, intellectual portion of the vehicle via research, design, engineering, and production. Canada and the United States deserve no less; the industry should accept no less. Even if we have the 60 percent rule of origin, and I believe we must have it, the market is still wide open to imports from third countries that I have already said captured 40 percent of the new car registrations in Canada in September 1987.

The Canada–US Free Trade Agreement that our heads of state have signed will require change on our part. They have made a significant start, but I think it is unacceptable for us to give up the fight until that agreement is made as good as it should be or must be. At 60 percent, the Automotive Parts Manufacturers' Association of Canada (APMAC) will support it, at 50 percent it will not.

The APMAC would support a proposal that met the concerns of the new, nontraditional manufacturers to reach 60 percent, while at the same time creating the objective for the North American industry to reach its real potential on the basis of fairness. The proposal is that the FTA, with its imperfections, including dispute settlement, be signed and implemented as it is now written, but with one change: effective January 1999 raising the level of direct cost of processing required to meet the rule of origin from 50 percent to 60 percent.

The 60 percent level of achievement will be important to all of North America and to our material suppliers as well as our parts producers. The 60 percent level is supported, or at least not opposed, by everyone in the North American automotive industry. Labor too will accept it, even though in the United States it might choose a higher number, while in Canada it tends to oppose the concept of free trade for many nonautomotive reasons. The 60 percent level is not perfect, but it is a compromise, and any agreement of such wide-sweeping proportions as this requires that we make compromises so that at the end of the day we may all be able to agree that we truly have a win-win situation.

Finally, we should also focus upon the impact of the abolition of duty drawback both in the United States and Canada. It is an issue because the tariff rates are not identical. For automobiles, the US rate is 2.3 percent, while in Canada it is 9.2 percent. If a company were choosing a North American site, and it would achieve only 50 percent North American value added with the balance coming from offshore, there would be an advantage of 6.9 percent on the 50 percent imported portion to skew that investment to the United States and away from Canada.

Issues like duty drawback and its impact upon North American automotive trade could be addressed by a select panel, as proposed for automotive issues in the FTA. The panel, if appropriately staffed at the secretariat and panel member level, could play a meaningful role in North American automotive policy development. I believe, and this is solely one Canadian's view, that no bureaucrats associated with the agreement's development should participate either directly or indirectly on the panel or its secretariat.

5

Implications of the Energy Provisions

Philip K. Verleger, Jr.

Energy policy has been one of the more contentious issues of the past 20 years in both the United States and Canada. Policies were adopted in each country only after prolonged battles between representatives of consumers, producers, and the environment. Frequently, the debate concerned the distribution of rents created by the increase in the world price of oil between consumers and producers.

Relations over energy trade between Canada and the United States reflected both these internal policy debates and the inevitable tensions encountered whenever trade takes place. Indeed, the record indicates that energy relations between the two countries have been extremely rocky. Viewed from the United States, Canadian actions have occasionally appeared unfriendly:

□ Canada temporarily cut exports of oil to the United States at the time of the Arab embargo in the early 1970s when shortages were occurring throughout the United States.

□ Canada adopted an energy plan in the late 1970s that sought to terminate exports to the United States by the early 1980s.

□ Canada pursued a program to reduce foreign investment in its energy industries.

□ Canada imposed a system of export taxes and export price controls that ensured that US consumers paid much higher prices than did Canadian consumers. These pricing schemes were then replaced by a system of volumetric discounts designed to displace domestically produced natural gas by Canadian imports when demand declined and prices collapsed.

□ Canada adopted measures that limited electricity exports to the United States and forced American consumers to pay higher prices.

Philip K. Verleger, Jr., is a Visiting Fellow at the Institute for International Economics.

Actions taken by the US government relating to energy trade between the two countries were undoubtedly viewed with equal dismay by Canadians:

☐ Government controls on the wellhead price of natural gas held prices below market levels, effectively denying Canadian exports access to the US market.

☐ The US mandatory oil import quota from 1958 to 1973 was implemented in a manner that prevented increased Canadian exports to the United States through "informal advice" or jawboning.

☐ The United States closed its uranium market to Canadian producers from 1964 to 1975 by denying foreign suppliers access to enrichment facilities.

☐ The United States denied potentially lower cost Alaskan crude to West Coast Canadian refiners, forcing them to purchase more expensive supplies.

☐ The United States proposed and then abandoned a pipeline to bring natural gas from Alaska to the lower 48 states after encouraging the Canadians to start construction on the Canadian portion.

☐ The United States pursued energy policies intended to increase the use of coal while failing to address the problems caused by sulphur dioxide emissions (primarily acid rain) on Canada.

☐ The United States allowed the Bonneville Power Administration to deny British Columbia Hydro access to the Northwest Intertie, effectively prohibiting BC Hydro from marketing electricity to California and forcing California consumers to pay higher prices.

☐ The United States imposed a higher Super Fund tax on imports of Canadian petroleum (as well as all imports) than was imposed on domestic producers.

☐ The United States occasionally imposed fees on oil exports from Canada to the United States.

The Canada–United States Free Trade Agreement (FTA) addresses many of these points of past disagreement. However, on balance it is of very marginal importance because it fails to address the vital long-term issue of development of Canadian energy supplies. In fact, the agreement sanctions the continuation of a Canadian investment policy that explicitly favors Canadian companies. US acquiescence on this point is deplorable, both because the Canadian approach has contributed to an unnecessary increase in dependence by major industrialized countries on insecure supplies of oil from the Middle East and because acceptance of bad Canadian policies weakens the United States' ability to oppose bad policies such as import fees in the United States.

This paper begins by examining the modest accomplishments of the agreement that will eliminate some historical sources of tension. It then examines the failings in the area of resource development. It concludes by recommending further negotiations to resolve the difficulties created by Canadian investment regulations.

What the Agreement Accomplishes

The agreement will resolve many of the problem areas noted earlier. These measures represent a useful first step in the elimination of the more egregious barriers to energy trade between the United States and Canada. The benefits of the agreement are discussed below.

Petroleum Exports

The agreement does break new ground in eliminating barriers to the importation and exportation of petroleum. This has been a sore spot in US–Canadian relations for more than 15 years. The problem first arose in 1973, when Canada rebuffed US efforts to find increased supplies of petroleum. It reached a momentary peak in December 1973, when supplies of industrial fuel oil from Canada to factories in Maine were temporarily suspended. Difficulties continued through the late 1970s as Canadian exports were gradually cut in order to meet growing domestic demand and conserve remaining reserves. The trend in petroleum exports to the United States is shown in table 5.1.

Tensions between the two countries peaked again in the early 1980s, when Canada adopted its ill-advised and ill-fated National Energy Program (NEP). Price controls, which had been imposed on Canadian oil to "insulate" the domestic market from price increases in 1973, were extended at a time when most other nations were removing their controls. Border taxes were imposed on exports of oil to the United States to ensure that American consumers did not benefit from these controls.

The low energy prices were intended to give Canadian manufacturers a competitive edge over manufacturers located in the United States, a point that was noted by US firms.[1] The imposition of price controls, limits on

---

1. These benefits turned out to be short-lived because of the collapse of world oil prices. In actuality, US manufacturers gained the greater benefit because decontrolled US prices declined while Canadian firms were saddled with high-cost contracts.

Table 5.1   US imports of petroleum and natural gas from Canada, 1973–87

Year	Petroleum (thousand barrels a day)	Natural gas (million cubic feet)
1973	1,325	1,027.2
1974	1,070	959.1
1975	846	948.1
1976	599	953.6
1977	517	996.7
1978	467	881.1
1979	538	1,000.6
1980	455	796.4
1981	447	762.1
1982	482	783.4
1983	547	711.8
1984	630	745.4
1985	770	926.2
1986	807	747.7
1987	833	994

Source: US Department of Energy.

exports, border taxes, and a quarrel between Ottawa and Edmonton over the distribution of the rents had the expected impact on Canadian exploration and development. Expenditures on exploration declined, the number of wells drilled plummeted, and oil rigs were moved from Alberta to the United States.

The United States practiced its own form of discrimination beginning in 1975 by prohibiting sale of Alaskan crude oil to Canada. Legislation authorizing the construction of the Trans-Alaskan Pipeline and the Export Administration Act of 1979 required that Alaskan oil be consumed in the United States. This requirement has forced producers to transport substantial volumes of North Slope crude from Alaska to the US Gulf Coast at much higher costs. At the same time, refiners located in British Columbia have been forced to acquire higher priced supplies.

Most of these difficulties would have been avoided had the FTA been in effect in 1973. The imposition of border taxes would have been prohibited as would limitations on exports. Refiners in British Columbia would have had access to more favorably priced Alaskan crude. Consumers in the United States would have benefited from Canada's ill-fated experiment with price controls. Thus, the agreement offers some clear benefits to oil consumers in both nations.

Natural Gas Trade

The relationship between Canada and the United States has been equally contentious and confused in the area of natural gas. Many of the problems may be traced to the byzantine natural gas market regulations adopted in the United States.

These tensions occurred when the Canadian National Energy Board (NEB) imposed a requirement that Canadian reserves equal at least 15 years of annual consumption before any exports were permitted. Exports were cut in the late 1970s and early 1980s as the growth in reserves lagged behind increases in consumption.

The relationship was further complicated by a policy that established a uniform border price for natural gas. Initially set at $1.60 per thousand cubic feet (mcf) in 1976, this price increased to a peak of $4.94 mcf in early 1981, a time when much price-controlled domestic gas sold for less than $1.00 mcf. These border prices were far higher than prices charged Canadian consumers.

The high Canadian prices coincided with development of surplus-producing capacity in the United States (the gas "glut" or "bubble") and led to a loss of sales by Canadian exporters. By mid-1987 prices on some exports had declined to $1.60 mcf. However, it appears that Canada's pursuit of high prices in the early 1980s and slow response to falling prices had prevented it from increasing sales until 1986 (see table 5.1).

Canadian efforts to capture an increased share of the US natural gas market in the 1980s have been further frustrated by a series of regulatory measures adopted by the US Federal Energy Regulatory Commission (FERC), the organization charged with regulating natural gas. In a series of orders issued during the mid-1980s, FERC adopted measures that had the effect of transforming the US market from a traditional cost of service industry into a commodity type market. Canadian exporters were less able to compete in this environment because they were still regulated.

The problems in the gas market arose with the adoption of FERC order 380. Order 380 relieved gas distribution utilities—local distribution companies (LDCs) that purchase gas from pipelines and deliver it to the ultimate consumer—of the obligation to pay for gas supplies not taken. Traditionally, these buyers had entered contracts with pipelines that required them to take a specified volume. Order 380 was followed by order 436 that effectively required pipelines to operate as common carriers. Prior to its adoption, pipeline companies had been able to deny LDCs access to low-cost gas by refusing to carry it for them.

Transactions in the US gas market quickly shifted from a long-term to a spot basis where a substantial portion of volume was sold under short-term spot contracts. This policy had two unintended negative effects on Canadian exporters. First, Canadian supplies that had been sold under long-term contracts were not taken because buyers were relieved of their obligation to buy. Second, requirements that exporters obtain federal approval of export contracts effectively prevented Canadian exporters from responding to the rapidly changing US gas market where buyers and sellers could execute agreements without government approval and begin service immediately.

The FTA will have only a modest impact on the ability of Canada to gain access to the US market because it fails to address the essential incompatibility of regulations between the two markets. Today the US market is essentially deregulated, the Canadian market is not. US buyers will not rush to buy Canadian gas until Canadian regulators adjust their regulations to match those in the United States or until the US supplies of gas begin to run short.

Uranium Trade

Canadian exports of uranium to the United States have been limited periodically since 1966. Although endowed with abundant reserves of uranium that can be extracted at very low costs, Canada lacks facilities for enrichment of these ores into uranium oxide, the fuel used in most reactors. Canadian exports were frozen out of the US market from 1966 to 1975 because the US Atomic Energy Commission refused to process foreign supplies. This exclusion was imposed under the Atomic Energy Act that prohibits enrichment of foreign uranium for domestic use when the domestic industry is threatened. Low-cost Canadian uranium began to displace American uranium in 1980.

US producers fought the enrichment of Canadian imports in court on the basis that Canadian imports threatened their economic viability. Federal district and appeals courts have supported the claim of US firms. Canadian uranium would again face exclusion from the market unless the Supreme Court reversed these opinions. However, this risk is eliminated because the FTA resolves the issue by according Canadian uranium the same status as domestically produced uranium.

Electricity Trade

Electricity exports from Canada to the United States have increased substantially over the past 10 years. Hydro Quebec has negotiated a long-term supply arrangement with a group of New England utilities to expand its hydro generation capacity and deliver the output of these facilities to New England through a new dedicated intertie. A second facility was proposed but temporarily stopped by Canadian officials because the output was not obviously surplus to Canada. At the same time, British Columbia has been frustrated in its efforts to sell power to willing buyers in California by the refusal of the Bonneville Power Administration to transmit the exports on the Northwest Intertie.

The FTA will eliminate some of these impediments to electricity exports. B.C. Hydro will be accorded the same treatment as any other non-Northwest utility and thus will be permitted to transmit electricity over the intertie under certain limited circumstances. Deliveries to US customers in the Northeast will not be subject to curtailments except to the extent that consumers in Canada and the United States will have to accept proportional curtailments in the event of shortage. Negotiation of future supply agreements may be made easier, although the National Energy Board in Canada still must certify that production to be sold under contract is surplus to Canada's needs.

What the Agreement Lacks

The FTA addresses many of the difficulties encountered between the United States and Canada over the past decade in the sphere of energy trade. However, it makes a negligible contribution to the improvement of the longer term energy market environment in the United States, Canada, or the free world.

The presumed goal of energy policy is to ensure an adequate supply of fuels produced (and used) in an environmentally acceptable fashion at relatively stable and predictable prices for the long term. If such an environment can be achieved, free markets will ensure that consumers make the optimal choice between conservation and consumption and that investments in exploration and development of resources will be allocated in an efficient manner. In this idealized world, US imports of energy materials would undoubtedly skyrocket as investment dollars previously allocated to US oil and gas fields were placed elsewhere, including in Canada.

The requirement for this ideal climate is particularly great in the energy sector because most investment projects are capital intensive, extraordinarily expensive, subject to long gestation periods, and long-lived. Thus, private investors are often unwilling to come forward with funds required for larger projects if there is any doubt about the political climate toward investment in the host country.

US–Canadian energy relations provide an excellent illustration of the problems encountered in obtaining the funds necessary to proceed with large and expensive energy projects. Canada is endowed with potentially enormous reserves of oil, gas, and coal. Most of these reserves, however, are found in extraordinarily inhospitable areas such as the Arctic or in the Atlantic off of Newfoundland. Other resources such as tar sands are located in more easily accessible regions, but require intensive processing to be converted from solid to liquid form. Development of these potential sources of supply requires a commitment of enormous capital by private investors—capital that cannot be generated in Canadian markets. Only a handful of companies—the 6 traditional major oil companies and perhaps another 10 or 12 large firms—have both the funds and the experience to find and develop these reserves successfully.

Canada is also endowed with an abundent supply of hydropower. Both the provinces of Quebec and Nova Scotia are endowed with many locations where very large hydro power generation facilities could be built. Although extraordinarily expensive, such facilities once completed would provide electricity at very low marginal costs and without the environmental risks associated with nuclear power or coal. Again development has been slowed by a shortage of indigenous capital.

Unfortunately, Canadian policy for the past decade has generally frustrated investment in resources by foreign firms. The Trudeau government sought to increase Canadian ownership of resources through the NEP. Canadian companies were encouraged to try to take over assets held in Canada by US firms. At the same time, the Foreign Investment Review Agency (FIRA) prevented US companies from bidding for smaller Canadian companies. Furthermore, the Canadian government took a 25 percent investment interest at no cost to itself in both future and ongoing exploration projects in Arctic and offshore areas at the time these projects went into development.

These actions had the predictable effect of stifling development of resources in Canada. The saga of Dome Petroleum is instructive on this issue. Encouraged by the call for increased Canadian ownership, Dome made a bid for part of the US company, Conoco, in 1981 in an effort to force Conoco to sell Dome its 53 percent share in Hudson Bay Oil and Gas. The bid succeeded. Conoco sold its share of Hudson Bay to Dome and was later forced to merge with Du Pont. However, the acquisition forced Dome to increase its long-term debt to C$6.2 billion, 70 percent of its capital. The company undertook a restructuring and slowed or stopped exploration and development. Moreover, its high debt level made it vulnerable to the collapse in oil prices. Finally, in the spring of 1987 Dome was forced to accept an offer to merge with an American company, Amoco, in order to avoid receivership.[2]

---

2. The merger had not yet been finalized as of February 1988.

The Canadian policy would appear to have had two effects. First, foreign investment has been discouraged. Second, Canadian firms like Dome have been forced to curtail expenditures on exploration and development because they have burdened themselves with debt incurred in the acquisition of assets previously owned by foreign companies. The experience of Dome over the past six years provides a vivid illustration of the second effect. The failure of Mobil to proceed with the development of the Hibernia field, a promising but deep field off of Newfoundland, offers an example of the first.

The agreement also fails to fully address the surplus tests imposed on exports of natural gas by the province of Alberta and the National Energy Board. Currently, Alberta prohibits exportation of natural gas from the province to the rest of Canada unless developed reserves are equal to more than 15 times annual consumption in the province. Until recently, the NEB imposed a similar type of test on exports from Canada to the United States, requiring that reserves be 25 times projected consumption. No similar tests were imposed by the NEB on sales to Canadians.

The NEB regulations were modified in 1987. The reserve test was removed. Instead, the burden of proof has been shifted to Canadians, who must show that a market for the gas exists in Canada in order to prevent the NEB from issuing a permit for the exportation of gas. The effect of this rule is to permit greater exports to the United States but to leave the United States as a decidedly second-class customer to whom "leftovers" from the Canadian market are allocated.[3]

The continuation of restrictive investment rules in Canada provide support for the view that the goal of free trade must be subordinated to the national need for secure supplies of energy. This "energy security" rationale has long been the dominant factor in the determination of energy policies in many countries including the United States and Canada. As the recent Canadian experience shows, however, such policies may inhibit new exploration and development. The question is: Can a country logically pursue a policy that is antithetical to free trade by imposing limits or restrictions on developments of its resources while receiving the benefits of trade in energy with a second nation?

Canada should allow market prices to dictate the rate of development of its resources if it wishes to enjoy the benefits of free trade with the United States. The benefits of trade to consumers are maximized only when the

---

3. The NEB and Alberta regulatory systems are actually far more complicated than described here. Petitioners desiring to export gas must also show, among other things, that the price will be at least as high as paid by Canadians, and at least as high as the cost of alternatives. I am indebted to Professor Leonard Waverman for explaining the details of NEB regulation to me.

barriers to the contemporaneous trade and development of resources are dropped. Otherwise, the consumer gains because prices are lower today, but loses in future periods because investments in new supply have been less than optimal, thus causing prices to be higher than would otherwise have occurred.

Some may argue that this view is impractical. Instead, each country should determine the rate of optimal development of its own resources and preserve that portion of its energy reserves that it determines to be appropriate for future generations.

Such views are rejected here because they are contrary to both the spirit and theory of free trade. Limitations on foreign investment in Canadian resources of the types applied by Canada and reserve tests are as inappropriate as are measures to limit oil imports into the United States through the adoption of an import fee or other quantitative restrictions on oil imports. Canadians have correctly deplored proposals of the latter sort. Americans should oppose limitations on investment with equal force. Unfortunately, US negotiators capitulated in the FTA negotiations.

The US failure to secure liberalization of Canadian restrictions on foreign investment in energy is doubly unfortunate because it increases the likelihood that the United States will pursue some form of protection for its energy sector—probably in the form of an import fee. Pressures for such a step are strong and growing.

Adoption of an import fee in the United States could be justified using the same arguments employed by Canada to defend its investment rules. Ironically, the result would probably be unacceptable to Canada and could give rise to serious conflicts between the two countries. Canadian producers would benefit from such an act under the FTA because Canadian exports to the United States would be exempted. Canadian consumers, however, would suffer because prices would increase to the level prevailing in the United States.

It is regrettable that the negotiators permitted such a situation to develop. Long-term energy policy goals were sacrificed for the short-term expedient of reaching agreement. To resolve the real issues, the two countries should expand the FTA to include US investments in Canada's energy sector and eliminate surplus tests for exports. Without such an agreement, future trade conflicts are inevitable.

The FTA will reduce the historical tension over energy supplies between the United States and Canada. However, much is left to be accomplished. Three areas of negotiation would appear to hold particular promise for both nations: harmonization of natural gas regulations, deregulation of electricity transmission, and elimination of investment barriers in both nations.

Consumers in the United States and Canada would benefit from the harmonization of policies and regulations relating to natural gas. At present, US consumers probably pay higher prices because Canadian producers are prevented by Canadian regulations from gaining complete access to the US market. Should these barriers fall, Canadian producers will be able to enjoy greater revenues and profits due to increased sales. These profits, in turn, should permit Canadian consumers to benefit from lower prices. Such an idealized outcome will be possible, however, only if US and Canadian legislators and regulators set aside their parochial concerns to establish a more coordinated system of regulation.

Deregulation of electricity transmission and possibly the separation of ownership of transmission facilities from generation facilities will also be required to facilitate free trade in energy. Currently, utilities such as Bonneville exercise monopoly power over access to interstate transmission facilities, power that is used to deny access to other generators such as B.C. Hydro. Only when access to transmission facilities is opened to all suppliers on an equal basis can free trade in electricity be achieved. This will require legislative and regulatory change in the United States.

Finally, elimination of investment barriers will foster a rational and faster development of North American energy resources. This more rapid development of North American resources would benefit consumers in both countries because increased supplies would lead to lower prices.

The free trade agreement really can lead to substantial benefits in energy trade in the long term if these additional steps are taken. As it is, the FTA is a beginning, but not the end.

Comments

Marshall Crowe

I am a little bit surprised by the remarks of Phil Verleger. For the past ten years I have had no obligation to defend the Canadian government or its policies or programs. My reaction, based solely on continuing experience in the industry and reading the Canada–United States Free Trade Agreement (FTA) and looking at what had been happening and what may happen, is that it is remarkably good both for Canada and for the United States. Without going into all the details where I may disagree with the speaker, I certainly disagree with the overall impression that he has given that this is a bad agreement with respect to energy or that it does not really achieve very much. I think on the contrary it achieves a great deal.

The basic structure of our energy relations over quite a long period of time has been that when energy supplies in Canada or worldwide were plentiful, and the United States was not hard up for energy, the United States not unnaturally tried to restrict Canadian imports. We had the US oil import quotas for a long time and various problems of getting natural gas priced in the United States at a reasonable price.* When the situation was reversed and there was a shortage, and the United States was anxious to get more energy, Canada was not so anxious to sell; we tried to raise the price and we got worried about our own domestic requirements and put on restrictions. Obviously, this is not a very mature way to conduct energy relations between two countries, one of which has over the long haul a very considerable need for imported energy.

If you look back over what both countries have done, and I will not try to go through all the gruesome details, there was, for example, a prolonged period when the United States was restricting Canadian oil imports; about the time the Americans decided they wanted our oil, in 1973, we decided that we were not so sure that we had that much to spare. All of a sudden positions were reversed and Canadians were saying, well, we may have to put on some restrictions, and the United States was saying just open it up and let the pipelines flow. When we had the whip hand a bit later with respect to natural gas, the government moved in very heavily—not the

---

Marshall Crowe is President of M.A. Crowe Consultants and former chairman, National Energy Board.

* From 1959 to 1971 the United States imposed a quota on total imports of oil. Overland imports from Canada were formally exempted for much of the period; however, intergovernmental agreements restrained the growth in such imports. Canadian access to the US gas market was inhibited not by trade barriers, but by the low price set for domestically produced gas by the Federal Power Commission.—Ed.

National Energy Board(NEB)—and raised the prices well beyond what the market would bear. These price increases were too grasping, and as a result we tended to destroy the market. In the 1970s we also brought in price discrimination with an export tax on oil and a two-price system for both oil and natural gas, trying to get the maximum the market would bear in the United States and maintaining lower prices to Canadian users. This was very popular in Ontario and very unpopular in the producing areas of the country. Incidentally, as Phil Verleger has suggested, if the United States imposes an oil import fee, which, inter alia, increases the price that Western producers can sell their oil, I do not think that would be any problem at all for Canada.

In recent years a natural gas glut has developed, and Canada has been ready to export more than the US market could take. The United States in response has become more restrictive, and Canada has faced regulations by the Federal Energy Regulatory Commission (FERC) that have made it hard to get its gas into the United States at a price that gave a decent return at the wellhead.

So on energy trade policy Canada and the United States have been at odds fairly often and over quite a long period of time, notwithstanding that the trade has grown. Canada is almost the only significant source of imported natural gas in the United States. Canada's exports are very important as a proportion of total Canadian production and not unimportant as a share of US needs, in total perhaps only 5 percent but much more than that in certain areas. In the past couple of years Canada has often been the single largest source of oil imports into the United States, even though it has never provided more than, say, 10 percent of US total imports. Exports of crude oil in the pre-Arab embargo period of the early 1970s reached a million barrels a day. After a sharp decline they are now back up to something like 800,000 barrels a day including crude and products. So it is an important and long-lasting trade. With regard to gas policy, Canada never restricted gas exports (although it raised the price) under approved contracts; once approved, long-term licenses were always honored. There was only one episode of export curtailment and that was as a result of physical production problems in a particular field in northern British Columbia and the Yukon. It had nothing to do with government policies about surplus.

This new agreement, as I read it, means that Canada can no longer put on quantitative restrictions. That includes, as I understand it, the traditional National Energy Board practice of having to find the energy surplus, and not allowing it to be exported if it is not found to be surplus, calculated on a very broad basis. The formula has changed over time, but the original arrangement for natural gas was that the NEB had to find that there were available proven reserves to meet 25 years of anticipated Canadian consumption plus existing exports before you could approve any new exports.

That is a quantitative restriction. The NEB can still do all the calculations it likes, and the agreement talks about continuation of surplus procedure as long as it is not inconsistent with the FTA. However, the procedure does not have any bite because it cannot prevent exports unless at the same time, in accordance with the General Agreement on Tariffs and Trade (GATT), there is restricted production and consumption in Canada—and if we do that the United States has a right to continue to get at least the same proportion of total production as it did in some preceding appropriate period, 36 months is suggested, for which there are some reasonable statistics.

Canada does not have the right to cut off the United States even if the gas, oil, or electricity is in short supply and needed at home. The customers who have built up a claim have a right to continue to get the same proportion of total production as they were getting before, and the patterns of trade have to be honored. Deliveries of gas would have to be spread out in accordance with the previous pattern of trade.

In introductory comments on the energy chapter of the FTA, the Canadian government asserts that both sides remain free to determine whether or when to allow exports and that they may continue to monitor and license exports. Canada can monitor and license but cannot restrict except within the terms laid down in the GATT. That means that Canada must provide for a pro-rata share to the United States, can restrict exports only if it is restricting at home, and must cite certain specific reasons that are allowed in the exceptions under the GATT. The same thing applies if Canada ever wants to go back to controlling oil exports. At the moment, of course, Canada is trying to sell all it can, but it did put oil under control in the 1970s and removed it again a couple of years ago.

In the case of electricity, the Minister of Energy has already announced in advance of this agreement that as far as he is concerned there should be fewer controls on the export of electricity, and if there are any they should probably be imposed by the provinces, not by the federal government. Electricity exports are well on their way to becoming completely deregulated, and maybe that is a good thing. I am not sure that from the point of view of successful sales they will do any better because regulation by the NEB at least was a kind of built-in guarantee against charges of dumping. (One of NEB's criteria was that you could not export electricity for a price less than the price at which it was offered to Canadians.) If you take that out of the picture, you make it easier for some of the opponents of too much Canadian power to argue that it is being dumped.

I think the FTA introduces quite remarkable changes in the pattern of US–Canadian trade, and I think they really go a very long way. In a sense, from the Canadian negotiators' side, it was not too difficult to reach this agreement. What Canada is agreeing to do is to stop shooting itself in the foot. On the US side, what it wanted to get, presumably, was access without tricks and games and restrictions, over the long term, to Canadian energy, and it has obtained that. What Canada wanted essentially was access to the US market, and it did not do quite as well on that as the US did on access to Canadian supplies. It may all work out, but whereas the National Energy Board and its program of quantitative restrictions or any possible discrimination on prices were clearly on the table—and the FTA means, in effect, eliminating Part VI of the NEB Act that allows the Board to restrict exports on a surplus basis—what Canada got out of the FERC, which was not on the table apparently, was that if it does not like what FERC is doing it can make a complaint and have some consultations. There is absolute prohibitions of "wrong doing" on one side, and a right to complain and have consultations on the other side. There is some lack of symmetry in that.

I think Phil Verleger agrees with me on one argument: it would be contrary to the agreement for the United States to impose on Canada any import charge or any import quota on oil. The defense and national security provisions are very sharply narrowed down with respect to energy in the energy chapter of this agreement, so I do not think that section 232 of the Trade Expansion Act could be used against Canada. And I do not think you can come at it any other way unless oil exports increased very dramatically, and it could be claimed that Canadian oil imports into the United States were the primary cause of trouble. That seems highly unlikely. Canada has never supplied as much as 10 percent of US imports, and 5 to 10 percent is said in the agreement not to be "significant." If the United States did go ahead with this, which I think is probably unlikely anyway, and it had the consequences of somewhat raising the wellhead price of Canadian oil—not only the price it can get in selling it to the United States, but the domestic price too—I would certainly not be concerned. I think it is long overdue.

James T. Jensen

In 1974, following the first oil shock, the Organization for Economic Cooperation and Development (OECD) initiated a major study for all the industrialized countries to consider what their energy picture had been before the shock and what they were going to try to do to reduce their dependence on international oil. The Canadian and US submissions were fascinating. If you read between the lines, you discovered that they were incompatible.

James T. Jensen is President of Jensen Associates, Inc.

Canada had decided that one of the best ways to eliminate its dependence on imported oil was to make better use of its own natural gas by diverting some of its exports to internal use. The United States, on the other hand, concluded that it needed to increase the market share for natural gas and to step up imports. Canada was the sole source of imported gas at that time. Imports were emphasized because of the pessimism then about domestic discoveries. Thus, two governments looking at the same problem in isolation concluded that the same volume of Canadian gas could be used by each to solve its problems.

We have come a long way since 1974, when the very idea that prices might determine oil and gas market shares was unthinkable. It was taken for granted that governments would intervene actively to reduce oil import dependence. The idea that each government could independently determine the extent to which it would import or export various fuels was also taken for granted.

Such a policy has turned out to be basically unworkable. Since 1974, Canada and the United States have experimented with price and volume intervention in both domestic energy markets and in energy trade. The two countries have probably made just about every mistake in the book. It is increasingly evident that there has been a very strong reaction against simplistic intervention both north and south of the border. As a result, what we are seeing now is a move toward freer markets, a move toward the idea of market-responsive pricing, and a definite trend toward freer trade.

In his paper, Phil Verleger said that he feels that the Canada–United States Free Trade Agreement (FTA) is of marginal importance. When I first read that statement, I was taken aback because I did not agree at all. But as I have reflected on it, perhaps he is right. The FTA is a document negotiated at the highest government-to-government levels. But the real progress toward freer energy markets and freer trade is being made at the working level by agencies and companies as they deal with the specifics of the problem. And I believe they are well ahead of the policymakers at this point. Thus, the FTA in energy may be best characterized as an insurance policy to guarantee that governments are not tempted to return to the bad old ways.

The fundamental issue in energy is the inherent conflict between free trade on the one hand and national security with its dependence on imported energy on the other. It was Winston Churchill who put the British government into the oil business to provide oil for the British Navy, giving rise to what is now known as British Petroleum. National security in energy will always be an issue in any energy trade debate. Clearly, in 1973 after the first oil shock, national security loomed large in the thinking of both countries.

Both governments did things in the name of security that substantially distorted trade patterns, but those distortions were not new in 1973. Both governments had policies in effect that intervened in energy price and volume within their countries and thus had an inevitable impact on trade.

What are some of these other policies? The regulation of oil conservation is commonly in the hands of the state or provincial governments, agencies such as the Texas Railroad Commission or the Alberta Energy Conservation Resources Board. These agencies inevitably influence price and volume as they attempt to regulate leasing, drilling and production.

In the name of national security, the United States instituted a mandatory oil import program in 1959. Had it not acted to control the volume of imports, low-cost imported oil would have caused either a collapse in US oil prices or a collapse in volume as the state conservation commissions shut in US production in the name of market demand pro-ration. While Canada was technically exempt, government jawboning was used to limit the growth of Canadian imports.

There is also tax policy. Oil and gas are commonly subjected to special federal tax treatment in both countries, but special state or provincial taxes also apply. Anyone who has watched the tug of war in Canada between Edmonton and Ottawa over taxation, and has observed the impact that it has had on the economics of exploration, can appreciate that Canada does not have a single coordinated tax policy.

Free trade implies free markets. But energy activities include a number of utility operations that are regulated as natural monopolies. Electricity, gas distribution, and until recently, gas transmission all fit that pattern. Inevitably, if governments regulate prices as if electricity and gas were monopolies, it complicates the pattern of crossborder trade.

When governments intervene in energy price and volume in an uncoordinated way, the resulting impact on markets and on trade can border on the absurd. Nowhere was this more apparent than in United States policies prior to 1973. The United States was supporting the price of US oil above international levels because of the mandatory oil import program by controlling the volume supplied to the market. We were, in the name of utility regulation, controlling natural gas prices below market-set levels. By holding down gas prices at the same time we were holding up oil prices, any pretense that market-responsive competition between the two existed was fiction.

For Canada, as an exporter of both oil and gas to the United States, the consequences of these policies were bizarre. Canadian exports were priced on a netback basis—that is, they accepted the US oil and gas price structure and deducted transportation costs to establish their own field prices. But since Quebec and the Maritimes depended on imported oil, a two-price oil system evolved in Canada. Oil prices east of the Ottawa River were at low international levels, while the rest of Canada paid higher prices based on US levels. In effect, Canada interfered with internal trade between Quebec and Ontario in order to preserve this dual pricing system. Gas prices, to the producing provinces' frustration, were netted back from US regulated prices at levels that Alberta, at least, regarded as much too low.

The first oil shock tore the delicate balance of these rather incompatible policies to shreds as national security became an overriding consideration. Both governments instituted oil price controls—but in different ways—to prevent their own energy prices from rising to OPEC-set levels.

Both governments controlled wellhead prices for natural gas. But Canada decided that it no longer needed to accept low regulated gas prices from the United States and thus unilaterally established an export price at the Canadian border that was much higher than that which producers would have realized from domestic sales. In retrospect, it was also much higher than workable markets would have set, although that was not so apparent at the time.

Both governments (and their state and provincial counterparts) made major changes in taxation structures so that the apparent cost structure of their respective industries was significantly altered.

Both governments reacted to the disruption of the earlier balance by a series of uncoordinated ad hoc policy responses. How free trade in the way we are discussing it today could have taken place in the energy environment of 1974 and 1975 is a mystery. I believe that many of the paper's examples of bad trade practices are simply a reflection of the chaotic government energy interventionism so characteristic of the mid-1970s. But in many ways those are the bad old days.

In oil and gas, we have increasingly been moving toward market-responsive pricing and also toward freer trade. Certainly, we are not there yet, but the momentum is there. By dismantling many of the earlier interventionist policies that have proved to be unworkable, the two governments are making free trade much easier.

The paper is very critical of surplus tests, particularly as they apply to natural gas. I do not share the author's condemnation of them as they apply to natural gas or electricity since neither of these energy sources can ever be a freely traded international commodity in the sense that oil can be. When a country begins to exceed the capability of its own resources, the marginal cost of replacing local supply with imports may be quite high. But I would agree that surplus tests, as they have been applied by Canada, have negatively affected trade. There are signs, however, that that is changing.

The natural gas surplus test, though changing in formulation from time to time, has always been comparatively mechanical. After setting aside some formula reserve for Canada, the surplus could be licensed for export. But the economic incentive to create a surplus was never very great, and thus the actual gas reserve on which an importer could rely to finance a pipeline was inevitably short. The largest capital expenditure for a natural gas pipeline ever made in the United States was for the Northern Border Pipeline. This was to be the prebuild leg of the Alaska Natural Gas Transportation System. The export formula initially permitted it only eight years of guaranteed gas reserves, by implication threatening this major investment if Canada could not find more reserves in surplus in the future.

With the recent revisions of the National Energy Board, the mechanical surplus test has been removed and the burden of proving that an export contract imperils Canadian consumers is placed on the intervenors. A Canadian long-term contract made under the new conditions can be honored. The same kinds of problems have existed in electricity. It has been difficult to buy firm power from Canada. But, as Canada expands its hydroelectric supply, it is willing to make "economy power" available south of the border. Economy power looks good in the short term, but there is always that "now you see it, now you don't" characteristic to it. If Canada is moving more and more toward a pattern in which both long-term and short-term contracts can be made and honored between willing buyers and sellers, the impact on free trade will be significant.

Phil Verleger also expressed some reservations about the agreement in that it ties Canada into a US pricing structure that could force Canadian consumer prices higher in the event that the United States turns protectionist and institutes an oil import fee. Marshall Crowe indicated that as a Canadian, he is not worried about that. Canada is an energy exporter, and therefore high energy prices are not necessarily all bad.

In conclusion, I am inclined to agree with the paper that the free trade agreement in energy may not be such a major step forward. But this is not because its provisions are poorly crafted. Rather, the momentum at the working level toward freer markets and freer trade is well ahead of the trade environment that the agreement promises. Thus, the great benefit of the agreement is that it provides guarantes that our respective governments will be constrained from reinstituting the chaotic interventionist policies of the 1970s.

6

Services and Investment

Jeffrey J. Schott and Murray G. Smith

The Canada–United States Free Trade Agreement (FTA) fills a major gap in bilateral economic relations and breaks new ground in international agreements by incorporating provisions that cover transactions in services and investment. Such issues are subject to limited multilateral rules and procedures, and US–Canada transactions in these areas take place without the benefit of the legal framework of a bilateral treaty of friendship, commerce, and navigation (FCN), which is common among industrial countries.[1] The FTA contains four chapters on these issues. They cover services, financial services, temporary access for business persons, and investment. The negotiations on financial services proceeded on a separate but parallel track from the general services agreement.

Services

Despite the fact that many service sectors are subject to government regulation, service transactions between the United States and Canada have been relatively unfettered. While restrictions exist that distort trade and investment flows, substantial trade and investment in services does occur across the border. Deregulation in some areas—notably financial services and telecommunications—promises even more activity in the future.

As shown in table 6.1 the United States has been running sizable and increasingly large surpluses in nonfactor services trade with Canada. The US surplus totaled $1.7 billion in 1985 and $2.3 billion in 1986; it ran at an annual rate of $2.6 billion through the first nine months of 1987. These

---

1. Canada is distinct among major industrial countries in not being a signatory to FCN or bilateral investment treaties.

Table 6.1 US trade in services with Canada, 1985–87
(million US dollars)

Services	1985			1986			1987		
	Exports	Imports	Balance	Exports	Imports	Balance	Exports	Imports	Balance
Travel and pas- senger fares	3,037	2,694	343	3,185	3,242	−57	4,183	3,632	551
Other transport	926	725	201	895	547	348	927	575	352
Royalties and fees	563	27	536	622	17	605	623	21	602
Other private services	1,467	749	718	1,956	524	1,432	2,137	944	1,193
Miscellaneous government	52	107	−55	32	97	−65	64	167	−103
Total nonfactor services	6,045	4,302	1,743	6,690	4,427	2,263	7,934	5,339	2,595
Total factor services	10,506	3,167	7,339	11,399	2,587	8,812	12,596	4,856	7,740

a. Data at annualized rate based on statistics for the first nine months of 1987.
Source: US Department of Commerce, *Survey of Current Business,* September and December 1986 and 1987, table 10.

figures include the transportation sector, which has been excluded from the FTA. The US surplus is strongest in areas where the FTA could have its greatest impact: tourism and private services.

The negotiations on services had a twofold objective: the establishment of rules or principles to guide future government policy regarding the provision of services by nationals of either country and the rollback or liberalization of existing barriers to trade in specific service sectors. The provisions on services, set out in Chapter 14 of the FTA and its annexes, indicate that the governments were more successful in rule making than in rollback.

The most significant achievement of the services chapter is that it imposes a "standstill" on services trade restrictions. This standstill sets a clear contractual obligation on both countries not to introduce new laws and regulations that distort bilateral service transactions.[2] The purpose is preemp-

2. The standstill in the services chapter means that all existing restrictions not eliminated in the agreement are grandfathered when the FTA comes into force on 1 January 1989. It should not be confused with the standstill obligation contained in the exchange of letters accompanying the signing of the agreement on 2 January 1988 that commits both sides to observe the spirit of the FTA while the ratification process proceeds.

tive: to forestall future attempts to impose protection in the service sectors. The standstill does not require changes in existing policies, laws, and regulations even if they have discriminatory effects. At the same time, the standstill obligation does not prevent either government from implementing changes in domestic policies and regulations, but it does require that any changes not mask protectionist intent nor discriminate against services provided by US and Canadian interests in either country. As a result, businesses should be able to better plan their trade and investment strategies.

Most of Chapter 14 deals with the elaboration of a set of principles to guide future government policy. The principles apply both to services that can be transacted across borders and to those that require local establishment for the production, marketing, or distribution of the services. Annex 1408 provides a schedule of covered services. It includes a broad range of services related to agriculture and forestry; mining and construction; the distributive trade; insurance and real estate; business, management, and other professional services; and tourism, computer, and telecommunications-network-based enhanced services.

The services chapter does not apply to financial services (covered exclusively in Chapter 17), transportation industries, cultural industries, and a range of government and social services. Some of the recent bilateral disputes over services trade have arisen in the cultural and transportation industries, but these industries will not be subject to the general dispute mechanism that applies to services in the FTA. In addition, the services chapter does not "apply to any taxation measure, provided that such taxation measure does not constitute a means of arbitrary or unjustifiable discrimination" (Article 1407), nor does it apply to government procurement.[3]

Interestingly, the FTA establishes meaningful obligations—more binding than the comparable GATT standard—regarding the policies of state, provincial, and local governments in the areas of services and investment (but not financial services). Article 103 of the FTA commits both countries to ensure that "all necessary measures are taken in order to give effect to its provisions, including the observance, except as otherwise provided in this Agreement, by state, provincial and local governments." This is a stricter obligation than Article XXIV:12 of the GATT: "Each contracting party shall take reasonable measures as may be available to it to ensure observance of the provisions of this Agreement by the regional and local governments." As such, subnational governments are more likely to pursue policies consistent with the country's international obligations than in the past.

---

3. However, the procurement provisions of the FTA apply the rights and obligations of the GATT Government Procurement Code, which does cover services related to goods trade.

The provisions of Chapters 14, 15, and 16 set out rights and obligations of particular relevance to services trade, including:

☐ national treatment, to prohibit new discrimination against foreign service providers in sectors listed in Annex 1408

☐ right of establishment or right of commercial presence, to provide appropriate market access guarantees to ensure that the national treatment obligation is meaningful

☐ licensing and certification procedures, to ensure that—with limited exceptions—government regulators judge providers of services solely on their competence

☐ procedures facilitating crossborder travel by business persons (Chapter 15)

☐ sectoral annexes that address specific restrictions and regulatory issues

☐ prospective rollback of existing restrictions that have been grandfathered under the FTA provisions.

The national treatment provision does not involve a blanket commitment to accord national treatment in all cases. Analogous to GATT Article XX, Article 1402.3 of the FTA notes that derogations may be necessary to meet "prudential, fiduciary, health and safety, or consumer protection" concerns; however, any derogation should provide for treatment that is "equivalent in effect" to that accorded domestic firms, and neither country should introduce any measure that "constitutes a means of arbitrary or unjustifiable discrimination" (Article 1402.8). In short, national treatment is the norm; where it is not applicable, the differential treatment of foreign firms should not involve implicit protection for domestic firms.

A national treatment obligation is only valuable if a foreign firm has effective commercial access to the domestic market. Some services can be provided at long distance, in which case an obligation for national treatment is sufficient. However, market access commitments are a necessary complement to the national treatment commitment for many other services. Depending on the service, market access may involve the need to establish a presence in the market, or the need to be able to have access to distribution channels, or the need to have equal access to operating licenses for activities in regulated industries, or the capability to relocate specialized management or technical personnel.

The FTA elaborates these aspects of the national treatment obligation in terms of a right of commercial presence or a right of establishment to ensure that transactions can be conducted across borders with access to the necessary distribution channels and in terms of commitments to nondiscriminatory licensing and certification procedures. The right of commercial presence accords access to marketing and distribution channels needed to provide a service across borders. It does not cover investments in local enterprises that would establish a legal presence in that market through a subsidiary or branch office. However, the FTA does accord such a right of establishment generally under Article 1602 of the investment chapter and under the sectoral annexes for specific service sectors.

The obligations in Article 1403 require that the ability to apply for licenses, and government decisions to grant licenses to provide services covered by the FTA, should be made "principally" with regard to the competence, not the national origin, of the provider. To limit possible discrimination, the FTA encourages regulatory bodies in both countries to adopt similar licensing and certification requirements. Voluntary harmonization or mutual recognition is a key objective for rule making for many aspects of regulated services industries.

FTA provisions on labor services (covered in Chapter 15) apply only to professional and technical services, investors and intracompany transferees, and not to the broader category of labor services. This may reflect the fact that the key *bilateral* issue in the area of labor services involves the temporary entry of business persons. Undoubtedly, it also reflects greater political sensitivity in both countries to temporary immigration of blue-collar workers.

Sectoral annexes to Chapter 14 of the FTA provide concrete illustrations of how the rules and obligations already noted would affect specific service activities. Sectoral annexes appended to Chapter 14 cover architecture, tourism, and computer services and telecommunications-network-based enhanced services. Efforts to draft a separate annex on the transportation sector failed because of the strong opposition of the US maritime industry.

The key point to make about the sectoral annexes is that while the framework of principles seeks to establish a standstill, the sectoral annexes provide for a rollback of services trade restrictions. In this way, the agreement seeks to deal with the particular services trade problems that beset both countries. The development and elaboration of sectoral annexes can be an evolutionary process within the framework of the services agreement. Indeed, the treaty provides for the extension of talks to an increasing number of service sectors.

Where appropriate, the annexes seek to develop common standards for the regulation of service activities. For example, the sectoral annex on architecture agrees to review recommendations that are being developed by the Royal Architectural Institute of Canada and the American Institute of Architects. It also agrees to "encourage" regulators at state and provincial levels to adopt complementary licensing and certification policies and requirements that provide national or most-favored-nation (MFN) treatment.

What was done in architecture could be applied to other professional services such as accountants, engineers, and consultants.

The sectoral agreement on tourism defines the types of activities covered by the general rules and obligations, including the "establishment of sales offices or designated franchises" and "access to basic telecommunications transport networks." The significance of this annex lies in the protection of unfettered access to the provision of tourism services. Travel and tourism account for more than $6 billion per year in transactions between the United States and Canada (see table 6.1).

The computer and telecommunications services agreement is the most detailed and significant sectoral pact. It contains important provisions with regard to establishment rights for enhanced services only and access guarantees to basic telecommunications transport services, including transborder data flows and access to databanks. The latter has been an issue in bilateral relations because of Canadian requirements in some sectors for local processing of data, in particular under Canada's Bank Act; those requirements have been grandfathered under the FTA, however. The FTA also includes a key commitment pertaining to public monopolies that ensures that state-owned entities do not engage in anticompetitive practices. Along with Article 2010 of the FTA, it establishes some discipline on the operations of such monopolies.

Overall, the main achievement of the services chapter is to spell out clear contractual obligations intended to preclude new discriminatory measures. Although only limited progress was made toward the liberalization of services trade, the FTA contains in Article 1405 a "best efforts" commitment to a rollback of existing restrictions. Such liberalization could result from periodic policy reviews, from the extension of the coverage of the FTA to additional services, and from the negotiation of new sectoral annexes.

Financial Services

Over the years, the United States and Canada have had substantial cross-border activity—mostly direct investment—in financial services. For example, at the end of 1985, Canadian bank assets in the United States totaled about US$40 billion; similarly, there were 17 subsidiaries of US banks and 4 representative offices in Canada with total assets of about C$11.8 billion. In addition, 19 Canadian firms or subsidiaries are members of US stock exchanges; 4 US firms are currently registered with the Ontario Securities Commission (they were grandfathered when foreign ownership restrictions were imposed in 1971), and several other US firms own a minority stake in Canadian securities dealers.[4]

These data understate the extent of bilateral and global interdependence in the financial services industries. As part of the growing globalization of financial markets, US and Canadian corporations are dealing in offshore securities and capital markets. In turn, the internationalization of financial markets is creating pressure for deregulation of financial services within the United States and Canada.

Deregulation of the financial service industry is proceeding apace in both countries. In December 1986, the Ontario government announced steps to open the securities industry to other Canadian financial institutions and to foreign ownership.[5] As a result, the Canadian banking and securities industries have become increasingly integrated. The five leading banks have acquired holdings in securities firms; foreign banks also have increased their participation in those firms subject to prescribed limits.[6] However, controls on foreign ownership of securities dealers are now being phased out; all limits are scheduled to expire in June 1988. At that time, foreigners will be allowed to acquire Canadian securities dealers or to establish subsidiaries in Canada. Some controls remain, however, on foreign ownership of the largest (Schedule A) Canadian banks, but under the FTA the restrictions on dominant shareholders will be applied equally to US and Canadian interests.

In the United States, efforts also have been made to push deregulation of financial markets and, in particular, to break down the barriers between commercial and investment banking enshrined in the Glass-Steagall Act. However, the recent developments on Wall Street have made Congress cautious about reforming this legislation. If reforms are made, they will likely include safeguards that maintain some restrictions on nonbank activities.

While Congress argues the merits of deregulation, the pressure for reform will, if anything, grow stronger. Indeed, this is already occurring at the state level. Bank regulators in several states have already authorized their state-chartered banks to engage in selective insurance, securities, and real estate transactions.[7] Moreover, if there are some notable failures in securities

---

4. US Department of the Treasury, "National Treatment Study: Report to Congress on Foreign Government Treatment of US Commercial Banking and Securities Organizations," 1986 update (December 1986).

5. The Canadian securities industry is primarily subject to provincial regulations.

6. See *Financial Times,* 22 December 1987, Section III, 3.

7. For further details, see Robert E. Litan, "Bank Revolution Won't Wait for Congress," *Wall Street Journal,* 10 November 1987, 36.

houses in the coming months as a result of the Wall Street developments, commercial banks—through their bank holding companies—may be forced to get into the securities business. As a practical matter, Glass-Steagall may then become increasingly irrelevant.

The agreement on financial services covers commercial banking, investment banking, and trust and loan companies. Insurance is primarily covered by the services and investment chapters.[8] The FTA provisions reflect both the substantial integration of the US and Canadian markets that already exists and the trend toward deregulation in both countries in recent years.

In most respects, the financial services agreement continues the trend toward deregulation in financial markets that both governments have pursued. Both governments commit to liberalize their financial markets, to extend the resulting benefits to the firms of the other country, and to establish a consultative mechanism to oversee the liberalization. As with the entire financial services pact, the consultative mechanism is not subject to the dispute settlement provisions of the FTA, and it is to be administered by the US Treasury and the Canadian Department of Finance. Furthermore, unlike the services chapter, there are no provisions regarding the regulatory policies at the state or provincial level.[9]

In essence, the agreement will free US-owned banks and other financial institutions operating in Canada from most of the current restrictions on market share, asset growth, and capital expansion imposed against foreign firms. In particular, US commercial bank subsidiaries will not be subject to the 16 percent ceiling set by the Canadian Bank Act on the foreign bank share of the total domestic assets of all banks in Canada, and restrictions on the establishment of intra-Canada branches by US-owned Schedule B banks will be removed. Moreover, national treatment will be accorded to new applications from US commercial banks to enter the Canadian market. In addition, the so-called "10/25 rule," which limits total foreign participation in Canadian Schedule A banks to 25 percent, will be dropped for US nationals or firms under the FTA. The 10 percent ceiling for individual holdings regardless of nationality still remains, however, for the Schedule A banks. Similarly, ownership restrictions are being removed for insurance, trust, and loan companies, allowing US firms to diversify by establishing or acquiring federally regulated insurance and trust companies, Schedule B banks, and securities firms.

---

8. The provisions of Chapter 17 that cover the right to diversify or establish Canadian subsidiaries through acquisitions also apply to insurance companies, however.

9. For a detailed analysis of the financial services chapter by two of the US negotiators, see Carl J. Lohmann and William C. Murden, "Policies for the Treatment of Foreign Participation in Financial Markets and Their Application in the US–Canada Free Trade Agreement," paper presented at a conference sponsored by the University of Ottawa Faculty of Law, 22 January 1988, processed.

The FTA also includes important commitments to safeguard the extensive US business operations of Canadian banks and to allow them to underwrite Canadian government securities in the US market. The agreement guarantees the right of Canadian banks to retain the multistate branches grandfathered under the International Banking Act (IBA) of 1978. Since the IBA is subject to review after 10 years, the FTA provides safeguards that those multistate branches will be maintained. The agreement also provides national treatment for Canadian financial institutions under prospective amendments to the Glass-Steagall Act. Although one cannot predict how that act will change in the near term, it will change and change dramatically. The FTA ensures that Canadian financial institutions will be protected so that they receive national treatment under any changes in the Glass-Steagall Act or related laws.

Investment Issues

Policies regulating direct investment have often been highly contentious in Canada–US relations; in most instances, disputes have arisen because of Canadian regulation of US direct investment. In large measure, this has resulted from the asymmetries in the level of bilateral investment and from Canadian ambivalence about the influx of foreign direct investment in the boom periods of the 1950s and 1960s. In the early 1970s, about three-fifths of the manufacturing and mining industries and three-quarters of the petroleum industry in Canada were foreign owned, principally by US firms. The value of US direct investment in Canada was about 10 times the value of Canadian direct investment in the United States.

These figures have changed dramatically in recent years. From 1982 through 1986, Canadian direct investment in the United States grew by 56.4 percent, while US investment in Canada expanded by only 15.3 percent (see table 6.2).[10] Most of the Canadian growth was in other private investment, including banking, finance, and real estate, which almost doubled to US$10 billion at the end of 1986. By contrast, the bulk of US growth was in investment in Canadian manufacturing.

Both the United States and Canada have long restricted investment in sensitive sectors of the economy. On the US side, the rationale for restricting or prohibiting foreign ownership frequently involves concerns about national security. Thus, aliens generally cannot get operating licenses for radio

---

10. Canadian data, which are calculated somewhat differently, show even faster growth in Canadian direct investment in the United States. See Alan M. Rugman, *Outward Bound: Canadian Direct Investment in the United States* (Toronto: Canadian-American Committee, 1987).

Table 6.2   Direct investment between the United States and Canada, 1982–86 (million US dollars)

| | Total[a] | Of which | | | |
		Petroleum	Manufacturing	Services[b]	Other
Canada in the United States					
1982	11,658	1,500	3,500	1,058	5,600
1983	11,434	1,391	3,313	1,040	5,690
1984	15,287	1,544	4,115	1,142	8,486
1985	17,131	1,589	4,607	1,532	9,403
1986	18,313	1,385	5,389	1,497	10,042
United States in Canada					
1982	43,511	10,421	18,825	6,083	8,182
1983	44,417	10,398	19,289	6,498	8,232
1984	46,671	11,156	20,986	6,600	7,929
1985	47,106	10,460	21,848	6,335	8,463
1986	50,178	10,936	23,759	7,017	8,466

Source: US Department of Commerce, *Survey of Current Business,* August issues, 1985–87.
a. Direct investment includes equity (capital stock, additional paid-in capital, and retained earnings) plus net intercompany debt.
b. In the case of Canadian investment in the United States, the data is for wholesale trade; in the case of US investment in Canada, it is for banking and finance.

stations in the United States under the Communications Act of 1934, and ownership of maritime shipping is restricted under the Jones Act. On the Canadian side, the concerns have focused on cultural and economic sovereignty matters.

Concern about the influence of foreign subsidiaries on the Canadian economy led the Canadian government to introduce the Foreign Investment Review Act (FIRA) in 1973. Under FIRA, new establishments as well as direct acquisitions by foreign firms and indirect acquisitions—involving transfer of ownership of foreign-based parent corporations—were subject to review to determine whether the transactions were of "significant benefit" to Canada. During the process, foreign firms were often encouraged to make undertakings about import and export performance, employment, local sourcing of inputs, research and development efforts, and investment plans.

Although FIRA was controversial when it was introduced, bilateral investment disputes came to a boil in the early 1980s.[11] The Liberal

---

11. For further details, see David Leyton-Brown, *Weathering the Storm: Canadian–US Relations, 1980-1983* (Toronto: Canadian-American Committee, 1985).

government of Pierre Trudeau instituted the National Energy Program, which included tax and subsidy measures that discriminated against foreign-owned energy companies, and it proposed more activist regulation of foreign investment under FIRA. The US government protested and subsequently brought a complaint in the GATT regarding Canada's performance requirements under FIRA. The GATT panel report on FIRA found that Canada had contravened the GATT by obtaining commitments from firms regarding domestic sourcing of goods, but that the GATT rules did not cover export performance requirements. Canada accepted the GATT ruling and ceased requiring firms to engage in import substitution for traded goods.

In 1984, the newly elected Conservative government of Brian Mulroney introduced new legislation that altered FIRA considerably and renamed it Investment Canada. Review of the establishment of new businesses ceased, except in the cultural industries, and thresholds of C$5 million and C$50 million were established for the review of direct and indirect acquisitions. Investment Canada's objective is to promote inward direct investment; it reviews business plans—which may include undertakings about import substitution for services, export performance for goods and services, research and development efforts, job creation, and other matters—in screening relating to acquisitions above the thresholds. In the absence of the FTA, future administrative practice could easily revert to more aggressive interventionist investment policies. With the FTA, future undertakings will be sharply curtailed (see below).

In contrast to the overall thrust of encouraging foreign investment, the Conservative government increased restrictions on firms in publishing and film distribution. Among the most contentious measures was a policy that forced divestiture on foreign subsidiaries in publishing in the event of indirect acquisitions. An incident involving Gulf & Western's acquisition of Prentice Hall and Gunn became highly controversial because the Prentice Hall acquisition had occurred prior to the promulgation of the new policies. A negotiated solution was reached in the Prentice Hall case, when the Prentice Hall transfer was allowed to proceed, and Gulf & Western agreed to divest the Canadian operations of Gunn.

The Canadian policy of compulsory divestiture in book publishing and film distribution remains in place and could be a source of friction at any time as a result of corporate restructuring in the United States. However, if this occurs, the government of Canada commits to "purchase the business enterprise from the investor of the United States of America at fair open market value, as determined by an independent, impartial assessment" (Article 1607.4). US firms thus receive some protection from compulsory divestiture in these industries, though US firms still remain at a disadvantage vis-à-vis Canadian firms when bidding for US publishers with Canadian subsidiaries.

Apart from the cultural industries, where Canadians are sensitive to the very high levels of foreign periodicals, movies, and television programming, the recent liberalization of Canadian investment policies seems to be a predictable consequence of Canada's experience with the National Energy Program and the greater stake of Canadian companies in the US economy. Certainly, rising Canadian investment in the US economy expands the Canadian constituency concerned about the effects of present or prospective discriminatory investment policies by federal or state governments in the United States. But in the absence of the FTA, and in those sectors not covered by the agreement, investment issues could easily reemerge as a source of bilateral tensions because of continuing Canadian sensitivity about US investments in Canada.

Implementation of the FTA will reinforce the recent trend toward liberalization of Canadian investment policies and provide more transparency to the investment restrictions that remain on both sides of the border. Except for cultural and transportation industries, future disputes regarding the investment provisions of the FTA will be subject to the general dispute settlement procedure.

The investment chapter of the FTA adopts an approach that parallels the services chapter. Existing discriminatory policies and restrictions affecting foreign investment are grandfathered, notably in the energy sector, but future policies and regulations must be consistent with national treatment. The investment provisions apply to goods-producing activities and all service activities not explicitly excluded. Sectoral exclusions apply to transportation services, basic telecommunications, and cultural industries. Investment issues relating to most financial services (except some insurance services) are exclusively covered in Chapter 17.

The national treatment obligation with respect to future investment policies applies to establishment of a new business, the operation of a business, and the acquisition or sale of a business, subject to provisions in the agreement. Specifically, Canada retains the right to screen certain direct acquisitions under the Investment Canada Act. Canada agrees to phase out screening of indirect acquisitions within three years and to raise the threshold for screening of direct acquisitions by US firms or investors to C$150 million (in constant real terms) by 1992 from C$5 million at present. As a practical matter, this will limit the screening requirements to the direct acquisition of roughly the top 600 nonfinancial companies and to sectors where investment restrictions are grandfathered (for example, energy). In addition, US firms obtain a "right of exit," where subsidiaries can be sold to investors from third countries as well as from the United States subject only to screening of direct acquisitions above the threshold.

The FTA explicitly precludes the imposition of new performance requirements on investments that affect trade with the other country. Thus, new export performance, import substitution, and domestic content requirements cannot be imposed on firms. Non-trade-related undertakings, such as those relating to employment, can still be obtained from firms. In addition, minimum domestic equity requirements cannot be imposed in the future, but are grandfathered for certain designated industries. Note, however, that the substantial reduction in prospective reviews by Investment Canada will limit the capability to impose or enforce any performance requirement.

The FTA provides for international law standards and procedures governing expropriation, ensuring due process and fair compensation. It also generally ensures free repatriation of earnings and capital. The cultural industries are excluded from the agreement, but in the event that Canada imposes compulsory divestiture of indirect acquisitions in any cultural industry (such as book publishing), the government will offer to buy the company involved at an independently determined, fair open-market value. Given the possible costs of such purchases, this provision will tend to discourage forced divestiture in these areas.

The FTA provides certain exclusions from, or qualifications to, the national treatment obligation on investment. Government procurement is explicitly excluded from the investment chapter, and the obligations on government procurement are limited to those in the GATT Tokyo Round procurement code and the procurement chapter of the agreement. Tax and subsidy measures are not subject to the investment provisions "provided that such measure (tax or subsidy) does not constitute a means of arbitrary or unjustifiable discrimination between investors of the Parties or a disguised restriction of the benefits accorded to investors of the Parties" (Article 1609).

Except for cultural and transportation industries, basic telecommunications, and financial services, the obligations under the investment chapter are subject to the general dispute settlement provisions of the agreement. This puts the investment rules on a firmer contractual basis than the vague commitments that presently exist between the two countries such as under the nonbinding 1976 OECD Declaration.[12]

---

12. Although Canada signed the 1976 OECD *Declaration on International Investment and Multinational Enterprises* that contained a national treatment provision, it qualified its participation with the observation that "elements of differentiation between Canadian and foreign controlled enterprises" existed in Canada and that Canada would "continue to retain its rights to take measures, affecting foreign investors, which we believe are necessary given our particular circumstances." When Canada's investment policies became contentious in the early 1980s, Canada simply provided an explanation of its policies to the relevant OECD committees, thereby fulfilling its obligation to consult.

Conclusion

The FTA creates a new legal framework governing bilateral services transactions and direct investment flows between the United States and Canada. It consolidates recent progress in liberalization of services trade and investment policies, provides more transparency for restrictions that remain on both sides, and establishes in most instances a standstill against new restrictions. The sectoral annexes to the services chapter and the prohibition of trade-related investment measures roll back selective barriers to trade. Furthermore, the agreement facilitates entry and temporary relocation of business persons, investors, professionals, and corporate transferees, thereby making it easier to conduct business in either country. Finally, the elimination of screening of indirect acquisitions and the higher thresholds for review by Canada of direct acquisitions will liberalize investment flows and remove an important source of bilateral tension.

Most importantly, the FTA creates a new environment conducive to bilateral economic relations. The FTA establishes for the first time contractual obligations on Canada and the United States with respect to services and investment issues. These obligations are subject to an expeditious rule-oriented dispute settlement mechanism. The innovations will provide a more predictable environment for the private sector to plan its business strategies and will help facilitate the resolution of disputes between the two governments.

Clearly, the services and investment chapters have been shaped by national sensitivities on both sides and by unique stresses on the world's largest bilateral commercial relationship, but negotiating these elements of the FTA provides useful experience and precedents for the multilateral negotiations in the Uruguay Round. The services and investment provisions in the FTA go further than previous free trade areas or existing OECD arrangements in defining specific international rules and dispute settlement mechanisms. At the same time, these provisions are much less sweeping than the Treaty of Rome in the European Community, which establishes broader national treatment obligations and provides greater mobility of capital and labor. The FTA achieves less in rollback of existing barriers to services trade and investment than some might have hoped, but the selective liberalization and focused obligations under these provisions offer guidance for multilateral efforts to develop rules and dispute settlement mechanisms for services trade and investment issues.

Comments

Harry L. Freeman

I am going to make some very general comments on the importance of the Canada–United States Free Trade Agreement (FTA). First, we already are seeing beneficial fallout from the Canada–US agreement. The other day there was a modest announcement that the US Securities and Exchange Commission had reached an agreement with its regulatory counterpart in Canada to monitor certain kinds of securities activities. Such an agreement would not have occurred had the US–Canada trade negotiations fallen apart.

Viewed another way, the costs of not having come to an agreement with Canada—or not achieving ratification by the Canadian Parliament and the US Congress—could be extremely high, particularly for financial institutions and other service organizations. Those costs could be experienced in a steady deterioration in relations between the two countries:

☐ increased Canadian nationalism and more virulent US protectionism

☐ repeated escalation of trade disputes

☐ a negative flow of investment funds from the United States to Canada

☐ emergence of new nontariff barriers

☐ a drop in US–Canadian trade and subsequent loss of US and Canadian jobs

☐ a fall in tourism in both countries and a consequent decline in air passengers between the two countries

☐ nullification of treaties

☐ even termination of joint staffing of sensitive military bases.

We have taken one another for granted for so long that we can only guess at the reaction to failure. This is the first time in years that our relationship has been put to a real test.

Second, the agreement is important as a model for other countries. The world is very interested in how the Canada–US agreement develops. During a recent trip to the Soviet Union, I met with the head of the US–Canada Institute in Moscow, Georgi Arbatov, and the head of the political section. They wanted to hear about the Canada–US agreement on services as well

Harry L. Freeman is Executive Vice President of American Express Company.

as the sectoral agreement on financial services, and the extent to which the agreement will set a precedent for agreements in the General Agreement on Tariffs and Trade (GATT). They asked whether America will push hard for a similar agreement in the GATT and did I think the USSR would be admitted into the GATT. They wanted to know what the agreement means for bilateralism and multilateralism. So, there are people everywhere closely watching the outcome of the FTA.

A third important achievement is that for the first time we can take a new look at business opportunities in Canada—not in a headlong rush, but in strategic niches. One of the most common questions I get from the media, particularly the Canadian media, is, do you think that Canada will be overrun by American financial institutions? In effect, would Canada be Americanized if the big US banks and nonbank financial companies go north?

I have always responded in the same way. If you are familiar with how Canada works and the position of the very large chartered banks, which are now in the process of buying most of the major securities firms in Canada, it is virtually impossible to envision an Americanization of the Canadian financial market. The sheer size, power, and sophistication of the Canadian financial institutions would inhibit that. As in downtown Frankfurt, downtown Toronto is dominated by five or six skyscrapers, all of which are headquarters of the major banks. I do not imagine that many US institutions would be able to take on Toronto Dominion Bank or Royal Bank of Canada, or any of the others.

What is more likely is that financial institutions and companies that already operate in Canada will have the option of thinking about additional niche strategies in the Canadian financial services market, which is roughly the size of California's. Unlike the unique US market with the many small banks and thrifts, the Canadian market as well as the European and Japanese markets are relatively sewn up by major financial institutions—banks and insurance companies. Until now, it has not been possible to justify looking for opportunities in Canada. Now it could be worthwhile. It may be a year or two before the right opportunity comes along, but at least there is the option of looking around. For these reasons, a US rush into Canada is an odd notion, and I think an erroneous one.

I am also pleased that the trade agreement will put pressure on the United States to broaden its approach to the powers of financial institutions. That, in my mind, is a very good thing.

Finally, the fact that there is a trade agreement that covers financial services and investment is a tremendous accomplishment. No other agreement has achieved what this one has. Some aspects of this one are covered in the US–Israel agreement, but the US–Canada pact will be the first major implemented agreement covering services, financial services, and investment. And covering investment as a trade issue has never, to my knowledge, been done before.

Furthermore, the US–Canada pact has immense value as a bilateral agreement. According to Treasury Secretary James Baker "[a] strategic employment of bilateral agreements can actually sustain and support GATT, or at least achieve economic liberalization where GATT cannot."[1]

I am optimistic about the GATT, but with Canada we have already arrived at an agreement, and it has been signed by the respective heads of state—a major achievement. Moreover, no other countries have negotiating teams with experience in the newly covered areas of services, financial services, and investment, and so we should be able to make a very important contribution to the GATT negotiating teams in Geneva. And the Canada–US bilateral agreement will help, in my view, push for a greater multilateral effort. In the process, it will help to strengthen a currently weak GATT—weak because it does not cover most of world trade, including services, agriculture, and investment, for example.

I am in favor of strengthening the GATT as rapidly as possible. The question is, who, besides the United States, really is interested in doing that and at what pace? The rate of change in financial markets and in the world at large is accelerating, and the rate of our negotiations is decelerating.

Let me close with a comment about the widely reported US–Canada dispute settlement provisions, some of which apply to services. I have not talked to anyone in the business world who is thinking about these provisions. Most of those who are interested are lawyers; to others, this is not a critical question. The critical question is, does this agreement mean I can do business in Canada? The fact that this is the question of greatest interest—that it can be asked and receive a positive response—is an excellent sign for our two countries and the international community.

J. H. Warren

I speak with some trepidation because I spent a lot more of my life on trade policy than I did on matters financed in my six years as Vice-Chairman of the Bank of Montreal. Even my brief experience in the Bank of Montreal suggests that the Canadian financial sector should not be lulled into any false sense of security by Harry Freeman's comforting words: "Don't worry. It takes a couple of years to get organized. Since Canadian banks and

---

J. H. Warren was chief Canadian negotiator in the Tokyo Round. He is currently Principal Trade Policy Adviser to the Government of Quebec.

1. James A. Baker III, "The Geopolitical Implications of the US–Canada Trade Pact," *The International Economy,* January/February 1988.

financial institutions are so strong, why would you ever worry about us?" We will see how the world in fact unfolds in financial services, but I believe you will find the Canadian banking community alert and determined to remain competitive with American Express and other US financial institutions as time goes by.

Specific Comments

The Schott-Smith paper indicates that, in the services sector, future changes in regulatory policies or their administration are not prohibited. A Canadian minister or official might express this a little bit differently by assuring his or her constituents that the capacity of government to regulate has been fully safeguarded. However, under the Canada–United States Free Trade Agreement (FTA) both countries have accepted mutual disciplines regarding discrimination in future regulation.

The paper seems to express an element of surprise—perhaps tongue in cheek—that the chapter in the agreement governing temporary entry does not cover the broader category of labor services. Although not a participant in the negotiations, I have the feeling that the main thrust was to help business travel and business-related travel—activities that enhance the processes of trade and investment. Both governments were fully aware of the serious political problems that would result if they tried to change the fundamental nature of immigration policy at the blue-collar level. Given the sensitivity of immigration issues, I believe the progress that has been made on freedom of movement for business persons is a remarkable achievement. No longer will it be necessary to lie about the reasons for a trip to Chicago or Toronto. And if somebody says he's a real professional, the authorities might, for a change, say "come on in."

Although touched on in the agreement, professional services continue to be governed by domestic regulation and certification procedures. I am inclined to agree generally with the paper that what has been accomplished is rather better on rule making and future self-restraint than on changing present policies and rolling back discriminatory barriers, most of which are grandfathered. But in professional services the agreement seeks to get architects to work together and to recommend to the provinces and to the states some kind of mutual recognition of qualifications and greater capacity to move and practice between the two countries. The paper suggests that this step might lead to broader agreements in this area, and indeed this is envisaged in the agreement. But if I am not mistaken, the reference in the paper could be construed as potentially embracing doctors, dentists, and lawyers. As I read the accord, the envisaged extension would apply to their business services—engineering consultants, management consultants, and so on. Our medieval guild friends—the doctors, the dentists, and the lawyers—managed to get themselves excluded and are not next in line for liberalization.

There is a point on guaranteed access to transborder data flows and data banks that is very important, not only to financial institutions but also to all large multinational companies. The paper infers that the enshrined freedom for transborder data flow and access to data banks could resolve a longstanding problem, the thorny issue of the Canadian requirements in some financial sectors for local record keeping. However, existing Canadian regulations in this regard are grandfathered; the FTA affects future changes in regulations, not present regimes. In any event, since banking data can flow back and forth across the border subject only to local record-keeping requirements for fiduciary reasons, and since such data can be processed elsewhere, the rule is not a significant trade restriction.

The paper refers to the cultural protection that Canada was able to build into the agreement. Specifically, it notes that problems could arise from the procedure that governs compensation if an American publishing company has to divest after an indirect takeover of a Canadian publishing house. However, the agreement provides that in the case of a forced divestiture, there is an underlying last-resort assurance: the Canadian government is obliged to buy out the new US owner, and the price for the purchase by the Canadian government is subject to independent commercial arbitration.

The observations in the paper about discrimination in the investment field warrant a comment to clarify which regulations and rules would have to be consistent with national treatment. As I read the FTA, the "standstill" applies only to new policies and new regulations. Existing regulations can be altered but only so long as the degree of discrimination is not increased.

Regarding performance requirements related to investment, it is clear from the FTA that, in the future, trade-related conditions for investment would be out of order. Other conditions would be permitted; indeed, the Canadian explanatory text regarding this section of the FTA mentions product mandates, technology transfer, research and development, and local employment as investment conditions that would not be precluded.

Finally, the paper raises the question of the subnational jurisdictions in the two countries and how the obligations of the agreement with respect to investment and services would affect them. As Harry Freeman has pointed out, a lot of the action in Canada, and in the United States as well, is at the state or provincial level. As Schott and Smith note, Article 103 provides that the two federal governments—the parties to the agreement—shall ensure that all necessary measures are taken to give effect to its obligations by subnational levels of government. The General Agreement on Tariffs and Trade (GATT) states the comparable obligations to require the taking of such reasonable measures as may be available to the party. The obligation of the two federal parties to ensure adherence by the subnational levels of governments appears to have been strengthened relative to the GATT, but we may not know the intended force of the obligation until we have seen how the implementation process works. In theory, the federal government could endeavor to put into force all the obligations and responsibilities of the agreement through legislation, which would, however, be offensive to the powers given to the provinces under the Canadian Constitution. I find it hard to believe that taking measures to implement the agreement that would purport to require involuntary constitutional change in the United States or in Canada would be a feasible approach.

General Comments

The services provisions of the FTA do not seem to have created too great a stir in Canada. Most Canadian policies that are discriminatory have been grandfathered; Canada has a comparative advantage in some of the areas covered, such as banking; both countries have joined together to further liberalize services in the GATT; and, in the professional services, it will be some time before detailed arrangements can be worked out whereby our professional colleagues must accept someone rolling in from the other country to practice alongside them.

On specific issues, there was some disappointment in Canada that the transport sector had to fall by the wayside. This sector was a last-minute withdrawal because of pressure from US maritime interests. If transportation had been included in the final agreement, however, there might have been some segments of the Canadian transportation industry concerned about increased competition, while others focused on anticipated opportunities.

By contrast, the tourism subsidiary agreement has been generally well received. I do not think it adds very much to the existing situation, but perhaps it will stop people from doing silly things about tourism allowances the next time the border weather turns rough.

The political opposition in Canada from both of the main opposition parties is not particularly focused on individual provisions. Instead, there is a vague sense that the Canadian government has entered an arrangement with the United States that it did not say it was going to enter when it was on the election trail and that this arrangement will tie the hands of future governments regarding the capacity to intervene in the economy. There also is a fear that market forces will dictate harmonization in policy areas that are not covered by the agreement. Others believe the content goes beyond the needs of a trade agreement under Article XXIV of the GATT. In sum, the FTA is considered an undesirable dilution of Canadian sovereignty.

For example, in financial services, the Canadian Bankers' Association has said that the banking industry supports the FTA because what is good for the Canadian economy is good for the Canadian banks. However, it goes on to say that Canadian banks were required to give more in terms of liberalizing the capacity of American banks to grow in Canada than they gained in that market (because the Glass-Steagall Act restricts what foreign banks are permitted to do and where). While individual Canadian banks may differ, on balance they seem to be prepared to live with the deal. The securities trade is in a state of dramatic change in Canada and a bit ahead of the United States in terms of the deregulation of several institutions. As has been mentioned, provincial financial institutions are not covered by the agreement. The insurance companies are happy that they worked out a mutually satisfactory deal with the US insurance companies: they are covered not by the financial services part of the agreement but by the general services provisions.

The investment chapter is seen by opponents in Canada as limiting Canada's sovereignty and right to intervene in its economy. However, that view is not shared by British Columbia, the prairie provinces other than Manitoba, or the Eastern provinces, excluding Prince Edward Island. The attitude of Ontario is negative to ambivalent. By contrast, Quebec sees this agreement as a very important opportunity to attract investment and supplement savings, which Quebec needs to take advantage of market opportunities and to move up in the ranks of the diversified, modern industrial economies.

In recent years Quebec has experienced a remarkable burst of entrepreneurial activity. Quebec is conscious that, whatever the net direct investment position may be between Canada and the United States, it has a considerable investment stake in the US economy and thus a marked interest in the protection that the FTA will offer in the sense of not permitting the Americans in the future to discriminate against Canadians. This is the counterpart of US investors' interest in what has been done to ensure future nondiscriminatory treatment in the Canadian market.

The agreement represents a very useful first step. It is a pioneering effort and a very worthwhile one. Without underlining too much the cost of failure in terms of multilateral progress in the GATT or in terms of a less promising evolution of Canadian-American economic relations, I would like to note two very positive aspects that are most important for the future, provided the FTA is ratified by both countries. One is that the FTA itself envisages the identification of further areas for liberalization. Even more important than that will be the practice of living and working together within an agreed framework. Once that framework is in place, business people will respond quickly; historically, they have not needed the full transitional periods to respond to trade reforms. Once the rules of the game are set, entrepreneurs move quickly to adapt.

Thus, I am very encouraged about the foundation that has been established for the two countries. It is an important positive achievement quite apart from the avoidance of the cost of failure, which I do not believe one can put a number on. Both Canada and the United States should put their shoulders to the wheel in Geneva, but it is going to take longer to strike a useful deal in the GATT. In the meantime and for the future, we must make this agreement work here in North America. I have great hopes that both countries are going to come out winners.

7

Implications for the Uruguay Round

Jeffrey J. Schott

The main objective of the Canada–United States Free Trade Agreement
(FTA) is to create an open market for trade and investment in goods and
services—with appropriate safeguards—between the world's two largest
trading partners. While the benefits of the FTA accrue primarily to the
United States and Canada, the talks were also designed to complement
efforts to launch a new round of multilateral trade negotiations under the
auspices of the General Agreement on Tariffs and Trade (GATT).[1] Indeed,
many observers regarded US–Canada agreements on services, investment,
and other issues as important building blocks for broader multilateral pacts
(Hufbauer and Schott 1985; Aho and Aronson 1985).

This paper will examine the implications of the FTA for the Uruguay
Round of GATT negotiations. Important lessons can be drawn from the
bilateral talks with regard to what was achieved and what was not. The
following sections will discuss the implications of the agreement both for
the overall climate for GATT talks and for the negotiation of specific issues
on the agenda of the Uruguay Round.

General Comments

The conclusion of the FTA provides a much-needed shot in the arm for
trade liberalization. GATT talks have been threatened by mounting protectionist pressures. The elimination of tariffs between the two countries over

---

1. In the event the GATT talks fail, the FTA was also seen as a precedent that could
be extended to allow trade liberalization to proceed among like-minded countries in
a "market liberalization club." This view was most recently espoused in Baker (1988).

the next decade and the liberalization of significant nontariff barriers should help reverse the alarming trend toward trade protection in the United States in the past few years.[2] If one subscribes to the bicycle theory that trade liberalization must maintain forward momentum or fall off into protectionism, then the FTA is a big boost to GATT efforts to reduce trade barriers and to reform the trading system.

While the FTA is valuable in and of itself, it is definitely not a substitute for the GATT. Indeed, key aspects of the bilateral trade relationship, relating to reforms of subsidies and agricultural programs, depend on the development of multilateral discipline in the GATT. Both Canada and the United States need a successful GATT round as much as ever to complement and reinforce the gains of the FTA. In any event, the prospects for additional free trade agreements with other countries are quite limited and probably just as well. The US–Canada and US–Israel free trade agreements were exceptions: most bilateral agreements result in "voluntary" export restraints, which promote managed trade rather than trade liberalization.

At the same time, the FTA provides a strong reason to resist protectionist provisions in the omnibus trade bill that is being considered by a congressional conference committee. Implementing legislation for the FTA will be taken up only after further consideration of the omnibus trade bill in spring 1988. Some of the most troublesome provisions of the omnibus bill—those relating to the administration of the antidumping and countervailing duty statutes and the definition of domestic subsidies—would upset the negotiated balance of concessions in the FTA; they will need to be revised or struck from the final bill to merit the president's signature. Without such revisions, the FTA could be in jeopardy, but without them the president is unlikely to sign the omnibus bill in any event. Concern about the FTA, along with sensitivity to the market reaction to the trade bill since the 19 October 1987 stock market crash, may moderate protectionist elements of the bill.

Concerns have been raised, however, that the Congress may hold the FTA bill hostage to passage of the omnibus bill. However, the compromise agreement reached in February 1988—which commits the administration to jointly draft the FTA implementing legislation with the Congress in return for a commitment that a vote on the FTA bill will be held by the end

---

2. Indeed, in defending its record against congressional critics of its trade policy, the Reagan administration has boasted that it has imposed more protection than any other administration in the past 50 years. See remarks by Secretary of the Treasury James A. Baker, III before a conference at the Institute for International Economics, 14 September 1987.

of the 1988 session—should substantially lessen that threat. The more likely risk is that a veto of the omnibus bill could generate a backlash of opposition to FTA implementing legislation.[3] Would the Congress reject an agreement that is generally considered trade-creating and in the best interests of both countries? While such action may be threatened, it would be perceived as throwing the baby out with the bathwater. Therefore, I believe that rejection by the Congress of the FTA is unlikely.

A residual benefit of the FTA is the experience gained by US and Canadian negotiators in the substance and tactics required to craft trade agreements in difficult new areas such as services and investment. Negotiators learn to negotiate by negotiating, to quote C. Michael Aho of the Council on Foreign Relations.

Implications for Specific Negotiations

The FTA does *not* contain agreements that can be transported directly to Geneva to serve as the basis for multilateral negotiations in the Uruguay Round. For example, nothing in the FTA is akin to the government procurement code, which was delivered in penultimate form to the Tokyo Round negotiators after years of talks in the Organization for Economic Cooperation and Development (OECD). However, GATT participants can learn from the experience gained by the US and Canadian negotiators and build on some of the precedents established in the FTA to develop better GATT agreements.

The main implications for the Uruguay Round lie in three areas (listed in order of descending importance): dispute settlement, services, and investment. In addition, GATT negotiations will be significantly influenced by US and Canadian positions in areas such as subsidies and antidumping/ countervailing duties, government procurement, and intellectual property, where the results of the FTA negotiations left much to be desired.

---

3. The Senate Finance Committee threatened to derail the US–Canada negotiations at the start in April 1986 by withholding fast-track authority for the FTA unless the President adopted a more cooperative approach with the Congress on drafting a new trade bill and resolving specific trade problems. In the end, the committee extracted a written commitment from the President "to press for an expedited resolution" of the softwood lumber dispute between the United States and Canada, and the fast-track authority was not withheld after a 10 to 10 tie vote by the committee.

Dispute Settlement

GATT dispute settlement procedures have often been unduly criticized as slow and inconclusive. The experience of most GATT disputes does not bear this out.[4] However, problems still arise for two main reasons:

☐ GATT rules and national obligations are vague in certain areas.

☐ GATT procedures can break down *after* the submission of panel findings if the disputants cannot agree on remedial actions.

The agenda of the Uruguay Round is designed to rectify the former problem. The latter could benefit greatly from the precedents set in the FTA for the resolution of disputes.

Reform of GATT dispute settlement procedures could be promoted by the adoption of two features of the FTA provisions. First, recourse to binding arbitration in prescribed situations could facilitate the adoption of panel reports and the implementation of policy reforms. Second, extending the terms of reference of panel reviews to cover the consistency of national measures with their own domestic trade laws as well as the GATT could reinforce multilateral discipline on national trade policies and thus preempt potential disputes. These could well be the most significant precedents set by the FTA.

GATT panel reports are supposed to be findings of fact and law on the specific issues subject to a dispute. The "law" referred to is the provisions and procedures of the GATT; in effect, the panel is supposed to rule on a country's obligations under the GATT. Such rulings can cause political problems when domestic law is inconsistent with the GATT or when the panel findings lead to demands for compensation or other remedial actions. In these instances, large countries often find it easier to "stonewall" than to respond to panel findings because the consensus rule of GATT allows them to block approval of panel reports in the GATT Council. Small countries are more receptive to GATT rulings given their vulnerability to trade retaliation.

In the FTA, Canada and the United States agreed to be bound by panel rulings in disputes concerning whether final antidumping or countervailing

---

4. From January 1948 to September 1985, 75 disputes were brought before the GATT. Of all the cases, settlements were reached in 72 percent; cases were not supported or pursued by the complaining country in an additional 16 percent; retaliation was authorized in 1.3 percent; and action was not taken or was pending in 10.7 percent. Recent problems, especially those regarding agricultural subsidy disputes, derive more from the vagueness of GATT obligations than from the functioning of the dispute mechanism. See United States International Trade Commission (1985).

duty rulings have been applied in a manner consistent with national statutes and in disputes regarding escape clause or safeguards measures. In addition, binding arbitration could be imposed for all other disputes arising from the FTA, upon mutual agreement of both countries.

Resort to binding arbitration would remove the political filter from the dispute *resolution* process. The GATT system would benefit in three ways. First, both developed and developing countries would be seen to be subject to GATT discipline. Second, an effective and timely dispute settlement procedure would obviate the need for vigilante actions where retaliation is pursued unilaterally without GATT authorization.[5] Third, disputants would no longer be able to block the adoption of panel reports by the GATT Council. As a result, panelists would be able to prepare more objective findings, and those findings would be implemented more promptly than under present procedures.[6]

The second aspect may be even more far-reaching in its effect. In certain situations the US–Canada pact provides for binational panels to rule on the consistency of national actions under domestic laws and regulations. If the GATT were given similar responsibilities, this would have several important implications for the functioning of both the GATT dispute settlement and safeguards systems.

For the GATT to evaluate the consistency of trade actions with regard to domestic law *and* international obligations, it must be able to improve its surveillance of national trade policies. Increased GATT surveillance of national trade policies was a key recommendation of the report of the GATT "Wisemen."[7] Such reviews—analogous to the Article IV consultations on economic policy conducted by the International Monetary Fund—would provide the basis for evaluation of the application of national laws and regulations and of their consistency with GATT obligations. The reviews would provide information necessary for the judgment of disputes, and they could help ward off potential disputes by alerting governments when existing or proposed policies risk violating international obligations. As the Wisemen suggested, these trade policy reviews should be conducted frequently,

---

5. Such action already has been taken in the US dispute with Japan on semiconductors, and similar measures are currently threatened against Brazil and Korea. They result from frustration over the pace and effectiveness of the GATT mechanism, and they breed a growing mistrust of GATT discipline.

6. Given the political sensitivity of ceding authority to review national practices to a multinational body, the incorporation of binding arbitration in dispute settlement procedures may need to be applied at the start to only a limited class of trade disputes. Like the FTA, the GATT could start first with disputes over safeguard actions.

7. See Leutwiler et al. (1985). The US representative on the seven-member group was Senator Bill Bradley (D-NJ).

perhaps annually, for the largest OECD countries, almost as often for the newly industrializing countries, and less regularly for the poorer developing countries.

Finally, trade policy reviews could help fortify new GATT discipline on safeguards measures. The reviews would provide a forum where countries would have to justify their trade policy measures against agreed international standards, and they could be part of a system to monitor compliance with a new safeguards code that, it is hoped, will result from the Uruguay Round negotiations. Indeed, a new safeguards code may stand or fall on the perceived ability of the GATT to specifically monitor national adjustment policies. As I argue elsewhere, this code should require adjustment by the industry benefiting from temporary protection.[8] GATT monitoring of such programs—whether set by the industry itself or by its government—is essential. The proposed trade policy reviews would be indispensable for this purpose.

Services

The US–Canada agreement on services elaborates basic principles that the United States has broached in bilateral and multilateral forums for many years. Many bilateral treaties of friendship, commerce, and navigation contain provisions on traded services. Moreover, discussion of trade in services has taken place for almost a decade in the OECD Trade Committee, complementing the OECD codes on invisibles and on capital movements that were developed in the 1970s. The US–Israel agreement provided a skeletal framework of rules for trade in services, and now the FTA has put some bones on that skeleton. Because so few agreements cover international services transactions, the provisions of Chapters 14 and 17 of the FTA set out some useful precedents for GATT negotiations.

The main value of the FTA for the GATT talks on services lies in the elaboration of rights and obligations regarding national treatment, establishment, and licensing and certification procedures. The provisions of Articles 1402 and 1403 are carefully crafted and could serve as a model for key elements of a code of principles for a GATT agreement on services. As will be discussed, however, elaboration would be needed to clarify the application of most-favored-nation (MFN) treatment and to spell out how these principles would be applied in the specific economic and regulatory context of each signatory—or, indeed, whether the principles would be

---

8. See, for example, Hufbauer and Schott (1985) and Chapter 9 of Bergsten et al. (1987).

applied to specific service sectors at all. Notable progress was made, however, in setting out a commitment to discipline regulatory policies at the subnational level.

In addition, the FTA coverage of labor services sets an interesting precedent for GATT talks. There has been some concern, especially among developing countries, that these services would be excluded from the GATT agenda and considered solely as an immigration issue. The FTA coverage of labor services is incomplete, however. The provisions of the architecture annex to Chapter 14 and of Chapter 15 deal exclusively with professional services and the temporary entry of business persons and traders—the main problem area in the context of US–Canadian relations. These provisions exclude reference to blue-collar labor services. Nonetheless, the distinction between professional and blue-collar labor services is drawn, setting useful parameters for a GATT negotiation.

In other respects, however, the agreement is less useful as a model for a GATT accord. The agreement is long on rules and short on liberalization. Most existing restrictions remain intact. The most significant reforms will take place in the financial services sector, which was specifically excluded from the general services agreement and incorporates reforms that in many instances would have proceeded unilaterally. A successful GATT negotiation will require some tangible results in the form of liberalization of specific trade barriers.

In addition, the agreement does not deal effectively with problems created by subsidized services, though the negotiators grappled long and hard to do so. Discipline on subsidies seems to have fallen victim to the overall failure to deal with problems of subsidized trade (see below).

The agreement establishes a comprehensive standstill on new services trade barriers. This was relatively easily arrived at by the United States and Canada, given the level of development and openness of their service sectors. But in a GATT negotiation, a standstill will be a much more difficult objective to reach.

Because a standstill is more likely to be one of the end results of a GATT negotiation instead of a starting point (as it is for merchandise trade as set out in the Punta declaration), the framework of a GATT for services will have to be a bit different from the US–Canada accord. First, the principles contained in the FTA concerning national treatment, right of commercial presence, establishment rights, and transparency of trade measures may not be universally applied. Many countries may not want to subject certain service sectors to *any* international discipline. Therefore, flexibility may be needed in the range of concessions that countries are able to offer. Some mechanism should be devised to allow countries to make commitments in some areas without opening up an entire service sector to international competition.

Second, the application of the MFN principle—which was not as relevant in the bilateral context—will have to be addressed. To preempt the free-rider problem, a GATT agreement needs to be applied on a conditional-MFN basis as between signatories and nonsignatories (see Hufbauer and Schott 1985). However, a question still remains whether the MFN principle should apply among signatories, if some countries assume more detailed obligations in particular sectors than do other countries.

Third, the US–Canada services agreement casts doubt on the efficacy of negotiating self-contained sectoral agreements. The failure to reach agreement on even minimal liberalization in the maritime sector is instructive: if two countries could not balance concessions in one sector, how could a larger group of countries come together? To be sure, a self-contained sectoral negotiation did take place regarding financial services. However, work on Chapter 17 of the FTA was conducted apart from the general negotiations on services, and it differed from the general rights and obligations spelled out in Chapter 14, especially with regard to the standard for national treatment, coverage of state and provincial bodies, rollback of existing barriers, and consultative and dispute procedures.

Should this bifurcated approach to services extend to the GATT talks? Negotiators were successful in separate talks in achieving a rollback of barriers in the FTA. However, one needs to ask whether finance officials have sufficient leverage to encourage the deregulation and liberalization of protected markets for banking, securities firms, insurance companies, and the like on a multilateral basis. Moreover, are the investment and data flow issues to be tackled in the GATT separable from the regulatory issues affecting the financial services sector? Important negotiations are being conducted by central banks that are seeking to establish a harmonized multilateral approach to regulatory guidelines,[9] but can a key objective of prospective GATT talks—the rollback of barriers on a multilateral basis—be achieved without the additional leverage gained from being able to trade off concessions between sectors covered by an overall GATT accord on services?

The best approach for negotiating services in the GATT would be to have countries negotiate a common set of principles to guide government policy and then spell out the economic activities to which the policy principles would apply. Instead of seeking to balance concessions within each sector, it would be better to get countries to negotiate commitments to the application of certain principles in various sectors. For example, one country might extend national treatment to insurance but not maritime, while another

---

9. Peter Norman, "Ways to Boost Global Banking Stability Proposed by 12 Industrialized Nations," *Wall Street Journal,* 11 December 1987, 10.

might accord establishment rights to banks but not agree to grant national treatment in the accreditation of doctors. Each country could define how the principle would apply, and the commitments would be bound in a schedule of concessions. Such negotiations would complement the work on a services framework agreement or "umbrella" code of principles. In this respect, the negotiations on the entity coverage of the government procurement code in the Tokyo Round provide a useful precedent.

Investment

A GATT agreement on investment needs to cover a wide range of trade-related investment measures, including rights of establishment. Such measures can have significant trade effects. Investment incentives and performance and trade balancing requirements often act as implicit domestic or export subsidies; compulsory licensing and technology transfer requirements often encourage domestic production and investment to substitute for imports. Similarly, exchange and capital controls affect the mix of domestic production and the sourcing of inputs, and subsequently influence the flow of exports and imports.

While the agenda for GATT negotiations on investment has not yet been clearly defined, the US–Canada talks, in combination with the experience of the OECD Codes on Invisibles and on Capital Movements, provide a solid basis for GATT talks. As in services, several of the provisions of Chapter 16 of the FTA set out useful models for a GATT accord, especially those provisions dealing with national treatment, performance requirements, remittance restrictions, expropriation, and domestic equity requirements (also covered in the chapter on financial services).[10]

The national treatment provision in Article 1602 of the FTA improves upon key aspects of the OECD codes by enumerating establishment rights for greenfield investments and by barring minimum equity requirements. The FTA does not remove all entry barriers, but in most cases where foreign direct investment is permitted, it is granted national treatment.[11]

The FTA also establishes obligations regarding performance requirements and expropriation that could serve as a model for a GATT accord. Article 1603 of the FTA prohibits trade-related performance requirements and local

---

10. Of course, the effect of these provisions is circumscribed by exceptions noted in the agreement—particularly the exemption of energy industries. The challenge to GATT negotiators will be to limit the scope of derogations as much as possible.

11. The FTA effectively grandfathers all existing investment controls, including the Canadian ownership requirement for energy development. Reviews by Investment Canada are amended, however, pursuant to the schedule in Annex 1607.3.

purchasing requirements. This article goes beyond the recommendations of a recent GATT panel report on the Canadian Foreign Investment Review Agency, which censured only domestic sourcing rules. As a practical matter, the sharp reduction in investments subject to screening by Investment Canada will make it more difficult to impose and enforce such requirements. Article 1605 reflects the international law standard for expropriation, limiting recourse to these actions and requiring prompt compensation at fair market value.

The FTA commitments also apply to an area where previous investment agreements have not provided substantial discipline—namely, the policies of state and provincial governments. For example, the United States and Canada have maintained annexes and specific reservations to the OECD invisibles and capital movements codes that effectively exempt policies under state and provincial jurisdiction.[12] In the FTA, Canada and the United States undertake a broader obligation in Article 103 to "ensure that all necessary measures are taken in order to give effect to its provision. . . by state, provincial and local governments." While the FTA contains some exceptions to this general rule, in most instances subnational bodies are to grant "most-favored" treatment to goods and services from the other country, in essence placing US and Canadian firms on the same footing in activities regulated at the subnational level.[13]

The main issue that the FTA does not cover is the thorny area of investment incentives. This is not surprising, given the total lack of agreement on disciplines on domestic subsidies and the fact that many investment incentives are granted by states and provinces. With the decline of barriers to both trade and investment, however, the use of subsidies to attract new business may occur more often in the future. A GATT agreement on investment will have to deal with the subsidies issue, either head-on or by reference to changes in the GATT Subsidies Code, to avoid a proliferation of new barriers to trade and investment.

---

12. However, if subnational practices contravene code rights, the national government commits to use its "best efforts" to change the practice. Indeed, in the financial services sector, the US government has obtained changes in specific state practices and laws in several instances to meet concerns of other OECD countries.

13. "Most-favored" refers to treatment *within* a state or province. Subsidiaries of US firms in a Canadian province, for example, would receive the same treatment as local firms, even if there is discrimination against firms from other Canadian provinces. Such a provision builds on the precedent of a little-noticed footnote to Article 7 of the GATT Subsidies Code, in which "signatories accept nonetheless the international consequences that may arise under this Agreement as a result of the granting of subsidies within their territories." To date, there has been little discussion of this provision in the code committee of signatories.

Other Issues

In some areas, the implications of the FTA for the new round are to be found in what was not negotiated as much as in what was included in the final agreement. This is particularly true regarding subsidies and the complementary area of antidumping (AD) and countervailing duties (CVD). It also holds for government procurement and intellectual property issues. In most instances, the buck was passed forward to Geneva with both countries committing to pursue multilateral accords in the GATT and other relevant bodies. These issues will be addressed in turn.

Subsidies and antidumping/countervailing duties. The agreement does not require any changes in existing antidumping and countervailing duty statutes. It does, however, establish an oversight and dispute settlement mechanism to review whether administrative rulings under existing laws are consistent with the requirements of *national* laws. The panel review supersedes recourse to judicial review of final findings under US law; the panel rulings are binding on both countries. In addition, any prospective changes in these national statutes would be subject to review, upon request, by a binational panel to ensure that national rights and obligations under the FTA and the GATT are not infringed by the new provisions. Changes would not apply to the other country unless specifically provided for in the legislation.[14]

The agreement fails to address the key issue of discipline on the use of trade-distorting domestic subsidies. Instead, the issue is shunted to prospective bilateral negotiations during the next five to seven years that will attempt to develop new disciplines on subsidies and to harmonize national unfair trade statutes. These talks could take place bilaterally and/or result from agreements reached during the Uruguay Round; the time frame for the talks set out in the FTA seems designed to accommodate both types of negotiations.

In a sense, the failure of the United States and Canada to reach agreement on new rules on subsidies and CVDs is not surprising. In some situations, discipline on subsidies could be effective only if applied to the trade of other major trading countries as well (clearly the case with regard to agricultural subsidies). Moreover, these changes involve some of the most substantial concessions that each country could offer in a trade negotiation.

---

14. The FTA *could* lead to preferential treatment for Canada under the AD and CVD statutes. Such a "two-tiered" system would complicate GATT efforts to negotiate reforms in these areas.

As such, the Uruguay Round acted as a disincentive to meaningful reforms in the context of the bilateral FTA. Each country will need a significantly higher "payment" for such changes than could be extracted in a bilateral deal.

As a result, the bilateral negotiations envisaged in the FTA will be driven by progress in the GATT talks on subsidies. The United States and Canada will be two of the main protagonists of the GATT talks, with the agenda of the negotiations likely set by the subsidy/CVD disputes between them (and between the United States, Europe, and Japan regarding agricultural subsidies). The convergence of policies sought by the FTA could well result from pressure to develop joint negotiating positions in Geneva, especially regarding agricultural and other domestic subsidies. Subsidy reforms, in turn, will facilitate the harmonization of CVD laws.

The harmonization of AD laws poses a different problem. Antidumping duties traditionally have not been applied to trade between partners in a free trade area. The FTA thus raises a question about whether continuation of current AD practices is justified for bilateral trade. The objectives of harmonization might be better achieved by the convergence of anticompetition/antitrust statutes, which would obviate the need for AD laws for bilateral trade.

Government procurement. The key lesson from the government procurement provisions of the FTA was not what was achieved, but what was not negotiated. The FTA lowers the threshold—for bidders from the other country only—above which government contracts must be subject to the open procurement rules set by the GATT government procurement code. The lower threshold itself should have a liberalizing effect on bilateral trade, opening up new trade opportunities for an additional US$3 billion in US contracts and US$500 million in Canadian contracts. To this extent, it would be a useful precedent for reform of the GATT code during the Uruguay Round.

However, the threshold issue is only one part of the procurement problem. The threshold and other provisions of the GATT code apply only to the purchases of those government entities listed in the agreement. As a result, the code does not regulate purchases of products such as urban mass transportation equipment and telecommunications and power-generating equipment. In addition, the code does not yet deal with purchases of services. Both the extension of entity coverage and the inclusion of services would have been significant breakthroughs for the FTA in the area of government procurement. The failure to achieve progress in either area is not a hopeful sign for progress in GATT talks.

Intellectual property. The protection of intellectual property rights (IPRs) is one of the key "new" issues on the agenda of the Uruguay Round. Despite the relative compatibility of legal regimes for the protection of IPRs in the United States and Canada, there was no agreement in this area in the FTA except for the hortatory charge in Article 2004 to pursue a GATT accord and the commitment in Article 2006 to compensate or otherwise protect copyright holders for retransmission of programs.

In Geneva, the United States has suggested that a GATT agreement on IPRs needs to harmonize enforcement provisions for patents, copyrights, trademarks, and semiconductor chip mask designs and to encourage the adoption of "standards and norms that provide adequate means of obtaining and maintaining intellectual property rights."[15] There is no international consensus, however, as to whether the GATT should deal with the latter issue of standards-setting or should focus solely on enforcement issues. The failure to adopt a chapter on IPRs in the FTA provides no guidance on this critical point.

An important area where progress could have been made was the development of standards for compulsory licensing. This issue has been an irritant in bilateral trade relations because of longstanding disputes in the pharmaceuticals sector; it is also an important issue for other countries. While legislation in Canada (Bill C-22) has been promulgated that resolves the controversy by granting patent protection for seven-to-ten years before compulsory licensing is required for pharmaceuticals, the issue is not subject to the bilateral enforcement procedures of the FTA because the bill was handled apart from the FTA negotiations.

The Near-Term Impact

Even before the FTA is implemented, the lessons learned from the bilateral negotiations can be applied in the Uruguay Round in Geneva. If trade ministers really are intent on accelerating the GATT talks in 1988, there is much to be learned from the negotiation of the FTA.

Rather than promoting bilateralism and weakening the GATT system, the FTA should provide a big boost for the GATT and ample grist for the negotiating mill of the Uruguay Round. GATT accords on dispute settlement,

---

15. "US Framework Proposal to GATT Concerning Intellectual Property Rights," as reproduced in Bureau of National Affairs, *International Trade Reporter*, 4 November 1987.

services, and investment should be facilitated by the precedents set by the US and Canadian negotiators; indeed, much of an "umbrella" code on services could be extracted from Chapter 14 of the FTA. Even in areas not handled by the FTA, GATT negotiations should receive additional attention because of the recognition that multilateral disciplines are needed to help resolve bilateral trade problems in areas such as agriculture and subsidies. In sum, the FTA contains a lot of "pluses" for the Uruguay Round and no significant "minuses"; it is a "win-win" agreement for the United States and Canada and for the GATT as well.

References

Aho, C. Michael, and Jonathan David Aronson. 1985. *Trade Talks: America Better Listen!* New York: Council on Foreign Relations.

Baker, James A., III. 1988. "The Geopolitical Implications of the US–Canada Trade Pact." *The International Economy,* January/February, 34–41.

Bergsten, C. Fred, Kimberly Ann Elliott, Jeffrey J. Schott, and Wendy E. Takacs. 1987. *Auction Quotas and United States Trade Policy.* POLICY ANALYSES IN INTERNATIONAL ECONOMICS 19. Washington: Institute for International Economics, September.

Hufbauer, Gary Clyde, and Jeffrey J. Schott. 1985. *Trading for Growth: The Next Round of Trade Negotiations.* POLICY ANALYSES IN INTERNATIONAL ECONOMICS 11. Washington: Institute for International Economics, September.

Leutwiler, Fritz, et al. 1985. *Trade Policies for a Better Future: Proposals for Action.* Geneva: GATT Independent Study Group, March.

United States International Trade Commission. 1985. *Review of the Effectiveness of Trade Dispute Settlement Under the GATT and the Tokyo Round Agreements.* Publication 1793. Washington, December.

Comments

John Whalley

Jeffrey Schott's paper is a very useful summary of many of the questions raised by the Canada–United States Free Trade Agreement (FTA) for specific issues in the new round. I thought it might be useful for me to make some broader and complementary comments on how the agreement might influence the general direction of both the round and the wider trading system as well as on the implications for Canadian and US behavior in the system in light of the agreement.

Will the Agreement Accelerate or Retard the Trade Round?

This is clearly a hard question to answer since the bilateral agreement represents a weakening of multilateral commitment by both countries, yet it also provides new codes and an impetus to trade liberalization that subsequently can be multilateralized. Also the emergence of a larger, more unified North American trading bloc puts more pressure on the European Community (EC) and Japan to come to the table.

From my conversations with "GATTologists," the precedent for the current situation seems to be the Dillon Round. It is generally agreed that the Dillon Round was significantly accelerated by the formation of the European Community since this generated a cohesive bloc for the United States to negotiate with and, in turn, forced the pace of negotiations because of US concerns to negotiate with this emerging larger power.

My sense, however, is that this time around things are likely to be somewhat different. Evaluating progress on the current trade round is difficult. On the one hand, one can look at the more than 140 proposals that have been tabled thus far in the 14 groups in the Group of Negotiations on Goods—the impetus given to the process by the meeting in Punta del Este—and convince oneself that this is indeed a major and significant event. On the other hand, one can argue that the current situation—growing EC–US trade tensions and the macro situation with the falling dollar, which the Europeans see as giving the US major improvements in access to European markets combined with the key role of agriculture and the EC proposal on agriculture—makes swift progress extremely unlikely. Moreover, the elec-

John Whalley is Professor of Economics at the University of Western Ontario.

tion year in the United States, the airbus controversy, the omnibus trade bill, and the expiration of US negotiating authority contribute to this chemistry of indecision, an inability to move forward, and a prescription for frustration.

Two points seem to be especially important. The first is that this agreement was initiated by the Canadians and, in part, represents a rejection by Canada of the use of the General Agreement on Tariffs and Trade (GATT) system for dealing with its economic interests. (I will return to Canada's wider middle-power interests, which will be discussed below.) Canada initiated this process because of the pressing need of its trade interests in the United States. One can argue about how far Canada has achieved its objective, but until 1982 it would have been unthinkable for any Canadian government to have taken such an action. The view within bureaucratic and political circles was that Canada was a committed multilateralist, that Canada needed the security of multilateral rules around any agreement with the Americans, and that even though it involved negotiating with many countries simultaneously, the GATT represented the best vehicle for Canada to deal with its economic interests in US markets.

Since 1982–83 that view has radically changed. The argument is that the GATT can no longer deliver, that it is an ineffective negotiating vehicle dominated by lowest common denominator outcomes, and that Canada can go farther and faster down the bilateral route. In my opinion, Canadian actions propelling the FTA demonstrate Canada's frustration with the GATT process. Unlike the Dillon Round that was accelerated by the formation of the EC, the bilateral agreement is partly a response to frustrations with the multilateral process.

In the case of the United States, it is much more difficult to say what this does to the way the United States views the round. How it appeared to an outsider to the process was that there was a genuine element of surprise in the United States when Canada took this initiative, and a certain degree of puzzlement remains as to why one of the United States' largest trading partners should actually approach the United States in a positive way with a concrete proposal for such an agreement. In turn, Canada's negotiating leverage may well have been the enormous difficulty the United States would have had in saying no. But the view that seems to me likely to become more pervasive in the United States, now that it has signed the agreement, is that even the United States, architect of the multilateral system, can obtain more bilaterally than it could in the past and elevate its bilateral activity. In the United States tension has clearly been increasing between a bilateral and multilateral focus for trade policies as evident in other recent trade policy actions. This agreement is the largest and most important manifestation of US bilateralism and as such, if anything, runs counter to efforts to accelerate the round.

What Does the Agreement Do to the Trading System?

This agreement, in and of itself, does not do a whole lot to the trading system. After all, it is compatible with GATT Article XXIV (plus or minus a few small items, which themselves are debatable). But it does seem to me that the agreement reflects what seems to be happening in the system generally, and what is important is that the United States, the pillar of the GATT system, has gone bilateral with its largest trading partner.

Within the system one has to remember that for European–US tensions the GATT is no longer the sole vehicle for resolving disputes. Much of the early drama on agriculture was played out in the Organization for Economic Cooperation and Development. The airbus, dollar, and other issues have all become bilateral issues. US issues with Japan over the years have largely been dealt with on a bilateral basis. In its dealings with developing countries the United States uses all sorts of bilateral tactics, including threatened graduation from the Generalized System of Preferences, and in recent negotiations with Mexico it has traded US steel quotas for reductions in steel duties in Mexico and quotas for apparel for improved access in fabrics.

If one asks why all of these bilateral actions are going on and why they are not being discussed multilaterally, the conclusion that I draw is that bilateral negotiation is largely unconstrained rather than constrained. Arrangements such as the Canada–US agreement are, of course, Article XXIV compatible, but in negotiating in this way one is not constrained by the most-favored-nation (MFN) obligation. Also, one is far less constrained concerning what one discusses. The items and topics covered by this agreement, including energy, investment, agriculture, and financial institutions, are of a type and range unthinkable for any negotiation in the GATT.

Unconstrained bilateral negotiation rather than constrained multilateral negotiation was clearly attractive to these two parties in negotiating this agreement. And, in my opinion, the agreement merely reflects what is happening more widely in the trading system. I also believe that ultimately there will be more, not less, drift toward regionalism and large power blocs, which could result in even more conflict and tension. This agreement, in and of itself, does nothing to reverse this process and possibly does something to accelerate it. To my mind, it goes a long way toward endorsing it.

What About Canada and US Behavior in the System in Light of the Agreement?

This agreement is of major symbolic importance to Canada and of significant but somewhat less importance to the United States. Nonetheless, it will have an impact on how they both behave in the system.

In the past there seems to have been two objectives that Canada sought through its participation in the GATT: to take care of Canada's economic interests, which have been largely equated with gaining improved and more secure market access in the United States, and to demonstrate, for domestic political reasons, Canada's active role as a global middle power. Canada frequently chairs working parties and committees, prepares summary documents, and so on.

My sense is that the first objective underlying Canada's participation in the multilateral process has now been severely undermined. There has been a clear and convincing demonstration of Canada's ability to negotiate directly to deal with its trading interests with the United States. The GATT is of less importance to Canada from the point of view of securing its economic interests. Indeed one could even argue on economic grounds that Canada's interest will be to maintain its margin of preference in US markets, so there will be some resistance to multilateral tariff cuts and multilateralization in general through the GATT.

On the other hand, the agreement's effect on internal politics has increased the pressure on Canada to elevate its middle-power diplomatic role. The need is to demonstrate that Canada's sovereignty has not been impaired by the agreement, that Canada is a separate country that takes foreign policy positions independent from the United States. Thus, from a Canadian point of view, I see far less concern with the first objective above and far more with the second.

From a US viewpoint the situation is much more difficult to gauge. In the past, two objectives seem to explain US participation in the GATT. The first is the international domestic process and the executive-legislative compromise coming from the 1934 Reciprocal Trade Agreements Act. The statute was the vehicle for containing domestic protection and resisting the spread of protection by tying reduction in US barriers to reductions in barriers abroad. After 1947, this was done multilaterally rather than bilaterally because of the complexity of the sequences of bilateral negotiations that resulted in the 1930s.

Second, there has always been a US geopolitical interest in the GATT. In the early days, this reflected concerns to help rebuild Western Europe and develop global institutions that would support efforts to contain communism, and the same concerns subsequently spread to the participation of the developing countries in the 1960s. However, with the subsequent growth in Japan and Europe and less perceived threat from the Soviet Union, US geopolitical interests in the GATT are less central than formerly and economic interests in trade policy are more important. As a result, we see the United States moving both bilaterally and regionally.

This agreement is in step with all of these developments. It demonstrates to US policymakers that they can advance their economic interests through bilateral negotiation, and it also shows other countries that they can negotiate bilaterally with the United States and achieve their interests. Whether 10 years from now this will be viewed as a cornerstone agreement that marked a major departure in both US and global trade policy remains to be determined. But these wider dimensions of the agreement are worth noting.

Julius L. Katz

From the beginning of the US-Canadian negotiations, I have been skeptical of the argument that such an agreement might be one of the building blocks for the multilateral negotiations under the General Agreement on Tariffs and Trade (GATT). This argument was suggested in the pamphlet by Gary Hufbauer and Jeffrey Schott on the next round of trade negotiations, referenced in Schott's paper for this conference.

For one thing, the case for the Canada–United States Free Trade Agreement (FTA) was compelling on its own terms because of the significant economic benefits it was likely to yield and because of the unique characteristics of US-Canadian geography, the existing high degree of integration of the two economies, the similarities of their political and economic systems, and the natural North-South attraction for trade and financial relationships. Free trade between the United States and Canada is something that has been waiting to happen for almost 150 years. That it has not happened until now has been primarily the result of political circumstances in both countries.

Another reason for doubts about the building block approach was a concern that an agreement with Canada would inevitably stimulate proposals for bilateral agreements with other countries or groups of countries. We have, in fact, heard proposals for such agreements, among others with Mexico, the Caribbean, and even Japan. Treasury Secretary James Baker recently suggested the possibility of pursuing other bilateral agreements as an element of US policy.

The United States has a fundamental, overriding interest in a world trading system based upon the principle of multilateralism. It is hard to see how a series of bilateral preferential agreements would further that US interest. Clearly, the US–Canada agreement would meet the test of conformity with GATT Article XXIV, which authorizes free trade areas. It does not

Julius L. Katz is Chairman of the Government Research Corporation. He is also Chairman of the Functioning of the GATT System negotiating group in the Uruguay Round.

follow, however, that agreements of the scope and depth of the US–Canada agreement could be negotiated with countries with disparate economies and economic policies, such as Mexico or with the countries of the Caribbean or the Pacific rim. The outcome of negotiations with other countries might not be agreements patterned after the US–Canada model but rather agreements tailored to the circumstances of individual countries. The result would be to erode further the most-favored-nation principle and seriously jeopardize the GATT as an instrumentality for multilateral rules and as a forum for multilateral negotiations.

In his paper, Jeffrey Schott focuses on the implications of the US–Canada agreement for specific issues in the Uruguay Round. I would agree with Schott that the US–Canada negotiations have provided valuable lessons for the Uruguay Round, in terms both of what has been achieved and what was not achieved.

The dispute settlement mechanism established in the FTA is in many ways path-breaking and provides elements that could well be incorporated in the GATT. The GATT is one of the few commercial agreements that does not provide for binding arbitration. What is surprising about the GATT dispute settlement mechanism is not that it has functioned so badly, but that, contrary to public perception, it has functioned so well. Where it has functioned badly, or not at all, is with respect to those issues, primarily agricultural subsidies, where the rules of the GATT lack precision. In those cases, GATT panels have not had a basis for clear-cut conclusion, and the governments involved in disputes have been unwilling to accept any conclusion not supportive of their own policies or positions.

Apart from the problem of imprecision of certain rules covering primarily agriculture, the GATT mechanism is deficient in that the role of the dispute panels frequently confuses the roles of mediation and adjudication. US proposals in the Uruguay Round would place the mediation role with the Director General of the GATT, limiting the role of the panels purely to adjudication of disputes.

The other problem in the GATT procedure is that GATT panel reports do not stand on their own but must be unanimously approved by the GATT Council. Thus, a party to a result has a veto over a report by a panel. It is not yet clear whether the US proposals in the Uruguay Round will alter this practice.

Clearly, the mechanism of the FTA, with its provision for mandatory binding impartial arbitration in some cases and binding arbitration in other cases by prior agreement, goes well beyond the GATT system. It remains to be seen whether the Congress will accept binding dispute settlement, but if it does, I would hope that the United States would be encouraged to introduce the idea of binding dispute resolution into the Uruguay Round of negotiations.

The other major achievement of the US–Canada agreement with positive implications for the Uruguay Round is in the area of services. The framework of the FTA is a good model for a multilateral agreement on services. I am not discouraged, as is Schott, by the fact that "the agreement is long on rules and short on liberalization." Rome wasn't built in a day, and in an area as complex as services, the achievement of a framework system of generally applicable rules is a notable achievement, even if it was necessary to grandfather many existing nonconforming practices. This, in fact, was the approach of the GATT, which set out rules and objectives and then in a series of negotiations has progressively reduced barriers to trade.

The other lesson coming out of the experience of the US–Canadian negotiations is that the task of liberalization of services trade is not a question of the United States against the rest of the world. In a number of service sectors, the United States is limited by legislation and politics from doing very much liberalization. The United States, for example, sought national treatment in the area of financial services, but it could not agree to the principle of reciprocity because of the provisions of the Glass-Steagall Act. It took some artful drafting for the United States to negotiate its way around that dilemma. Similarly, the lesson of the abortive attempt to include the transport sector in the FTA will not be lost on other nations negotiating in the Uruguay Round. In the end, even a promise to provide national treatment to Canada in the event of any future change in US cabotage law (the Jones Act) had to be abandoned in the face of a threat from the maritime lobby, which could have scuttled the entire agreement.

With regard to objectives not dealt with by the FTA, the greatest disappointment was the failure to agree on some sensible and workable rules for subsidies. The apparent reason for the failure is that the two sides simply ran out of time. This is perhaps why they committed themselves to spending the next five years, and two additional years if necessary, to find agreement on a problem they could not solve in 18 months.

The failure to deal with the problem of subsidies demonstrates that the complexity of the issue, both in terms of substance and politics, is greater than commonly supposed. What becomes clear as one reviews the course of the negotiations, is that subsidies is another area where US limitations and inhibitions are as great as those of other countries. The notion that only if the rest of the world stopped subsidizing turns out to be naive, to say the least. Hopefully, the US–Canada negotiations will prove instructive as these issues are confronted in the Uruguay Round.

Finally, I would like to make note of Jeff Schott's observation that the FTA will provide a shot in the arm for trade liberalization. I hope he is right, but all the returns are not yet in. Personally, I have believed from the outset that the US–Canada negotiations would succeed and that the agreement would be supported by the Congress. One must recognize, however, the major hurdle in the way—namely, the omnibus trade bill. It takes a great leap of faith to forecast, as has Schott, that the free trade agreement will help temper the protectionist provisions of the trade bill and increase the chances that the President could sign the bill. In the final analysis, it is the fate of both the trade bill and the legislation to implement the free trade agreement, rather than the agreement itself, that will directly influence the future course of the Uruguay Round.

8

Political Perspectives

Barbara McDougall

In Canada, the free trade agreement with the United States has been debated at a visceral level that we have not experienced since the referendum on Quebec independence in 1980. At meetings of the Parliamentary Committee, set up to examine the preliminary outline of the agreement, not only did the captains of Canadian industry appear to express their views and, in most cases, their support for the initiative, but Canadian artists, writers, intellectuals, union leaders, social activists, regional spokespersons, and just about anyone else who could get a hearing before the committee also expressed passionate views on what free trade might or might not do *for* Canada and *to* Canada.

Independent groups, for and against the agreement, have formed, using millions of dollars of sophisticated advertising to win the hearts and minds of Canadians to their particular points of view. A series of debates has sprung up across the country, and every service club has added "free trade" to the top of its program agenda.

And "free trade" has made some very strange bedfellows indeed. Canada's newest Premier, Frank McKenna, a Liberal, has thrown his support behind free trade, despite the pressure of two other Liberal premiers who oppose free trade (David Peterson of Ontario and Joe Ghiz of Prince Edward Island). Robert Bourassa, Premier of Quebec and a Liberal, is one of the agreement's staunchest supporters. Even the New Democrats, who are traditionally aligned with "big labor," find themselves in a difficult position with recent polls showing that slightly more trade unionists support the deal than oppose it!

Overall, the polls show a moderate trend toward support for the agreement in principle, with the greatest support in Quebec, Western Canada, and on

Barbara McDougall is the Canadian Minister of State (Privatization), Regulatory Affairs, and Minister Responsible for the Status of Women.

This is the revised text of comments presented at the conference.

both coasts. Opposition is still strongest in Ontario, but even in Ontario that opposition is beginning to weaken as the details of the agreement become better known and understood.

Ontario's basic objectives reflect the major areas in which there has been considerable public debate. Ontario set up six conditions that had to be met before it would support the agreement:

☐ There could be no unfettered right of investment; there isn't.

☐ The Auto Pact was to remain intact; it has been improved.

☐ Agricultural marketing boards were to remain; they will.

☐ Regional development powers were to continue untouched; they do.

☐ A binding dispute settlement mechanism had to be established; it was.

☐ Canada's cultural sovereignty was to remain intact; it has.

Essentially Ontario was saying, "Right now things are going pretty well here. If you can get us a better deal, fine. But don't mess with what makes us what we are."

We think we got a better deal. In fact, we know we did. Ontario stands to be one of the prime beneficiaries from the growth and renewal that will come from the free trade agreement. And so will the rest of Canada.

Canada is a confederation; federal-provincial differences are the norm rather than the exception. Toronto comedian Dave Broadfoot once called Canada "a collection of ten provinces with strong governments loosely connected by fear." But that does not mean that the federal government must be deterred every time there is a regional or interest group that disagrees with the prevailing national will. In fact, it is the strength and ability of federal parties and leaders to hold to national visions that determine their success with the electorate.

Free trade is a natural extension of the vision and direction for Canada that Brian Mulroney and the Progressive Conservative Party promised when it swept to power in September 1984. I believe that our record and history will show that we stuck to a broad national strategy for economic renewal. It was a strategy based on four basic principles.

First, we knew that national progress required national unity—that we could hardly compete with those from abroad if we were not cooperating at home. And we knew that there were two major threats to national cohesion—the estrangement of French-speaking Quebec and growing regional economic disparities.

Second, we accepted the reality of growing global interdependence; that our national prosperity could be achieved only by setting policies that met our international needs, not just our domestic wants. And that meant challenging entrenched interests and reforming many aspects of our regulatory policy framework.

Third, we recognized the worldwide trend from natural to human and technological resources, with its clear implication that our economic future lay more and more with manufacturing and a growing services economy. And fourth, we understood that full employment and sustained growth was a pipe dream without a sound currency, lower interest rates, and investor confidence.

Over the past 40 months, we have implemented a wide range of initiatives based on these principles, including:

☐ a constitutional rapprochement with Quebec (the so-called "Meech Lake Accord")

☐ a decentralized approach to regional development and the establishment of specific regional agencies to assist development and diversification in the West and in the Atlantic provinces

☐ tax reform to ensure internationally competitive rates; to better balance taxation in the resource, manufacturing, and services sectors; and to allow individuals to spend, save, or invest more of their own money as they see fit

☐ reform of our transportation, communications, and financial regulations

☐ policies to encourage more applied research and greater cooperation between government labs, universities, and the private sector

☐ a more positive environment for foreign investment

☐ a systematic strategy to reduce our budgetary deficit over the medium term based on expenditure control *and* tax increases.

I mention these initiatives because trade policy has always been an integral part of this broader economic strategy. We acknowledged the Catch-22 of our small population. In order to produce goods that can compete in world markets, our industries must invest in modern plant, equipment, and technology on an efficient scale. Yet in order to justify that investment, they needed access to a potential customer base larger than our own. That begged the question, how to gain such access?

One way would have been to rely solely on multilateral negotiations in the General Agreement on Tariffs and Trade (GATT). The GATT is important and remains a cornerstone of our trade policy, but we recognized that GATT negotiations take time. We also recognized that GATT rules have increasingly been set to meet the needs of the Big Three economic powers—the United States, the European Community, and Japan.

A second option to secure access was to revive the bilateral sector negotiations with the United States initiated by our predecessors, who are now the great opponents of this free trade agreement and the self-proclaimed defenders of multilateralism. But we recognized that the two governments had failed even to agree on the sectors, let alone sectoral rules. And we further recognized that, even if we could achieve sectoral agreements, such a process might require a series of GATT waivers and undermine the multilateral system.

That left a third alternative—a two-track approach of more GATT negotiations plus a GATT-compatible free trade agreement with the United States, which, in any event, represents 80 percent of our multilateral trade.

The rationale was again straightforward. Because of past negotiations, Canada and the United States were already close to meeting the GATT test of a free trade area. And if we could get over that threshold, we would accomplish two things. First, we could design more specific rules tailored to the needs of our *two* countries. Second, bilateral rules might spur progress in the GATT. In addition, both countries could improve their competitiveness to seize opportunities in third markets if such GATT negotiations proved successful.

Obviously, we chose the third option. And I believe we have chosen well.

The phase-out of tariffs in the FTA will mean not only lower consumer prices; it also will give Canadian industries an advantage over the rest of the world in the US market. It will allow integrated North American industries to become more competitive against overseas competition. And it will end a major barrier to value-added processing prior to export, as we sought in the Tokyo Round.

The agreement to open up government procurement means a new C$4 billion market for Canadian business, with the potential for further liberalization in the GATT or future bilateral negotiations.

I believe we have struck a good balance in the automotive sector. Products that were outside the Auto Pact will flow duty-free, and we have addressed the difficult issue of North American transplants with what is effectively a 54 percent content rule.

From our perspective, these rules mean that both of the key reasons for our automotive success—the tariff incentives for the Big Three to produce in Canada and our significant cost advantage over US plants—remain. We have struck a reasonable balance between the traditional North American automakers and the new entrants. And by moving to tariff-free status, we can pass the GATT free trade area test and gain preferential tariff access for products like petrochemicals—tariff concessions that were denied us in the Tokyo Round.

In agriculture, we have preserved our Article XI marketing board powers, and we have taken a first step in ending the insane global grain war.

In the energy sector, we have secured access for our hydroelectric, uranium, oil, and gas exports. This is a critical step in ensuring our own energy security because after price, the economies of scale made possible by secure access to the US market are the most important factor in allowing us to develop our huge hydro, tar sands, and frontier resources.

In other areas of the agreement, we have built on the GATT Standards Code, attacking some of the most devious nontariff barriers to trade, like artificial health standards. It is hoped that this will stimulate further progress in the global negotiations.

We have also created greater certainty for Canadian and US investors, essentially putting our past commitments in the Organization for Economic Cooperation and Development on a contractual basis. Canada has retained the right to review significant direct investment proposals. Current restrictions in key sectors remain, and the special status of cultural investments has been entrenched. Just as important is the fact that Canadian investors will be protected from potential US restrictions—clearly important when you consider that for the past decade Canadians have invested C$3 in the United States for every C$1 flowing north.

In terms of future investment patterns, the greater access for Canadian goods made possible by the agreement will limit the need for Canadian companies to jump US trade barriers and set up shop in the United States. We believe as well that it will allow third-country investors to contemplate Canada as a location for North American facilities as well.

The services agreement is a global precedent and in the long run perhaps the most important element of all. The agreement is practical, leaving current laws and regulations intact while setting out principles to govern future laws. And it is accompanied by an equally practical agreement on temporary work access. Once again, we believe it will strengthen Canada's GATT bargaining position in this sector. And in financial services, Canada's commitments are tied to progress on US regulatory reform, which is accelerating in the US Congress.

Finally, we have devised a better way to avoid and settle our inevitable disputes. The new joint commission will assist in preventing and resolving future disagreements. We have agreed to exempt each other's products from emergency actions when our exports are not the problem—an intelligent approach to global safeguard actions. A joint panel will act as a binding court of appeal on antidumping and countervailing disputes. And we will be negotiating new and better antidumping and countervailing duty laws over the next few years.

All in all, I believe the agreement makes good common sense. It is both practical and farsighted. And we are confident that it will stand the test of time and prove beneficial to both our countries for many years to come.

But first it must be implemented. And I know both sides are eyeing each other with a livelier interest than usual.

Many of you will be scrambling for the nearest Canadian political science text to see what recourses the provinces may have to block the agreement or what hurdles a Liberal-dominated nonelected Senate could create to thwart the public will. We believe that the opponents to free trade have already taken their best shots and will recoil as public approval of the agreement continues to grow. The Canadian government will do everything in its power to ensure the speedy progress of this initiative through Parliament.

On our side, we will be looking south, following both the congressional fast-track process and the omnibus trade bill. It is no secret that the passage of such protectionist legislation would, to say the least, give us pause. We shall have to see whether ways and methods can be found to resolve our concerns (for example, by the amendment of Section 113 of the House version to cover free trade agreements entered into on or before 2 January 1989).

We certainly welcome the view of the *Wall Street Journal* on 5 January 1988 that President Ronald Reagan and Prime Minister Mulroney are setting "the world on a promising new strategy for trade liberalization." Major newspapers in Canada such as the *Globe and Mail* and the *Financial Post* have taken the same strong stand, recognizing that even with minor imperfections, the free trade agreement represents fundamental progress toward eliminating the hidden costs of self-interested protectionism. Interestingly, the *Wall Street Journal* editorial is titled "A Test for *Fair* Traders," calling into account the ethical values that are so necessary for any contractual arrangement to be valid and binding.

The free trade agreement is *not* a devolution of national sovereignty, as some of the more strident critics in Canada would try to make people believe. Nor is it an economic union between Canada and the United States. The free trade agreement is a commercial agreement between friendly and ethical partners, between two countries who already have close to 80 percent of their trade free of tariffs.

Free trade is fair trade. Fundamentally, Canadians know it and Americans know it. There are millions of people on both sides of the border waiting impatiently for the diplomatic and political negotiations to conclude, so that together we can establish a solid foundation to welcome the twenty-first century.

M. Peter McPherson

I would like to discuss the Canada–United States Free Trade Agreement (FTA) in general terms and then highlight a few areas that I find particularly interesting, areas that in some cases might otherwise be overlooked. As a participant, I would also like to communicate the flavor of the final hours of these historic negotiations.

It should be clear to everyone that a free trade agreement between Canada and the United States makes sense. We are each other's largest trading partner and will benefit from the removal of trade restrictions between us. In addition, and perhaps not as obvious, the agreement will enhance the international competitiveness of both countries. Canada and the United States are stronger and better able to meet international competition as an integrated market than as separate markets.

From a Canadian perspective, ensured access to a major market is clearly important. It creates an environment conducive to the investments necessary to achieve economies of scale and to meet global competition. For some time, thoughtful Canadians have expressed fears that if the Canadian market were to become too isolated, Canadian products would become increasingly disadvantaged internationally. From a US perspective, the economic case for the agreement may not be quite as strong. It is true, however, that a combined, larger market helps US international competitiveness as well.

Key Concerns

This agreement does not simply eliminate trade barriers such as tariffs and import quotas, as one might find in a traditional free trade area. It contains additional elements, some of which were added because of particular political concerns within Canada or the United States. Each country brought to the negotiations its own list of issues that it believed to be essential if the agreement were to be salable to its people.

The Canadian negotiators had a number of objectives. Most important, they wanted to stop what they perceived to be a growing protectionist movement in the United States and to gain security of access to the large US market. Specifically, they wanted discipline on the use of US laws governing unfair trade practices, particularly the countervailing and anti-

---

M. Peter McPherson is Deputy Secretary of the Treasury, and former head of the Agency for International Development.

This is the revised text of comments presented at the conference.

dumping statutes. They wanted to guarantee that, in the future, the Government of Canada could take actions it considered necessary to protect Canadian cultural identity. They wanted the Auto Pact to remain in place.

The US negotiators' general objectives were trade and investment liberalization. They needed an agreement that opened trade between our two countries and that was in the United States' overall economic interests. The United States needed liberalization of Canada's investment policy, which historically has been a source of much bilateral tension and concern to US investors. Without commitments on investment, the benefits of trade liberalization could be undercut.

Negotiating Process

US negotiators worked under a trade law that provided for congressional approval of a trade agreement with a quick vote and no congressional amendments. The law was due to expire 2 January 1988. To use the fast-track procedure, the President needed to notify the Congress on or before 3 October 1987 that we had achieved the basis for an agreement, and the President needed to sign the agreement on or before 2 January 1988. Needless to say, the Canadian negotiators also considered these deadlines real.

In the months preceding October 3, Ambassador Peter Murphy, the chief negotiator in the Office of the US Trade Representative (USTR), had worked endless hours, days, and months to make substantial progress toward an agreement. He had settled many aspects of the agreement.

Despite this, the negotiators remained unable to pull together the pieces of the agreement and to resolve certain key issues. It became clear in the final days that the negotiations required higher level political involvement.

The senior Canadian team for these final, hectic days included Derek Burney, the chief of staff to Prime Minister Mulroney; Mike Wilson, Minister of Finance; and Pat Carney, Minister for International Trade. They met with Jim Baker, Clayton Yeutter, and me in the corner of the Treasury Building that houses the Secretary's suite of offices. That area became a beehive.

The six of us met in the conference room, and the Canadian and US officials responsible for specific subjects jointly came before us, bringing with them unresolved issues. The six of us struggled with these issues. Most issues took more than one short meeting. It is in this context that we worked on the major issues for Canada and the United States.

Unfair Trade Laws

The Canadian negotiators wanted to address Canadian concerns about US unfair trade laws by setting rules that defined fair and unfair actions (for example, fair and unfair subsidies). Under their proposal, a binational dispute settlement system would enforce the rules and would be binding on the two governments. In prior meetings, Canadian and US negotiators exchanged papers trying to develop rules on subsidies.

The US negotiators wanted to write rules designed to discipline Canadian use of subsidies, while providing the Congress and the states considerable flexibility to subsidize. This seemed appropriate because Canada is rarely a major destination for subsidized US production, while the United States is frequently a major destination for subsidized Canadian production. We did recognize, however, that US subsidies are not insignificant and do affect bilateral trade.

The Canadian negotiators could not accept rules that had a greater actual impact on Canadian subsidies than on US subsidies. Furthermore, they had problems with the specific subsidy rules proposed by the United States. We were deadlocked, and we began to look for another tack.

The approach we developed was based on a proposal by Congressman Sam Gibbons (D-Fla.). Under it, each country would maintain its national law on countervailing and antidumping duties. In the case of bilateral disputes, however, either country could ask a binational panel to review decisions for consistency with the domestic law of the importing country. The panel would replace rulings by national courts.

On October 3, we struggled with this issue. By midnight, the President had to notify the Congress of his intent to enter into a trade agreement. Yet at 9:30 that night, the Canadians decided that there was no resolution of this issue and no agreement. The Canadians were concerned that, under the new approach, the United States could change its domestic law. We, in turn, could not accept an agreement that precluded the Congress from changing US law.

That was an unhappy period. We had agreed on so many issues that an agreement seemed within reach, but we were stymied. Alan Holmer (then USTR General Counsel), a group of excellent USTR and Commerce officials, and I sat down with a group of Canadian negotiators. We went back and forth over the issues for the next hour and a half. During this period, we developed the wording contained in the elements of agreement. These elements were subsequently fleshed out by the lawyers into the text of the agreement on countervailing and antidumping duties.

The text is elaborate. The bottom line is that, if an FTA panel finds that an amendment to national countervail or antidumping law is inconsistent with the GATT or the FTA, the inconsistency must be eliminated within nine months or the other country may retaliate.

In my judgment, this arrangement addresses the concerns of both countries. The Congress can amend US law; the Canadian government has recourse if it considers an amendment inappropriate.

At about five minutes to midnight that night, we called the messenger who was standing by at the Capitol to inform him that the President had decided to notify the Congress of his intent to enter into a trade agreement with Canada. With four minutes to spare, the messenger delivered the presidential notification.

Culture

That was dramatic, but is was not the only dramatic moment. We had an agreement in principle, but we did not have a written legal text. We had started by drafting agreed summaries—the elements of the agreement.

On October 4, however, the Canadians raised objections to the summary of the cultural agreement. They took the position that they should have a free hand in discriminating in favor of Canadian cultural activities. We recognized that the Canadians would not sign an agreement unless they were satisfied that it adequately addressed Canadian cultural concerns. Many Canadians fear that the US entertainment industry can swamp Canada's market, causing Canada to lose its cultural identity. Their view is a political reality for the Government of Canada and must be addressed. Nonetheless, we could not agree to give Canada a completely free hand. We had to be able to protect US industries from commercial harm.

We finally reached an agreement that excluded specified cultural industries from the FTA except as designated. (For example, tariffs will be eliminated on products of cultural industries despite the exception.) This agreement authorizes the United States to take measures of equivalent commercial effect against Canadian actions that would be inconsistent with the FTA, except for the cultural exception. This is a good compromise that balances the concerns of both countries. Canada can protect its cultural concerns; the United States can protect its commercial interests.

Automobiles

Because of national political concerns, the Canadian negotiators preferred not to discuss the Auto Pact in the FTA, but this was not tenable for the

United States. The United States would have liked to end the safeguard requirements that Canada uses to decide which firms are eligible to import automotive products into Canada duty free. These safeguard requirements are performance requirements that set domestic production requirements and so can distort automotive trade and investment. Since the Canadians initially refused to discuss the pact, the first real discussion of the issue took place in the final days immediately preceding the October 3 agreement.

The results of these discussions are, on balance, quite helpful to both countries in the long run. Under the FTA, Canada agrees not to expand the list of firms whose imports are eligible for duty-free access contingent on meeting the safeguard requirements. Therefore, while the safeguard requirements remain, Canada cannot expand them to new firms. This approach limits the potential investment distortions caused by the safeguards. In addition, the FTA provides a way for US automotive exports to enter Canada duty free without being affected by the distortionary safeguard requirements.

The agreement also addresses automotive issues not covered by the Auto Pact. It sets a timetable for the elimination of Canada's duty-remission programs for automotive trade. These programs waive at least a portion of the Canadian duty on automotive imports by firms that do not meet Canada's safeguard requirements but do meet other export or production requirements. Also, with limited exceptions, the agreement ends duty drawback for bilateral trade on 1 January 1994. This means that import duties must be paid on third-country inputs incorporated in products traded between Canada and the United States. Moreover, the FTA includes a tough rule of origin that ensures a product is of US or Canadian origin to be eligible for FTA tariff treatment. For the United States, this rule will apply to all Canadian automotive products, even those imported under the Auto Pact.

In the United States, we have received more comments on the automotive section of the agreement than on any other. Those who criticize the FTA should recognize that it phases out or limits the harmful effects of Canadian measures of historical concern to the United States.

The automotive issues were the subject of tough negotiations, not only on October 3 but also in the days following as the legal text of the agreement was drafted. The FTA is an improvement over the status quo. The choice is not between the total elimination of objectionable Canadian programs and the status quo. The choice is between the FTA and the status quo.

Investment

As I said earlier, the United States considered an improvement in Canada's investment policy essential to selling the FTA in the United States. Canada's investment policy was the source of numerous bilateral disputes in the past.

In the FTA, Canada and the United States agreed to accept a number of key principles. Both countries made assurances to provide national treatment on entry and after establishment for future investments of the other country. National treatment ensures equal treatment with local investors. Both countries preserved existing restrictions for certain sectors. The United States, for example, retained domestic ownership requirements for atomic energy facilities.

Canada agreed that Investment Canada will not screen indirect investments or most direct investment by Americans, after a phase-in period. New (or greenfield) investments by Americans will remain free of screening or scrutiny by the Government of Canada. US investors will be able to sell most investments in Canada to other US investors or to third-country nationals without screening.

The agreement prohibits, in the future, most performance requirements set as a condition for establishing investments. Specifically, it bans requirements on exports, import substitution, domestic content, and local purchasing, including such requirements applicable to third-country investments that could significantly affect US–Canadian trade. Moreover, where screening is prohibited, all performance requirements are effectively prohibited. This is true because the leverage provided by screening is necessary to apply performance requirements.

In short, the investment section of the agreement is a very positive development. While it addresses issues of concern to the United States for some time, the agreement on investment should not be viewed solely as a benefit to us. These provisions will mean greater prosperity for Canadians. It will help ensure that investment decisions in Canada are based on economic considerations. This will result in increased plant efficiency, lower priced goods that are globally competitive, and a greater number of higher paying jobs.

Other Areas of the FTA

I would now like to give you my perspective on a few other areas of the agreement. Tariffs and the rule of origin, which deal with traditional trade issues, are being largely ignored. Yet these areas may contain the most significant day-to-day benefits for businesses. In the case of energy, I am concerned that many people do not recognize its importance to both Canadians and Americans. In the case of the general dispute settlement and services provisions, I raise them because they are innovative.

Tariffs

Consider first tariffs. By 1998, the FTA will eliminate all tariffs for products of Canada and the United States. Some tariffs will be eliminated on 1 January 1989; some after five equal, annual cuts; and some after 10 equal annual cuts. When one sifts through the tariff area, one can find some valuable nuggets.

A few of my fellow Michiganians have criticized particular aspects of the agreement. I have been able to respond by pointing to the benefits of the FTA provided by tariff elimination. I tell them, for example, that the huge furniture industry in the western side of the state will gain from the five-year phase-out of furniture tariffs. This will particularly benefit our industry since the Canadian tariff is significantly higher than ours.

Of course, the furniture industry is but one example. The elimination of tariffs benefits many industries on both sides of the border. Economists estimate that the agreement will mean $1 billion to $3 billion per year in overall economic gains, most of them from tariff elimination.

Rule of Origin

The rule of origin for eligibility for FTA tariff treatment is a bit esoteric. But I would like to discuss this issue to show the innovation the FTA provides in another traditional trade area. To date, the United States has used the criterion of "substantial transformation" into a new and different article of commerce to determine the origin of a product. The Canadians objected to basing the rule of origin for the FTA on substantial transformation. They argued that it is a subjective determination made case by case. They wanted a rule based solely on North American value content, which would have imposed burdensome record-keeping requirements on business and would have been difficult to verify.

The United States developed a good and innovative compromise. It is a rule based on processing third-country products sufficiently to result in a prescribed change in tariff classification under the internationally agreed harmonized system of tariff nomenclature. There is no general rule. Instead, the FTA rule of origin spells out product by product the classification changes required for eligibility for FTA tariff treatment. For most assembled goods, the rule of origin also includes a requirement that US–Canadian materials and processing account for 50 percent or more of the manufacturing costs. The FTA rule provides greater certainty and predictability to traders, and it should be simpler for business to use and for government officials to administer.

Energy

The energy section is another part of the agreement that provides substantial benefits to the United States and to Canada as well. I would like to start with the benefits to the United States. The agreement basically gives the United States equal access to Canadian oil, gas, and electricity. The importance of this arrangement is often overlooked.

When I returned from the final negotiations in December, a US senator from a farm state called me to complain about a provision affecting a small amount of agricultural trade. After addressing the issue he raised, I asked him if he had considered what implications access to Canadian energy supplies, including access to gas, fertilizer, pesticides, and insecticides might have for farmers in his state. I pointed out that the United States has plenty of gas now, but we both remembered the shortages of the 1970s.

While it is easy to focus on the immediate interest at hand, we should take a long-term perspective. In this light, the energy provisions of the FTA are clearly in the interests of the United States. Some people find a particular provision of the FTA and say its contents could be improved. They lose sight of the agreement as an improvement over the status quo and that other provisions contain benefits that may be more important than the imperfections they first find.

While I have touched largely on the benefits to the United States, the energy provisions are also beneficial to Canada. The FTA not only gives the United States greater assurance of supply, but it also gives Canada greater assurance of access to the US market. As a result, we should see more long-term contracts between our two countries. This will help provide the incentive for Canada to explore and develop further its energy resources, especially gas. The people of western Canada have no doubt of this benefit.

General Dispute Settlement Procedures

The FTA provisions for resolving disputes, besides those disputes over countervailing and antidumping duties, contain innovations as well. These provisions, which build on procedures set out in the General Agreement on Tariffs and Trade (GATT), establish:

☐ a binational commission headed by the Canadian and US trade ministers to settle disputes

☐ a time frame for settlement of disputes

- a means for ministers to elect the use of arbitration

- a mechanism whereby panels of experts are used to provide guidance

- a requirement that objections to panel reports be made in writing, followed by reconsideration by the panel.

These provisions improve on the GATT procedures. They provide for faster dispute resolution and make it more likely that panel findings will be accepted. If these procedures are used successfully to resolve frictions between Canada and the United States, they may become a model for other agreements, providing a way to reduce tensions between trading partners.

Services

The FTA contains the first international trade agreement governing trade and investment in services industries. Although Canada and the United States now have relatively open markets for services, neither government is constrained from imposing new restrictions on services. In the FTA, the governments of Canada and the United States pledge that future laws and regulations affecting trade and investment in a wide range of service industries will not discriminate between service providers of the two countries.

The services provisions are not as extensive as the United States would like, but they are a step in the right direction. We should take this agreement and move forward on this important issue in the GATT Uruguay Round.

Conclusion

The FTA negotiations were tough and long. Many people slept little those last few days. Both sides tried hard to understand the other's difficulties and to figure out practical solutions. While neither side got everything it wanted, each came away with a good, balanced agreement that will put both Canada and the United States in stronger positions in international economic competition.

Appendix

Conference Participants
Washington, 11 January 1988

Sponsored by the Institute for International Economics and the Institute for Research on Public Policy

Philippe Adhemar
Embassy of France

Ray Ahearn
Library of Congress

C. Michael Aho
Council on Foreign Relations

Mary Alexander
Citizens for a Sound Economy

Kristen Allen
Resources for the Future

William Alpert
William H. Donner Foundation

Stuart Auerbach
Washington Post

Ian Austen
Maclean's

Dragoslav Avramovic
Bank of Credit and Commerce
    International

Thomas Axworthy
Charles P. Bronfman Foundation

Robert Ayres
World Bank

Rolf Bachmann
Alusuisse of America

Martin Bailey
US Department of State

Carol Balassa
Office of the US Trade Representative

Harvey Bale
Hewlett-Packard

William Barreda
US Department of Treasury

Gil Barrows
Canadian Cattlemen's Association

Thomas O. Bayard
Institute for International Economics

Carl Beigie
Dominion Securities

Donald Belch
Stelco, Inc.

John Bennett
Korea Economic Institute

C. Fred Bergsten
Institute for International Economics

Thomas Bernes
Department of Finance Canada

Robert Bertrand
Canadian Import Tribunal

Henri Blanc
Embassy of France

John Bohn
US Export–Import Bank

Doreen Brown
Consumers for World Trade

John Browning
The Economist

Lynn Buckle
Canadian Bankers' Association

Ravi Bulchandani
Goldman, Sachs & Company

Kenneth Button
Economic Consulting Services

Peter Calamai
Southam News

Michael Call
Mitsubishi

Donald Cameron
Mudge, Rose, Guthrie, Alexander &
  Ferdon

Stephen Canner
US Department of Treasury

Steven Charnovitz
Office of the Speaker of the House

Peggy Clark
US Department of Commerce

William R. Cline
Institute for International Economics

Calman Cohen
Emergency Committee for American
  Trade

Robert Cornell
US Department of Treasury

Maureen Crandall
US Department of State

Robert Crandall
Brookings Institution

Frank Crawford
Nissan

Marshall Crowe
M. A. Crowe Consultants

Joseph Damond
US Department of Commerce

Peter Dawes
Canadian Importers Association

Chris DeCure
Embassy of Australia

Ferry deKerckhove
Department of External Affairs
Canada

Germain Denis
Trade Negotiations Office
Canada

Roy Denman
Delegation of the European
  Communities

Cameron Duncan
House Committee on Small Business

James Dupree
Burns Bureau

Duncan Dwelle
American Fair Trade Council

Robert Ebel
ENSERCH

Michael Ebert
Office of Congressman Philip Sharp
  (D–Ind.)

Kimberly Ann Elliott
Institute for International Economics

Lewis Engman
Winston and Strawn

Guy Erb
Erb & Madian

Thomas Farmer
Prather, Seeger, Doolittle & Farmer

C. David Finch
Institute for International Economics

J. Michael Finger
World Bank

Pamela Fleming
C-SPAN

Pierre Fortin
Pharmaceutical Manufacturers
  Association of Canada

Isaiah Frank
Johns Hopkins University

Roberto Jorge Frasisti
Embassy of Argentina

Harry L. Freeman
American Express

Robin Gaines
US Department of Commerce

Raymond Garcia
Rockwell International

Gene Godley
Bracewell & Patterson

Lee Goldberg
Inside US Trade

Carol Goodloe
US Department of Agriculture

Robert Grayner
Business Fund for Canadian Studies in the US

Norma Greenaway
Canadian Press

Joseph Greenwald
Former Assistant Secretary of State for Economic Affairs

Arthur Gundersheim
Amalgamated Clothing and Textile Workers Union

David D. Hale
Kemper Financial Services

David Hall
British Embassy

Robert Hampton
Agriculture Council of America

Blair Hanley
Embassy of Canada

Graham Hardman
Business Council on National Issues

Anthony Harris
Financial Times

Ann Marie Havrilko
BP America

William Hawley
Citibank

C. Randall Henning
Institute for International Economics

Robert Herzstein
Arnold & Porter

Ann Hollick
US Department of State

In-Kie Hong
Daewoo

Wm. C. Hood
Former Director of Research, International Monetary Fund

Gary N. Horlick
O'Melveny and Myers

Fusen Hu
Coordinating Council for North American Affairs

Robert E. Hudec
University of Minnesota

Gary C. Hufbauer
Georgetown University

George Ingram
House Foreign Affairs Committee

James T. Jensen
Jensen Associates

Robert Jerome
Capital Strategy Research

Betsy Johnson
Office of Congressman Philip Crane (R–Ill.)

Julius L. Katz
Government Research Corporation

Osamu Kavaguchi
Cornell University

William Kelly
Former Deputy Director-General, GATT

Bogdan Kipling
Kipling News Service

Peter Kirby
Ginsburg, Feldman & Bress

Jay Kohn
Office of Congressman Richard Cheney (R–Wyo.)

Mike Kostiw
Texaco

Stephen Lande
Manchester Associates

Sheila Landers
O'Melveny & Myers

Warren Lavorel
Office of the US Trade Representative

Richard Lawrence
Journal of Commerce

Lisa Learner
Office of Senator Donald Riegle (D–Mich.)

Allen Lenz
US Department of Commerce

David Leyton-Brown
York University

Robert E. Litan
Brookings Institution

Peter Lo
British Embassy

O. Victor Lonmo
Automotive Parts Manufacturers'
 Association of Canada

Paul Macwhorter
Arnold & Porter

Sunder Magun
Economic Council of Canada

Greg Mastel
Office of Senator Max Baucus (D–Mon.)

James Matkin
Business Council of British Columbia

Barbara McDougall
Minister of State, Canada

John McKay
Broadcast News

Robert McNeill
Emergency Committee for American
 Trade

M. Peter McPherson
Deputy Secretary of the Treasury

Allen Mendelowitz
General Accounting Office

Paul Meo
World Bank

James Merrill
Marine Midland

Patrick Messerlin
World Bank

Seigen Miyasato
Johns Hopkins University

Mustafa Mohatarem
General Motors

Richard Money
New York Times

Peter Morici
National Planning Association

Bailey Morris
London Times

Robert Morris
US Council for International Business

Patrick Mulloy
Senate Banking Committee

William Murden
US Department of Treasury

William Niskanen
Cato Institute

Stephen Nordlinger
Baltimore Sun

Janet Nuzum
House Ways and Means Committee

Craig Oliver
Canadian TV

Mancur Olson
University of Maryland

Stephen Parker
Congressional Budget Office

Eliza Patterson
US International Trade Commission

Joseph Pelzman
George Washington University

Derick Plumby
British Embassy

Donald Pongrace
Akin, Gump, Strauss, Hauer & Feld

Lee Price
Joint Economic Committee

Harold Quinlan
Government of New Brunswick

Myer Rashish
Rashish Associates

Claire Reade
Arnold & Porter

Alfred Reifman
Library of Congress

William Reinsch
Office of Senator H. John Heinz III
(R–Pa.)

Mary Ann Richardson
Office of Senator Brock Adams
(D–Wash.)

Keith Rockwell
Journal of Commerce

Miguel Rodriguez
Institute for International Economics

Rita Rodriguez
US Export–Import Bank

David Rohr
US International Trade Commission

Dan Romanik
Bankers Association for Foreign Trade

Daniel Roseman
Institute for Research on Public Policy

Daniel Rosenblum
Office of Senator Carl Levin (D–Mich.)

Seymour Rubin
American Society of International Law

David Ruth
American Express

Yoshiaki Saegusa
Nissan

Andrew Samet
Office of Senator Daniel Patrick
Moynihan (D–N.Y.)

Leonard Santos
Verner, Liipfert, Bernhard, McPherson
& Hand

Jeffrey J. Schott
Institute for International Economics

Nancy Schwartz
US Department of Agriculture

Richard Self
Office of the US Trade Representative

Jack Sheehan
United Steel Workers Union

Jeremy Shen
Coordinating Council for North
American Affairs

David Shiles
Embassy of Australia

Peggy Simpson
Hearst Newspapers

Murray G. Smith
Institute for Research on Public Policy

Debra Steger
Fraser & Beatty

Michael Stein
Dewey, Ballantine, Bushby, Palmer &
Wood

Hugh Stephens
Department of External Affairs Canada

Paula Stern
Carnegie Endowment for International
Peace

Frank Stone
Institute for Research on Public Policy

S. K. Suri
London Life Insurance

Ulrich Suter
Alusuisse of America

Seiichiro Takagi
Brookings Institution

Margaret Tebbutt
Embassy of Canada

Patrick Templeton
Templeton & Co.

Sergio Thompson-Flores
Embassy of Brazil

Debra Valentine
O'Melveny & Myers

Robert Varah
DOFASCO

Philip K. Verleger, Jr.
Institute for International Economics

Ron Wall
Embassy of Canada

J.H. Warren
Advisor to the Government of Quebec

Phillip Webber
Congressional Budget Office

Leonard Weiss
Trade Advisory Panel, US Atlantic
  Council

Jim Wesley
World Beat

John Whalley
University of Western Ontario

John Williamson
Institute for International Economics

Arlene Wilson
Library of Congress

Gilbert Winham
Dalhousie University

Paul Wonnacott
University of Maryland

Ronald J. Wonnacott
University of Western Ontario

Barry Wood
Voice of America

Jeremy Wright
Canadian Federation of Labor

Jungho Yoo
Korea Economic Institute

David Zorb
AT&T

U124 R
2A.
set 2

X
tuks
+
erach.

2 Drs